The Great Beginnings Baby Name Book

The Great Beginnings Baby Name Book

Illustrious Names
from the Arts,
History, Literature, Sports,
Mythology, and Cultures
Around the World

SARA L. WHITTIER

CB
CONTEMPORARY
BOOKS
CHICAGO

Library of Congress Cataloging-in-Publication Data

Whittier, Sara L.
The great beginnings baby name book : illustrious names from the arts, history, literature, sports, mythology, and cultures around the world / Sara L. Whittier.
p. cm.
Includes index.
ISBN 0-8092-4445-4
1. Names, Personal—Handbooks, manuals, etc. I. Title.
CS2377.W55 1989
929.4'4—dc19 89-699
CIP

Data on the most popular boys' and girls' names in 1986 from The Sinrod Marketing Group Inc., Hicksville, NY. Reprinted by permission.

Most popular baby names in Canada from *The Gazette* (Montreal), © 1988 *The Gazette*. Reprinted by permission of *The Gazette.*

The ten most popular boys' first names and girls' first names announced in *The Times* from an article by Helen Beard, *The Times* (London), January 1, 1988. © Times Newspapers Ltd 1988.

Interior Illustrations by Anne Feiza

Published by Contemporary Books, Inc.
180 North Michigan Avenue, Chicago, Illinois 60601
Manufactured in the United States of America
Library of Congress Catalog Card Number: 89-699
International Standard Book Number: 0-8092-4445-4

Published simultaneously in Canada by Beaverbooks, Ltd.
195 Allstate Parkway, Valleywood Business Park
Markham, Ontario L3R 4T8 Canada

For the two who gave me my name,
Robert McClintock Whittier and
Mary Antoinette Whittier

CONTENTS

1 Great Beginnings, Great Expectations *1*
2 How to Select a Name *5*
3 Creators *13*
4 Leaders *85*
5 Discoverers *119*
6 Athletes *137*
7 Fictional and Mythological Characters *153*
8 Biblical Characters *183*
9 International Favorites *197*
10 Great Places *219*
11 More Names for Great Beginnings *225*
12 News from the Top *241*
Index *251*

1
GREAT BEGINNINGS, GREAT EXPECTATIONS

An astronaut. A United States president. A singer. A painter. A scientist. Captain of the school softball team! It is amazing to imagine all the wonderful possibilities that lie before your son or daughter. Yet before the events of a long and happy life begin, a child gets a unique gift: a name.

As you search for a name for your child, many images, feelings, and questions may run through your mind. What sort of person will he or she be like? What kind of name would suit him? Should she have a name that is currently popular or a more traditional one? What would be the *best* name?

Fortunately, there is no *single* answer.

For centuries, parents have wished the best of love, luck, opportunities, friendship—the best of life—for their children, and they have given them all kinds of names. What the names in this book have in common is that they are all associated with successful and famous people. Of course, great names and great people are not all alike. Thus, the names are divided into six main groups: creators, leaders, discoverers, athletes, fictional and mythological characters, and biblical characters. As you browse through this book you may find yourself gravitating toward one or two of the main groups while you search for a name that fits your values, personality, and hopes for your child. You will also want to check out the chapters "International Favorites," on popular names from around the world, and "More Great Beginnings," with its information on jewel names, flower names, Mayflower names, CEO names, and more.

With the names, you will find descriptions of their linguistic origins and meanings. Just as important, you will find information on their subliminal or hidden meanings. These are the underlying associations that make a name "say" something, that make someone picture a Liz as a different sort of person from a Betsy (though both may be officially named Elizabeth), or a Sean as different from a John (though both names have the same Hebrew origin).

USING THIS BOOK

Many names are related to other names, or are mentioned in several places in this book. When a name is mentioned that is described more fully elsewhere, it will appear in all capital letters. By looking up an all-capitalized name in the index, you can find the other page or pages on which the name is described.

BOY OR GIRL?

Many names have at some time in history been used for both men and women. Those that have a strong tradition for both sexes (for instance, Jackie) are listed separately, among boys' names *and* girls' names. It is very rare for a girl's name to be adopted for boys, but the reverse is very common. You might be surprised to know that Stacey and Florence were once commonly used for men! Names like these are listed where most people would expect them—with other female names.

NAME FASHIONS

A big concern for many parents is whether or not a name is fashionable. Many people do not want to seem to be *following* trends, but they do not want to be too far out of the mainstream either. Others want a truly original name, but not one that will mark their child as unusual in any negative way. All this is not new, for name fashions have come and gone since the time of Adam.

Among the Puritans in colonial America, Old Testament biblical names were in vogue. The major biblical figures provided popular names (Abraham, Isaac, Samuel, Sarah, Rebecca), but names of obscure biblical figures (Ichabod, Enoch, Mehetabel) were used as well. The Puritans also invented names, giving their children the names of Christian virtues (Charity, Patience, Mercy) and biblical admonitions (Increase, Treadwell). With the eighteenth and nineteenth centuries came an American fashion for classical names (Augustus, Hannibal, Julius, Horace, Lavinia, Julia). Then, with the rise of Romanticism, a number of aristocratic surnames came into use as first names (Percy, Sidney). At the end of the nineteenth century, flower names such as Rose and Daisy came into style. Throughout America's history, immigrants from all over the world added names to the melting pot as well (for instance, Eric, Max, Gretchen, Bridget).

In the late twentieth century, many of the old standard names such as John, William, Charles, Anne/Anna, Elizabeth, and Mary, which stood near the top of the popularity lists for several hundred years, have dropped dramatically on the lists of the most popular names for new babies. Some parents have turned to other traditional names to replace these, particularly names from the Old Testament (Joshua, Nathaniel, Sarah). Other trend-conscious parents are using traditional English surnames (Addison, Gray, Berkeley) as first names for their children. Still others seem to be picking up on more imaginative trends, choosing names of places (Brittany, Jersey) or even coining their own.

From London to Tokyo, from Ivy League schools to Hollywood, the world is full of interesting, evocative names. The purpose of this guide is to provide a useful sampling. Included are famous names from history, mythology, sports, the Bible, the arts, and the sciences. Some are popular now, others were fashionable in the past. They come from all over the world, but each has become known in English-speaking countries.

Choosing a name for another person is an awesome responsibility with no clear-cut right or wrong result. Whether you revive an old-fashioned name or choose a name that sounds up-to-date; whether you choose a name for its history or because you like its sound: take your choice seriously. But as you ponder your choices, there is just one more very important thing to do: have fun!

2
HOW TO SELECT A NAME

NAME MEANINGS

Many people faced with the task of naming a baby are curious about the original meanings of names. For some parents, the meaning may even be a very special part of the name. One couple, after years of wishing for a child, were introduced to a tiny infant who needed a home. When his foster mother explained that she had been calling him Jonathan because that means "gift of God," they felt at once he was meant for them. They adopted him, and Jonathan became his real name.

Day to day, however, few people spend much time thinking about the true origins of names. The fact that the name Paul comes from a Latin word meaning "small" does not detract from the basic strength and masculinity of the name. The fact that Elizabeth means "oath of God" is probably not a major factor in parents' choice of that name for a daughter. This aside, a pleasant meaning will always seem preferable. One reason Andrew ("manly") is more popular than Adrian ("of the Adriatic coast") may be the parents' preference for Andrew's meaning.

The meaning of Andrew is based on the linguistic origin of the name. The name has been traced to the Greek word *Andreas*, which means "manly." In the pages that follow, you will find many linguistic meanings of that kind. In some cases, however, a name is so ancient and has changed so much from its original form that scholars are at a loss to determine what it originally meant. In other cases, experts disagree. In these situations, several possible meanings are listed, or the meaning is given as unknown.

The subliminal meaning of a name may be even harder to pin down, for it is made up of nuances and associations that have accumulated over centuries. A name's association with a biblical character, TV character, saint, king, president, or movie star affects what it means to people. The name Clint conjures up the image of a handsome, tough, masculine man, largely because of the roles played by actor Clint Eastwood. The name Jeremiah sounds strong and trustworthy to many people because of its association with the biblical prophet Jeremiah. Other names are not so strongly linked with one particular person, but they have equally strong subliminal meanings. The feminine, old-fashioned, creative air of the name Emily comes partly from its association with poet Emily Dickinson, novelist Emily Brontë, and perhaps even etiquette writer Emily Post. Interestingly, the name Colette sounds coquettish and Carla sounds brisk and businesslike, even though one may not consciously recall a famous Colette or Carla. In the following chapters, you will find reasons for these and many other subliminal meanings. These may be related not only to famous people but to the name's country of origin, its linguistic meaning, or even the way it sounds to the ear.

Because of differences in personal taste and past experiences, people may disagree about a name's subliminal meaning. A person who went through school with a nerdy kid named Mel may feel differently about the name than a fan of the actor Mel Gibson. In the pages that follow, the intent is to summarize the *best-known* associations of each name—the most famous people, mythological characters, etc., that are linked to it. Naturally, every reader will have additional memories and knowledge about many names. The interpretations in this guide can be best used as a spark to your memory and imagination—to get you thinking about what a name really means to you and others—and ultimately to help you find a name that says what you want it to.

SOUND

Just as important as what a name means is how it sounds. Most names sound agreeable alone; the problems begin when one tries to match first, middle, and last names.

Consonants are the first and easiest element to consider. As a general rule, many people try to avoid repetition of first letters. Consonants *within* names are another story. Judicious repetition of consonant sounds within a name can actually help it seem to flow. For example, most people would agree that Ginger Rogers is a more attractive name than Ginger Rodney, and that Dustin Hoffman has a better ring than Dustin Hoffer.

However, there are a few consonant sounds that can work against a name if they are repeated excessively. Too many sibilants (s, f, z, sh) can create an unattractive hissing sound. Some people might go so far as to say that even more than one sibilant can somehow "weaken" a name (though this is not necessarily undesirable). Notice how the name Boris Becker sounds tougher than Boris Spassky and Melissa Manchester sounds more delicate than Cyndi Lauper. All four names are attractive, but the names with only one sibilant sound more vigorous than those with several.

The consonants "d" and "g," especially together, should also be used sparingly. Though Douglas is a popular name, to many people it sounds best when paired with a "light" last name with one or more sibilants—such as Fairbanks. As another example of what "d" and "g" can do, picture a millionaire named Donald Gump. Then picture Donald Trump, whose name sounds like coins jingling. The presence of both "d" and "g" in feminine names like Gertrude and Hedwig make them unattractive to some people, but can also create an impression of strength.

Like repeated consonants, repeated vowel sounds can help a name flow and create a nice ring. The names Eugene O'Neill and Randy Travis both use repetition of vowel sounds to achieve an attractive, lyrical effect. Faye Dunaway is a beautiful name that actually rhymes (though to some tastes this effect is too theatrical). For a strongly masculine effect, repetition of vowel sounds is perhaps best avoided entirely. Compare the masculine strength of the names Ryan O'Neal and Tip O'Neill to Eugene O'Neill.

RHYTHM

The number of syllables and the placement of emphasis on them make up the rhythm of a name. Perhaps the most common type of name in the English language is composed of a first and a last name, each with two syllables, each accented on the first syllable. For example: Michael Jackson, Joni Mitchell, Ronald Reagan, William Shakespeare, Isaac Newton, Harry Truman, Alice Walker . . . the list could go on and on. It is hard to go wrong with this combination. However, people with longer or shorter last names will naturally have to consider other options.

A one-syllable name combined with a two-syllable one may be the next most common combination. Bruce Willis, Fred Astaire, Demi Moore, and Sally Ride are examples of this type of name. A pair of one-syllable names can also be effective, though it is not very common for women. Names of this type include George Bush, Bart Starr, and Sean Penn.

Last names and first names with three or more syllables each generally do not mix well. Mahalia Jackson, Elizabeth Taylor, and Abraham Lincoln are all extremely appealing and powerful-sounding names. By comparison, a name like Abraham Saperstein sounds a bit awkward.

However, the sheer number of syllables is not the only factor at work. The more subtle key is the number and placement of accented or stressed syllables. Although the name Gloria Vanderbilt includes two words of three syllables each, it is easy to say and agreeable to hear because it has only two strongly stressed syllables, which are separated evenly by lightly stressed syllables. Thus the overall rhythm of the name is simple and symmetrical: GLO-ri-a VAN-der-bilt. By contrast, awkward-sounding names tend to have traffic jams of stressed syllables. A-bra-HAM SAP-er-STEIN and EN-gel-BERT HUMP-er-DINCK are two names that suffer from stress build-up. Locked in syllable-gridlock is Picasso's controversial biographer Arianna Stassinopoulos Huffington (A-ri-AN-NA-STASS-in-O-pou-los HUFF-ing-ton). A two-syllable first name like Daphne would break up the stressed syllables. Like Arianna, Daphne is elegant and of Greek origin, but Daphne Stassinopoulos Huffington (DAPH-ne-STASS-in-O-pou-los HUFF-ing-ton) is not quite such a mouthful.

NAMES WITH AN INTERNATIONAL FLAVOR

A name is a great place to show off your ancestral heritage. Or, if you wish to downplay the character of your surname, you can do that with a first name. As an example of how a first name can affect perceptions of a last name, imagine the tennis stars Gabriella Sabatini and Steffi Graf trading names to become Steffi Sabatini and Gabriella Graf, or Boris Becker and John McEnroe becoming Boris McEnroe and John Becker.

Parents considering names that are unfamiliar in English may also wish to choose a relatively simple one, which English speakers will not mangle in spelling and pronunciation—for example, Ari rather than Amnon, Cécile rather than Mireille.

NICKNAMES, DIMINUTIVES, AND SHORT FORMS

Many names have natural diminutives and short forms that go along with them. A boy named John will not necessarily be called Johnny, but it is almost a guarantee that at some point a boy named William will be called Will or Bill. Will and Bill then may become the diminutives Willy and Billy. Many men and boys favor the use of nicknames and short forms and much prefer to be known as Andy rather than Andrew, Matt rather than Matthew, Ken rather than Kenneth, Jim rather than James, and so forth. Whether or not as a parent you intend to call your child by a short form of his name, it is important to keep in mind the nicknames and shortenings that may inevitably be formed from a boy's name. The situation is similar for girls' names, though not as extreme. A child named Elizabeth who wishes to be called Elizabeth, not Liz, Beth, or Betsy, may occasionally have to make her preference known to teachers and friends.

Many names that originated as diminutives and short forms have become accepted as independent names. For example, Bart can be considered an independent name, or a short form of Barton, Bartlett, or Bartholomew. Sally originated as a diminutive of Sarah but has long been considered an independent name.

INITIALS

As you narrow down the choices for your child's name, one final consideration is initials. Make sure they are suitable for monogramming! Most people will want to avoid initials such as RIP, GOD, SOD, or SAP. Initials such as VIP, ESP, or ELF might be considered a lucky bonus.

The more ambitious may wish to take up an additional challenge: to devise a truly elegant set of initials. The number of famous people who are known by their initials is surprisingly large. They include F. Scott Fitzgerald, J. R. R. Tolkien, A. A. Milne, C. S. Lewis, T. S. Eliot, W. E. B. Dubois, F. Lee Bailey, and I. M. Pei. Aside from the snob appeal of being known by an initial or two, parents may consider this a way of passing down a traditional family name or the name of someone they admire while actually calling the child something else. For example, Fitzgerald's full name was Francis Scott Key Fitzgerald, but he went by Scott. (He was named for Francis Scott Key, the lawyer and poet who wrote "The Star-Spangled Banner.")

PUTTING IT ALL TOGETHER

As you narrow down your choices, you will doubtless want to compare your options, keeping in mind the considerations of sound, metrics, nicknames and diminutives, and initials. Even a name that meets all these criteria may sound great to you one day and not so good the next. For this reason, it is a good idea to keep your name ideas together in a notebook, on index cards, or on a pad of paper.

To keep track of the many variations inherent in any name (John Kenneth Galbraith, John K. Galbraith, Johnny, etc.), make a simple list for each name like this:

John Kenneth Galbraith = JKG
John K. Galbraith
John Galbraith = JG
John = Johnny

or:

Sarah Margaret Ferguson = SMF
Sarah M. Ferguson
Sarah Ferguson = SF
Sarah = Fergie?

When you think of a name you like, write it down in the format above. Then come back to it a few days or a week later and see if you still feel the same way about it. When you find a name you keep coming back to—a name that, over and over, seems to radiate a special happiness, integrity, and style—you'll know that is the name for your child.

3
CREATORS

A name in lights. A Pulitzer Prize. A gold record. An Academy Award. They are all symbols of success of a special kind: in the world of the arts. If a solo exhibit at a museum sounds more attractive to you than a seat on its board of directors, consider the names that follow. They belong to some of the world's top painters, poets, novelists, film directors, dancers, composers, actors, and musicians, and they are all names that cast a creative glow. The fact that many actors change their names to reflect their aspirations should be enough to convince you that in the arts, names can count a great deal. Yet to *any* creative spirit, in any walk of life, to have a good name—one that seems to fit—is a simple but enduring pleasure.

That this chapter is the longest in the book is no accident. Many people are creative, yet they will not become famous. Creativity is the most prevalent human characteristic of all. . . .

GIRLS' NAMES

Adrienne Creativity and strength of character are bound together in her name, with its echoes of the Adriatic Sea and ancient Greek and Roman civilization. Adrienne means "of the Adriatic coast." (Hadrian and ADRIAN are the masculine forms.) Adria comes from the same root and, while less familiar, sounds more contemporary. Poet and feminist Adrienne Rich and fashion designer Adrienne Vittadini are the twentieth century's standard-bearers for this name.

Aimee, Aimée Admiration and adoration may be in store for the one who bears this French name, which means "beloved." It is usually pronounced the same as Amy, but if the accent is used that would indicate the French pronunciation, eh-MAY. One creative and famous Aimee was the evangelist Aimee Semple McPherson, whose theatrical stage and radio performances made her a unique celebrity in the 1920s.

Alana See LANA.

Ali, Ally She could be the girl next door, or she could just be starring in the Hollywood version. Ally Sheedy and Ali MacGraw have helped give this name a popular, modern slant. Ali and Ally can be considered independent names, or they could be used as short forms of ALEXANDRA, ALICE, or Alison.

Alice Smart, and often wise and magical, is the popular image of Alice. There are Pulitzer Prize–winning writer Alice Walker, and English poet and essayist Alice Meynell to keep up this image. Alice is a variation of Adelaide and was a popular name in the Middle Ages.

Alicia When she puts on her first pair of toe shoes, the ballet world may have a sudden sense of *déjà vu*. Ballerinas Alicia Markova and Alicia Alonso have put this name in front of the footlights. In any field, it seems to combine beauty, femininity, and artistry. Alicia developed from ALICE.

Allegra Light and lively, alive to music, passion, and art: all this is said just by saying her name. Ballerina Allegra Kent brought the name to the stage with the New York City Ballet. Longfellow used it in his poem "The Children's Hour," referring to one of his daughters as "laughing Allegra." In music, the direction *Allegro* means "in rapid tempo" or "lively."

Anaïs Keen perception, curiosity, and talent seem to go along with her name. Like Anaïs Nin, she may write novels and diaries that make her famous. Anaïs is a French form of ANNE and thus can be said to mean "grace."

Anita This pert and sprightly name belongs to English author Anita Brookner and to the screenwriter and novelist Anita Loos. Anita originated as a Spanish diminutive of Ana (Anna). See also ANNA.

Anna Determination, passion, and creativity combine in her sensible-sounding name. Great Annas include: Anna Pavlova in ballet; Anna Mary (Grandma) Moses in painting; Anna Akhmatova in poetry; Anna Freud in psychoanalysis; Anna Sokolow in choreography. Of Hebrew origin, like HANNAH and ANNE, Anna means "grace." In the New Testament, Anna was a prophetess who recognized the infant Jesus as the long-awaited Messiah (Luke 2:36–38).

Annette Even if she is not a star like Annette Funicello of "The Mickey Mouse Club," she is apt to be popular. This name is a variation of ANNE, with a French twist. Like Anne, it means "grace." Diminutive: Nettie.

Anouk Exotic and appealing is the subliminal meaning of her name. The talented actress Anouk Aimee, the well-known bearer of this name, appeared in Fellini's *8½*, among other films. Anouk is a form of ANNE, thus meaning "grace."

Aphra She might be independent, resourceful, and creative—perhaps bohemian—and her life story may turn out to be as interesting as her art. In the seventeenth century,

Aphra Behn was the first Englishwoman to make her living as a writer. She also served her country as a spy. The name comes from Hebrew and means "dust."

Aretha Her name brings to mind a strong, creative personality, and the rich voice of a soul-R&B-gospel angel like Aretha Franklin. The origin of this name may be the Latin *Arethusa*, the name of a nymph and now also a variety of orchid.

Astrid, Astred The popular children's author Astrid Lindgren (creator of Pippi Longstocking) has helped this delightful Scandinavian name become well known. It comes from an Old Norse name meaning "divine beauty." It may also bring to mind the Greek name ASTRAEA, meaning "starlike."

Audrey Vivaciousness melded with talent and an outgoing nature combined with an innate sophistication—that is the character suggested by her name. Of Teutonic origin, Audrey means "nobly strong." As the princess in the movie *Roman Holiday*, Audrey Hepburn was pure Audrey.

Augusta, Augustina, Augustine In a muffled Victorian drawing room, Augusta is the lady to bring in a bit of gusto. In the nineteenth century, Augusta Maywood was an American ballerina, known as a striking and racy character and the first American dancer to become famous on an international scale. Like the masculine form, AUGUSTUS, Augusta means "exalted, sublime, venerable." Diminutive: Gussie.

Ava Even if Hollywood is not in her future, she'll share some of the natural glamour of actress Ava Gardner, along with her subtly evocative name. Ava may be a variation of Avis (Latin, meaning "bird") or of EVA.

Beatrice, Beatrix Her gift, if she's true to her name, is to make others happy—perhaps as an artist and children's author like Beatrix Potter (whose full given name was Helen Beatrix); as a comedienne like Bea Arthur; or as a writer like English socialist Beatrice Webb. The name comes from Latin and means "she who blesses or makes happy." Nicknames: Bea, Bee, TRIX, TRIXIE, Trixy.

Beryl Beauty, artistry, and adventure combine in the popular image of Beryl. The name has been used more frequently in Britain than in the United States, and it brings to mind two accomplished Englishwomen: aviator, adventurer, and writer Beryl Markham (author of the memoir *West with the Night*) and ballerina Beryl Grey. Beryl is one of the most subtle "jewel" names. The name comes from the mineral beryl, which comes in shades ranging from white to yellow to green and blue. Emeralds and aquamarines are forms of beryl.

Bette She may well be an actress at heart, in the great tradition of Bette Davis and Bette Midler. Interestingly, Bette Midler was named by her mother for Bette Davis. This name may be pronounced with two syllables (like Betty) or with one syllable (like "bet"). Bette is a variant of ELIZABETH.

Bonnie, Bonny In Scotland, "bonnie" is the word for "pretty" or "fair," and natural beauty and charm may belong to Bonnie. The Scottish word actually comes from the French word *bon*, meaning "good." This sympathetic name is also associated with the popular singer-guitarist Bonnie Raitt.

Bridget, Brigid, Brigit, Brigitte High energy and good looks are part of the popular image of Bridget. She might be either Irish or Swedish, for Bridgit is the name of a patron saint of both those countries. The French form, Brigitte, recalls the kittenish glamour of Brigitte Bardot (whose real name is Camille Javal). The original Brigit (who lived before either of the saints) was a Celtic fire goddess. The name is said to mean "strength." Irish forms of the name include Brighid, Brigid, and Brigit. Swedish forms include Birgitta, Brigitta, Birgit, Britt, Brita, and Britta.

Candace, Candice Elegance and sophistication are associated with Candace. If she is an actress she might be like Candice Bergen. If she is talented in the visual arts, she may be a textile and interior designer like Candace Wheeler. Diminutive: Candi, Candy.

Carol, Carole Friendly, sympathetic, efficient, hard-working: all these are part of Carol's popular image. The name brings to mind comedienne Carol Burnett, actress Carol Channing, and singer Carole King. In Eastern Europe, Carol is actually a masculine name, which is what one would expect from its origin. It comes from Carolus, the medieval Latin form of CHARLES.

Carson This lively, interesting name is a last name that has been used as a first name. In the past, such family names were often given to boys only—except in the South, where it was also common to give them to girls (such as the Georgia-born novelist Carson McCullers). In the 1980s, this practice of giving family names to girls has become fashionable all over the United States.

Cecilia, Cécile, Cecily, Cicely The dignified, yet musical, sound of her name links her with integrity and beauty. Saint Cecilia was a Roman Christian martyr, who, according to legend, sang as she was tortured for her faith and was later named the patron saint of music. Actress Cicely Tyson is a famous modern bearer of this name, which comes from an ancient Roman clan name.

Charlotte She is likely to be proper, feminine, with an artistic bent—and perhaps a hidden darker side. Charlotte Brontë, author of *Jane Eyre*, became one of the most famous Charlottes. Another literary Charlotte was English poet Charlotte Mary Mew. The name originated as a feminine form of CHARLES. Italian version: Carlotta. Diminutives: LOTTIE, Lotty, Lotta, Lotte. Charleen and Charlene are modern variants, and as such they sound less stuffy and old-fashioned, but they have not yet achieved the same level of acceptance and respectability as Charlotte.

Chere, Cher, Shere She may be a star, a maverick, or both—like the indomitable actress Cher. Cher took the name as a stage name (her given name is Cherilyn), but those given the name by their parents may always feel especially loved, for *chère* in French means "dear" or "darling." (*Cher* is actually the masculine form in French.)

Cheri, Cherie, Shari, Sheri, Sherry A sweeter, more gentle version of CHERE. Cheri and Cherie are the French spellings; Shari and Sherry are the more modern American variations, which may bring to mind television actress and puppeteer Shari Lewis. Shere (as in sex researcher Shere Hite) is an unusual variant spelling.

Cheryl A modern outlook seems to go with this modern name. A Cheryl may have an eye for design, fashion, and trends—or she may *be* the fashion, like beauty idol Cheryl Tiegs. Cheryl may have developed either from CHERE or CHARLOTTE. Cheryll, Cherrill, Sheryl, and Sherrill are alternative spellings.

Cindy, Cyndi, Cyndy She may be like CYNTHIA, except a lot more down to earth. She may use her talent to become a rock star, like Cyndi Lauper, or to rise on the fast track (perhaps in advertising, marketing, or promotion). All of these are short forms of CYNTHIA.

Clara Generous, accomplished, attractive—count on Clara to spread some cheer on a gloomy day. Clara Schumann was a composer, pianist, and beloved wife of composer Robert Schumann. Saucy Clara Bow was the " 'It' Girl" of silent films in the Roaring Twenties. The name comes from the Latin word *clara*, meaning "bright."

Claudette, Claudine Gorgeous, alluring, a bit campy, and fun is the image of Claudette. For the evidence, look no farther than Claudette Colbert in the 1934 Hollywood extravaganza *Cleopatra*. This French name is the feminine diminutive of CLAUDE and has an in-built European sophistication. Minus the "ette" diminutive, Claudette becomes Claudine. CLAUDIA is the more sober, Latin form.

Colette, Collette Charming, a bit decadent, and thoroughly entertaining is the popular image of Colette. Most of this comes from French novelist Colette (author of *Gigi*), which was the professional name of Sidonie-Gabrielle Colette. This French name (from Latin) means "a collar" or "a necklace." It can also be a short form of Nicolette.

Crystal A precious beauty: that is the stereotype of Crystal. Known to many people because of country-and-western singer Crystal Gayle, the name brings to mind a valued and fragile possession, like a crystal goblet or chandelier.

Cybill See SIBYL.

Cynthia She may be incredibly beautiful, poised, talented, kind—and a bit unreachable—if she is true to her name. Like Cynthia Gregory, she may make a splendid ballerina. Cynthia was another name for ARTEMIS, the Greek goddess of the moon. Poets have used this lithe and silvery name as a personification of the moon.

Daryl She could be as darling as a girl named Darlene, but with a bit more sophistication. Actress Daryl Hannah (*Splash*, *Wall Street*) has made this name well known. Like Darlene, it means "beloved" or "dear."

Demi Popular, artistic, and good-looking is the popular image of Demi. The name is well known because of actress

Demi Moore. It could possibly be a short form of DEMETER or DEMETRIA. In French, the word *demi* means "half."

Denise, Denice Pleasure is part of the meaning of this name, which comes from the name of the Greek god Dionysus, the god of wine. Whether or not she becomes a pop singer like Deniece Williams or an acclaimed poet like Denise Levertov, artistic pursuits could be her pleasure. Denise is the feminine form of DENNIS. Alternative spellings: Denyse, Dennise, Denese, Deneice, Deniece.

Dinah, Dina Beauty combines with toughness in this name, which is best known for the elegant Dinah Shore. The name's meaning comes from the Old Testament story (Genesis 34) of Jacob's beautiful daughter Dinah, whose abduction by a young ruler was brutally avenged by her brothers. Thus the name is said to mean "judged" or "avenged." Dina, if pronounced DEE-na (as in Dina Merrill, the actress), might also be considered a short form of Deanna or DIANA.

Dione, Dionne Lovely, talented, and original is the way most people would describe Dionne. Singer Dionne Warwick brought the name into the forefront in the 1960s, with hits like "I Say a Little Prayer," "Do You Know the Way to San Jose," and "I'll Never Fall in Love Again." In Greek mythology, Dione was the mother of the goddess of love, Aphrodite.

Djuna Inventive, exotic, cultured, and a bit eccentric is the image of Djuna—created by the celebrated writer Djuna Barnes (*Nightwood*). The name is pronounced "juna."

Dolly, Dollie She is apt to be as cute and sweet as her name, and like Dolly Parton she could have bushels of talent and gumption as well. Dolly is sometimes a nickname for DOROTHY or DOROTHEA.

Donna Attractive and feminine is the popular image of Donna. The name may be most often associated with singer

Donna Summer and movie and TV star Donna Reed. The name comes from the Italian word for "lady."

Doris This name suggests a lively, precocious child. Who knows where her talent will take her? She could end up a novelist like Doris Lessing, a movie star like Doris Day, or a tennis star like Doris Hart. In Greek mythology, Doris was a sea nymph and the name of a region of ancient Greece.

Dorothy She may be as clever as English detective novelist Dorothy Sayers and as witty as writer Dorothy Parker if she fits her gracious, somewhat grand-sounding name. The name comes from Greek and Latin and means "gift of God." Diminutives: DOLLY, Doll, Dot, Dottie. See also DOROTHEA.

Drew Attractive, likable, and privileged is the popular image of Drew. The name is known today for the actress Drew Barrymore, who played the little girl in *E.T. the Extra-terrestrial.* Drew is a family name, known especially for the Drew acting family, brought into use as a first name.

Edith, Edie In the late 1980s, her name sounds old-ladyish, but it has a distinguished and colorful past that could eventually inspire its revival. Famous Ediths include novelist Edith Wharton, singer Edith Piaf, poet Edith Sitwell (also famous for her love of exotic costumes and publicity), and Hollywood costume designer Edith Head, winner of many Academy Awards. The nickname Edie is reminiscent of heiress Edie Sedgwick, who in the heyday of 1960s pop culture was part of Andy Warhol's retinue. The name is Old English and refers to "one who fights for the family possessions."

Edna With this name there is a chance she could make her mark in the world as a writer. Ever since poet Edna St. Vincent Millay was born in 1892, the name's literary reputation has been assured. Edna comes from the Hebrew for "delight," a word similar to Eden.

Ella This simple musical-sounding name could herald a wonderful singer, like Ella Fitzgerald. Scholars disagree on the meaning of this name, but it is of Germanic origin and may mean "elfin" or "all."

Emily, Emilie She is diligent, artistic, quietly ambitious, and has a kind and generous nature, if she fits the popular image of Emily. Many Emilys have excelled as writers, including Emily Dickinson, Emily Brontë (author of *Wuthering Heights*), and Emily Post. This name originated as a Roman family name, Aemilius.

Erica, Erika Interesting and unpredictable, she could do about anything—except what's already been done. Writer Erica Jong left her mark on the world with her bestselling novel *Fear of Flying*. Erica is a feminine form of ERIC.

Erma, Ermina Her name may sound like a cross between a yawn and a groan, but there's still no stopping Erma. She may even end up as famous and popular as writer Erma Bombeck. Erma is a short form of Ermina, from Latin, meaning "noble." These names are also sometimes used as short forms of Hermione. Irma and Irmina are variant spellings.

Estelle Her name may currently sound a bit middle-aged, but Estelle is still likely to be beautiful and starry-eyed. The name is familiar because of actress Estelle Parsons, or Estelle Getty (Sophia of "The Golden Girls"). It comes from the Old French word "estoile," meaning "star."

Ethel What better place for Ethel than on the stage? In theater and music, this name has a great tradition, from Ethel Barrymore to Ethel Waters to Ethel Merman. Ethel comes from Old English and means "noble."

Eudora Her rather exotic classical name could be the beginning of a brilliant literary career—such as that of Eudora Welty, whose fiction, set mostly in her native Mississippi, won her the Pulitzer Prize and many other honors. This name, from the Greek, means "good gift."

Fay, Faye, Fae Her delightful, whimsical-sounding name comes from the Old French word "fae," meaning "fairy." Fay Wray was the name given to a baby girl born in Canada, fated for film immortality opposite King Kong. The name also belongs to the actress Faye Dunaway.

Flannery Like CARSON, this distinctive name is a family name brought into use as a first name. It too has been made famous by a Southern writer, Flannery O'Connor.

Georgia, Georgiana She might be brilliantly creative, with a flair for the dramatic—like the great American artist Georgia O'Keeffe. Georgia is the feminine of GEORGE, but the painter Georgia O'Keeffe helped give the name a resonance all its own. The variation Georgiana sounds more old-fashioned. It is often associated with the great stage comedienne Georgiana Drew Barrymore, mother of the famed Barrymore family of actors.

Gertrude She may be strong willed and sharp witted if she is true to her name's meaning, "spear strength." This Germanic name brings to mind the writer Gertrude Stein (*Four Saints in Three Acts, Autobiography of Alice B. Toklas*); the German feminist Gertrude Baumer; and the American heiress and sculptor Gertrude Vanderbilt Whitney. Diminutives: Gertie, Trudy.

Gilda Energetic, tough, and very funny is what the world expects Gilda to be—like comedienne Gilda Radner. The name is said to come from the Celtic, meaning "servant of God."

Ginger A home-baked cookie with a touch of spice . . . and Hollywood's wonderful dancer and actress Ginger Rogers, kicking up her heels with Fred Astaire: these are the beloved images of Ginger. The name is traditionally a nickname for VIRGINIA.

Gladys Whether she's got the Pips singing backup, like Gladys Knight, or a Welsh church choir, as one might expect from her Welsh name, Gladys can be hot. To some people her name may sound middle-aged, but that is not something to stop a determined Gladys from achieving her dreams. Of Welsh origin, the name's meaning is uncertain.

Grace Blessings seem to fall naturally on the typical Grace. More than simply graceful, beautiful, or talented, Grace is someone like the actress Grace Kelly, who married a prince; Grace Slick, who led the Jefferson Airplane to the top of the pop charts and West Coast hippie culture; comedienne Gracie Allen paired with George Burns; Gracie Mansion, starting the hottest new art gallery in New York City; Grace Jones photographed in her very wildest guise. Grace was a popular name in the American colonies, in remembrance of the grace of God. Later it came to be identified with secular meanings as well, such as physical grace and the Three Graces of Greek mythology.

Greer Her rather masculine-sounding name could be a plus in many fields. It has become associated with the talented (and feminine) actress Greer Garson. It is a form of the masculine name Gregor, which is a version of GREGORY used especially in Scotland.

Greta Gorgeous is one way of describing Greta, especially if her last name is Garbo. In unforgettable films like *Anna Karenina* and *Ninotchka*, the radiantly expressive Greta Garbo made this simple German name world famous. It is a short form of Margarete (MARGARET), which means "pearl."

Gwendolyn, Gwendolin, Guendolen Her Welsh name has an air of mystery and romance, and a literary flavor as well. It may bring to mind the Pulitzer Prize-winning poet Gwendolyn Brooks. In Welsh, "gwen" means "white"; what the rest of the name once signified is not known. Shorter variations: Gwen, Gwenn, Gwyn, Gwynne.

Heather Her name comes from a pretty but hearty plant, and it suggests a person of similar nature. Her healthy good looks and exuberance could take her far. For dancer Heather Watts, that meant as far as leading roles with the New York City Ballet.

Hedy Glamour and beauty are associated with her name, along with an appealing candor and simplicity. This formerly humble name gained star status in the 1930s and 1940s because of Hollywood actress Hedy Lamarr. Hedy originated as a diminutive of Hedwig, a German name that means "refuge in battle."

Hilda Her name has not been much used in recent years, and it has an Old World feel. This ancient English name might bring to mind acclaimed poet Hilda Doolittle ("H.D."). Hilda is of Anglo-Saxon origin, from a root meaning "combat" or "war."

Holly Industrious, plucky, and even a bit spiky like the pretty Christmas plant she's named for, she may excel in some aspect of the dramatic arts—perhaps like actress Holly Hunter, the star of *Raising Arizona* and *Broadcast News.*

Hope An aura of calm and goodwill surrounds her name. This name was a popular girl's name among Puritans in colonial America, along with names like Charity and Faith. It is associated today with actress Hope Lange.

Hortense A bit flowery, but with a classical strength and beauty, is the impression created by her name, which comes from Latin and means "gardener." It brings to mind writer Hortense Calisher.

Imogen, Imogene Perceptive, independent, and original, perhaps she will be one of America's great photographers—like Imogen Cunningham—or a TV comedienne like Imogene Coca. The meaning of the name is uncertain; it may come from the Latin word for "innocent."

Ingrid Whatever she does, in her off hours she can enjoy seeing a fellow Ingrid—Ingrid Bergman—in classic films such as *Notorious* and *Casablanca.* Art critic Ingrid Sischy is another notable Ingrid. This sophisticated-sounding Scandinavian name comes from Norse mythology and includes the name of the god Ing. Scholars disagree on the name's exact meaning.

Irma, Irmina See ERMA.

Isadora, Isidora This aggressively artistic name makes her seem destined to do something exotic, somewhat shocking, but very successful—like Isadora Duncan's barefoot dances in revealing Greek tunics and veils. Isadora is the feminine form of Isidore, the name of two esteemed Spanish saints. The name comes from Greek and means "gift of Isis."

Ivy Charming yet mysterious as an old house covered with vines is the image of Ivy. She could be a writer, like Ivy Compton-Burnett. The Victorian sound of her name seems to indicate that whatever she does, it will be civilized.

Jasmine See JESSAMINE.

Jennifer Her name can sound both artistic and analytical, as if she could be an engineer, architect, fashion designer, sculptor—or perhaps a brilliant painter like Jennifer Bartlett, or an acclaimed stage-lighting designer like Jennifer Tipton. The first syllable of this Welsh Celtic name means "white," and the meaning of the rest is unknown. Another form of the name is GUINEVERE. Diminutive: JENNY.

Jenny, Jennie Popularity seems to be a natural part of

this friendly-sounding name. In the nineteenth century, Jenny Lind was a wildly popular soprano from Sweden who became known as "the Swedish Nightingale." In the 1980s artist Jenny Holzer brought electronics, language, and flashing lights into her popular paintings. Jenny originated as a diminutive of Jane or Janet. It is also used as a diminutive of JENNIFER.

Jessamine, Jessamyn, Jasmine An attractive blend of strength and femininity surrounds her name, along with a touch of the exotic. The name is known in the arts for writer Jessamyn West. Jessamine, Jessamyn, and Jasmine are also names of a plant known for its fragrant yellow flowers. Its origin is Persian.

Jessica With actresses Jessica Lange and Jessica Tandy, newscaster Jessica Savitch, and author Jessica Mitford before her, Jessica seems to promise only the best. In the 1980s this name suddenly became very popular, maybe because Jessica sounds vaguely aristocratic but not snobbish. Neither the origin or meaning of the name are clear. It can be traced back to the Hebrew name Iscah (Genesis 11:29), which means "God beholds," and it was used by Shakespeare for a character in *The Merchant of Venice.* Variations: Jess, Jessie.

Jessie See JESSICA.

Joan She may be a woman of strong character and charisma—who can, if she wishes, hide behind a seemingly ordinary name. Joan Crawford, Joan Collins, Joan Baez, Joan Didion, and Joan Sutherland all show that this is no name for lightweights. It is a feminine form of JOHN.

Joanna, Johanna This name has a more gracious, old-fashioned sound than JOAN, JANET, or JEAN, to which it is related. The Scottish poet Joanna Baillie is one example of a highly accomplished Joanna from the past. Like JOAN, et al., Joanna originated as a feminine form of JOHN, which means "gift of the Lord." Joanne (as in the name of the actress Joanne Woodward) and Jo Ann are modern variations of this name.

Jodie, Jody You might find Jodie in jeans and pigtails in the backyard treehouse—or starring in the latest movie. The name is often associated with actress Jodie Foster. It is sometimes used as a masculine name, which gives it a tomboyish slant. As a feminine name, Jodie originated as a diminutive of JUDITH.

Joni Creative, interesting, but with a popular touch, she could become a popular singer-songwriter like Joni Mitchell. The name is a variation of JOAN.

Judy Expressive and creative, she is apt to be well liked wherever she goes. She could even be wildly popular, like actress Judy Garland or author Judy Blume—or popular and a bit controversial, like artist Judy Chicago. Judy originated as a diminutive of JUDITH.

June Her name seems to combine both beauty and strength. It comes from the lovely springtime month of June, which is named for the stately Roman goddess Juno, a patron of marriage and a special protectress of women. It is often connected with actresses June Lockhart and June Allyson.

Karen With its pleasant, uncomplicated sound, her name can serve her well in almost any setting. It is known to many people because of singer Karen Carpenter or Baroness Karen Blixen, the Danish author of the famous memoir *Out of Africa* (written under the nom de plume Isak Dinesen). Karen is a Scandinavian form of KATHERINE. Variant: Karin.

Kathleen She may have a classic glamour, like actress Kathleen Turner—or her own special style. This romantic, lyrical-sounding name is an Irish form of KATHERINE.

Kim She may have the type of beauty that lingers in the

mind, like Hollywood actress Kim Novak. Novak's success made the name popular for girls. Until she took it as a professional name, it was known mainly for the boy hero of Rudyard Kipling's famous novel *Kim.* The name Kimberley or Kimberly is accepted as the "full" name, though in fact it was not originally related.

Kiri She is bound to be delightful and popular with a name like Kiri. She may even become a beloved opera star like soprano Kiri Te Kanawa. Te Kanawa was born in New Zealand of Maori parents, the reason for her unusual name. (The Maori are the aboriginal people of New Zealand.)

Kirsten, Kristen The many variations of this name may boggle the mind, but what they have in common is their bright, attractive, and currently popular sound. Kirsten is a Danish and Norwegian form of Christine, associated with famous Norwegian soprano Kirsten Flagstad. Like CHRISTINE, it comes from Greek and means "Christian." Though it sounds like a Scandinavian name, Kristen is not used in Scandinavian countries. It came into use in English-speaking countries as a variation of Kirsten or Kristina (the Swedish form of Christine). Alternate forms include Kristen, Kersten, Kerstin, Keirstan, Kirsteen, Kirstin, and Kirstyn. Additional variations on these names are Kirsty, Kirsti, Kirstie, and Kerstie, which are Scottish forms of Christine. For more on another option, see KRISTY.

Kitty Her sweet-sounding name has a tough side too, and her strength and grit should not be underestimated. The name is known in TV-land for actress Kitty Carlisle and in theatrical history for Kitty Clive, an acclaimed eighteenth-century English actress. Kitty is a diminutive of KATHERINE, long used as an independent name.

Kristy Her vivacious-sounding name is popular nowadays because of actress Kristy McNichol. It seems to have originated as a diminutive of KRISTEN or of Kristina, the Swedish form of CHRISTINE. Alternative spellings: Kristi, Kristie.

Kyra Grace and beauty seem a natural part of this lyrical name. Kyra might be a ballerina, like Kyra Nichols. This name comes from the Greek word *kyrios*, meaning "lord."

Lana Movie-star beautiful, perhaps a bit indolent, with a come-hither look, Lana may even be as glamorous as film star Lana Turner. The name is a short form of Alana, a feminine form of ALAN.

Laura, Laurie Her pretty, old-fashioned, traditional name is full of positive connotations. One Laura—Laura Ingalls Wilder—grew up as a pioneer on the American prairies and later wrote beloved children's books based on her memories (the "Little House" series). Acclaimed composer/performer Laurie Anderson may be the most popular Laurie of the 1980s. The name is a feminine form of LAURENCE.

Lauren She could be a true American beauty, with a healthy dose of self-assurance, wit, and charm. Movie star Lauren Bacall became famous for her stunning performances, her green eyes, her low voice, and her marriage to Humphrey Bogart. The name is derived from LAURA or LAURENCE.

Lee An attractive, self-assured, and talented woman is the current image of Lee. Take, for instance, actress Lee Remick and artist Lee Krasner (who was also the wife of the painter Jackson Pollock). The name comes from the Anglo-Saxon family name Lee, which means "meadow." Leigh has the same meaning. The name is also used for men, for more on which see the listing under "Boys' Names."

Lena, Lina She may seem to glow with talent and creativity, if she is true to her name. She could be a great singer like Lena Horne, or an acclaimed film director like Lina Wertmuller. Both Lena and Lina originated as short forms of HELENA, which means "the bright one." They could also be short forms of CAROLINA, PAULINA, and other such names.

Leontine, Leontyne Powerful, sensitive, determined, artistic: all these are qualities of the typical Leontyne. She may be something like Leontyne Price, the soprano from Laurel, Mississippi, who became an acclaimed star of the Metropolitan Opera and the best Verdi soprano of her time. Leontyne, from the Latin, means "lionlike."

Lili, Lille, Lillie, Lily Her light-hearted name sounds full of grace and life. The name is associated with acclaimed nineteenth-century actress and society figure Lillie Langtry (called "the Jersey Lily"), and with the French composer Lili Boulanger. Lili and Lillie are variations of LILIANE.

Lillian, Liliane One may think of Lillian as a bit flowery and old-fashioned, but in bygone days, Lillian could be something else again—like playwright Lillian Hellman or silent film star Lillian Gish. The name is frequently said to mean "a lily" (Latin for "lily" is *lilium*). It has also been suggested that it developed from ELIZABETH. Liliane is the French spelling. Diminutives: Lil, LILY, LILI, LILLIE, LILLE. The last four are also considered independent names. Other variations: Lila, Lilah.

Lina See LENA.

Linda Her name sounds both attractive and intelligent. It was especially popular in the United States from the 1940s through the early 1960s, and famous Lindas include actress Linda Evans and television newscaster Linda Ellerbee. Linda comes from the Spanish word for "beautiful."

Lindsay In the 1980s, this name—with its upscale ring—became one of the most popular names for newborn girls. Actress Lindsay Wagner is one well-known Lindsay. The name is a Scottish surname that in the past was used mostly for men. Variations include Lindsey, Lynsey, Lyndsey, Lindsy, Linsey, and Linsay.

Lisa Creative, talented Lisa could do about anything. She could even become a popular television actress like Lisa Bonet (Denise Huxtable on "The Cosby Show"). This variation of ELIZABETH first became popular in the 1950s.

Liv Her name combines a sense of beauty and a strong will. It is best known because of Norwegian actress Liv Ullmann, star of many of Ingmar Bergman's films. Liv may be an independent name, or used as a short form of LIVIA or OLIVIA.

Liza Good humor, fun, and sparkling beauty combine in the popular image of Liza. If she is not a stunning singer/dancer/actress like Liza Minnelli, she's bound to be a showstopper at whatever she does. Liza is a short form of ELIZABETH.

Loretta, Lorette Her name may have a slightly plaintive sound, but on the inside Loretta is both talented and tough—if she is like country-and-western star Loretta Lynn or actress Loretta Swit. There is no consensus on the meaning or origin of this name, which seems to have come into popular use in the twentieth century.

Louise, Louisa Gentility, creativity, and a stylish flair may combine in the typical Louise. In the arts, famous Louises include silent film star Louise Brooks and modern sculptors Louise Bourgeoise and Louise Nevelson. The popular image of Louisa is someone a bit more old-fashioned and literary, perhaps like Louisa May Alcott, author of *Little Women.* Louise and Louisa are feminine forms of LOUIS.

Lucille One should not expect every Lucille to be as funny as Lucille Ball on "I Love Lucy," but she may be a good old-fashioned, nice person and have a better than average sense of humor. Lucille is a French form of LUCY.

Lucinda Her name suggests that she might have been raised on an English manor, complete with a nursery and a nanny—or at least in a house full of antiques and books. When she grows up she could be an illustrator, editor, classical musician, dancer—or perhaps a modern choreographer like Lucinda Childs. The name is a form of LUCY, perhaps combined with BELINDA, dating back several hundred years.

Lynn, Lynne A simple charm surrounds her name, which seems to leave open many options. She could even become an acclaimed actress like Lynn Redgrave. The name may have come into use as a short form of CAROLYN. Lynn is also a surname of Celtic or Anglo-Saxon origin, meaning "cascade" or "pool."

Maeve Gracious, colorful, charming: that is the impression created by her name. This traditional Irish name is familiar to readers of contemporary fiction because of writer Maeve Binchy. It comes from the name of a first-century Irish queen. Maven, Mavin, and Mavine are variations of this name.

Mahala, Mahalia She could be strong, sensitive, and expressive—and a great gospel singer like Mahalia Jackson. The name comes from Hebrew and means "tenderness."

Marcia, Marsha Her name suggests a successful, fighting spirit, ready to climb to the top in any field. The name is from Latin; like MARK and MARCUS, it is linked to Mars, the Roman god of war. Marsha is a modern variation, used by the Pulitzer Prize-winning playwright Marsha Norman (*'Night, Mother*).

Margaux Beautiful, elegant, and perhaps a bit decadent is the popular image of Margaux. This name is associated with actress Margaux Hemingway. Before Margaux Hemingway made it famous, it was not used as a first name and was known only to wine lovers as the name of a very fine French wine.

Margo, Margot She has creativity, dramatic flair, and plenty of get-up-and-go, if she is a typical Margo. She may use her talents to become a designer, architect, skater, gymnast, or a great ballerina like Margot Fonteyn. Or she may become an actress like Margot Kidder (Lois Lane in the *Superman* films, among other roles). The name is a French diminutive of MARGARET, famous in history because of Margaret of Valois, called *la reine Margot* ("Queen Margot").

Marguerite A Parisian cafe, a world-class library, a modern science laboratory, a field of flowers: they are all places one might find Marguerite. Author Marguerite Yourcenar was the first woman to be elected to the French Academy. Writer and filmmaker Marguerite Duras is yet another beautiful and brilliant Marguerite. The name is a variation of MARGARET, and in French it also means "daisy."

Maria Generous and warm-hearted is one common image of Maria. The name brings to mind Maria Callas, the great dramatic soprano. In Spanish and Italian, Maria is one of the most popular names. Often given in honor of the Virgin Mary, it is the Latin form of MARY.

Marian, Marion A leading artist, or an artistic type of leader, is what Marian might be. Marian Anderson became the first black singer to perform with the Metropolitan Opera. The name originated as a diminutive of MARY and dates from the Middle Ages. In the United States it has occasionally been used for men.

Mariel Sophisticated and beautiful is the image of Mariel, characteristics of the fashionable actress Mariel Hemingway. Mariel is a variation of MARY or MARIE.

Marilyn A suggestion of glorious beauty and unforgettable appeal are a part of her name, which is known the world over because of Marilyn Monroe. The name was created by combining MARY and LYNN.

Marlene, Marlena A sultry femme fatale, probably a shimmering blond, she might be found dangerously close to the wrong man, the front lines, or Hollywood's brightest lights. Actress Marlene Dietrich made this German name famous. (It is pronounced mar-LAY-nah in German.) It comes from the name Magdalena, the Latin name for St. Mary Magdalene.

Marlo Vivacious, creative, modern, and fun is the impression created by her name. Most often associated with actress Marlo Thomas, this unusual name has the advantages of a simple spelling and an attractive sound. It may have originated as a form of the surname Marlowe. Its similarity to the name MARGO suggests another reason for its appeal.

Mary Her simple, attractive name is one of the most popular of all time, used around the world at every level of society. The name came into use in honor of the Virgin Mary, mother of Jesus, and it has never lost its implication of pure goodness. It is linked with successful women in every walk of life, but in the arts it is associated especially with TV star Mary Tyler Moore, silent-film star Mary Pickford, impressionist painter Mary Cassatt, and author Mary Shelley (*Frankenstein*). Originally from Hebrew, the meaning of the name is not known. It has been variously interpreted as "bitter," "rebellion," and "star of the sea." Variations include: MARIA, MARIE, MIRIAM, MARIEL, and Moira (Scottish). Mary's many diminutives, often used as independent names, include MAE, MAMIE, MINNIE, MOLLY, and POLLY.

Mary Ann, Mary Anne, Marianne Energy, optimism, and goodwill all seem part of her name. This combination of MARY and ANNE was used in the eighteenth century, then became especially popular following World War II. The name is associated with journalist and writer Mary Ann Dolan, poet Marianne Moore, and English painter and traveler Marianne North.

Maven See MAEVE.

Mavis Her name sounds cheerful, industrious, and bright, even if one does not know that "mavis" is also a name for the song thrush. She might be a clever and esteemed writer, like Mavis Gallant, or perhaps a fine musician, painter, professor, or researcher. As the name of the bird, the name comes from Middle English (twelfth through fifteenth centuries).

May, Mae Her name sounds sweet and flowery, but she could be much more than that—like comedienne Mae West. This name is commonly thought to refer to the month of May, but it may have originally been a short form of MARY or MARGARET, a variation of MAIA, or a use of the Middle English noun "may," meaning "maiden." Though some may think of this as an old-ladyish name, its traditional sound and allusion to springtime may make it appealing to others.

Meredith With this name she may be a leader in the arts, or a creative leader in business, law, or almost any other field. Originally a masculine name, Meredith gradually came into use for women, perhaps because it sounds like it could be a form of MARY. Well-known female Merediths include actress Meredith Baxter-Birney, singer Meredith MacRae, and performance artist and composer Meredith Monk. The name is of Welsh origin, meaning "great chief." Alternative spellings: Merideth, Meridith.

Meret This delicate, unusual name is famous in the art world because of Meret Oppenheim, the surrealist artist who created, among other things, the world's only fur-lined tea cup (collection of the Museum of Modern Art, New York City).

Merle Distinctive and successful: that is one image created by her name. It recalls the glamorous Hollywood actress of the 1930s and 1940s, Merle Oberon. The name comes from the French word for "blackbird." For more on Merle as a masculine name, see the listing under "Boys' Names."

Meryl Her name implies both warmth and sophistication,

and it could take her about anywhere—such as from Yale to Hollywood, the path traveled by actress Meryl Streep. Meryl is a form of MURIEL.

Mia She could be as charming as a sparrow—and a popular actress like Mia Farrow. Mia might signify someone who is much doted on and desired, for in Italian "mia" means "my."

Miles She could be daring, dashing, creative, and inspiring—like Australian writer and feminist Miles Franklin, author of *My Brilliant Career.* The name may come from Latin, meaning "soldier," or it may come from the Old English name Milo, meaning "mild." Traditionally, it has been a masculine name. For more, see the listing under "Boys' Names."

Muriel Witty, sharp, stormy, gentle: Muriel could be any and all of these things. The name is associated in literature with Scottish novelist Muriel Spark, and Muriel Rukeyser, an American poet, feminist, and political activist. Muriel probably originated as the Old Irish name Muirgheal, meaning "sea bright," though it is sometimes said to mean "myrrh" (one of the gifts of the Magi to the baby Jesus).

Nadine Her name has a rather somber sound, and an international character. It is the French form of the Russian name NADIA, meaning "hope." It is known in literature because of South African writer Nadine Gordimer.

Natalie, Natala, Natalia She is bright and cheerful as Christmas morning, if she lives up to her name. It comes from the Latin word for "Holy Nativity," and is often said to mean "Christmas child." (The words *natal* and *native* come from the same root.) Actress Natalie Wood (whose given name was NATASHA) helped familiarize the United States with this French name. Natalia is the Spanish, Italian, and Russian version, best known for the ballerina Natalia Makarova.

Natasha, Nastassia, Nastassja She may be almost magnetically attractive, and have a European flair no matter where she is born. Actresses Nastassia Kinski and Natasha Richardson share the name. It is a Russian diminutive of NATALIA.

Nina, Ninon Her sprightly name has a particularly European flair. Nina Vyroubova was a well-known Russian-French ballerina; Ninon de Lanclos was a much celebrated French courtesan and cultural figure of the seventeenth century. Both Nina and Ninon are variations of ANNE or ANNA. Nina is Russian; Ninon is French.

Nora, Norah Her name sounds simple and straightforward, but she may well have a uniquely creative side. The name is associated with Nora Ephron, a popular contemporary writer and with Nora Joyce, who was a lifelong inspiration to her writer husband, James Joyce. This traditional Irish name originated as a short form of Honora. Noreen is a diminutive of Nora, sometimes used independently.

Noreen See NORA.

Olivia A grand elegance and delightful sophistication surround her name. It is well known because of the glamorous movie star Olivia de Havilland and the popular singer Olivia Newton-John. A more humble variation of the name is Olive. The name comes from the olive tree; the olive branch signifies peace.

Oprah Wise, warm, funny, and open-armed friendly is the popular image of Oprah—after TV talk show host Oprah Winfrey. Her wonderful name actually came about by chance. She was supposed to be given a biblical name, Orpah, but it was misspelled on her birth certificate as Oprah.

Paloma Her name has the beauty and grace of a work of art. The great artist Pablo Picasso gave the name to his daughter Paloma Picasso, who later became famous for her exquisite and luxurious jewelry designs. Paloma in Spanish means "dove," a symbol of peace.

Pauline, Paulina, Paulette Attractive, feminine, with an interesting personality: that could be a typical Pauline. Paulette may be similar, but more intriguing, and Paulina may project a hidden, inner strength. All these names are feminine forms of PAUL, which comes from the Latin word for "small." Pauline is French; Paulette is the French diminutive; and Paulina is Latin. They are often connected with actress Paulette Goddard, film critic Pauline Kael, and gorgeous supermodel Paulina Porizkova.

Pearl Precious, subtle, classic: that is a string of pearls, and it might be what Pearl is like too. However, two of history's most famous Pearls have been a bit more exotic. Pearl S. Buck won the Nobel Prize for her novels set in China. Pearl Primus was an acclaimed Trinidadian dancer and choreographer, noted for her use of anthropology and ancient ritual in her dances.

Peggy, Peg Creative, energetic Peggy might be a champion ice skater like Peggy Fleming, an art collector like Peggy Guggenheim, or a classical actress like Dame Peggy Ashcroft. Peggy and Peg are diminutives of MARGARET.

Raquel An adorable child in ribbons and bows . . . a voluptuous, attractive, sexily dressed woman . . . either could be Raquel. Naturally, her name brings to mind the beautiful Raquel Welch. Raquel is the French and Spanish form of RACHEL.

Reba Strong-willed and down-to-earth, she could even be a musical star like country-and-western singer Reba McEntire. Reba is a short form of REBECCA.

Rita She is attractive, colorful, and glamorous, if she is a typical Rita. The name is familiar because of the actress Rita

Hayworth, whose given name was Margarita. Rita, with its Italian or Spanish flair, is a short form of Margarita or MARGARET.

Roberta Her name seems to promise an interesting character. Roberta is the feminine form of ROBERT, but unlike many other feminizations of masculine names (Andrea, CARLA, CAROL, JOAN, JANE), Roberta has not been used enough to develop many variations The name is known in the arts because of Metropolitan Opera soprano Roberta Peters and pop singer Roberta Flack. The friendly sounding diminutive is Bobbie.

Rosanna She can be sweet and old-fashioned, and lively and modern too, if she is true to her name. She might be a popular actress like Rosanna Arquette, or simply look like one. The name is a combination of ROSE and ANNA.

Roz Smart, irreverent, and irresistibly funny is the ideal Roz. She might become a popular and hilarious cartoonist like Roz Chast. The name may be a form of ROSE, ROSA, ROSALIND, ROSALYN, ROSANNA, or particularly of Roza, a Slavic form of Rose.

Sandy Casual good looks and a likable, popular personality are part of the typical Sandy. She could be an actress like Sandy Duncan. The name was originally used as a diminutive of ALEXANDRA. It is now best known as a diminutive of SANDRA, or an independent name.

Shari See CHERI.

Sheena Beauty and glamour are associated with this exotic-sounding name which is familiar because of stylish singer Sheena Easton. It is an adaptation of the name Sine (pronounced SHEE-nah), which is a Scottish Gaelic form of JANE or JEAN.

Shelley She might be vivacious, funny, and friendly—and

she could be an actress like Shelley Winters or Shelley Duvall. The name comes from an old Anglo-Saxon place name.

Shere, Sheri, Sherry See CHERI.

Sheryl See CHERYL.

Shivaun, Sian, Siobhan This ancient Irish name has enjoyed a popular revival, so now it actually sounds very contemporary. Siobhan is the original form, but many variations are used that reflect the pronounciation (sha-VON), including Shivaun, Shavon, and Shavonne. The name is an Irish form of JOAN, as is Sian, another variation. It is associated in the theater with Shivaun O'Casey, actress, director, and daughter of playwright Sean O'Casey. Sian is pronounced like the masculine name Sean.

Sibyl, Sybil, Cybill She is gifted with a keen and sensitive intuition, if she fits her name. In Greek and Roman mythology, the sibyls were women who prophesied, with divine insight, into the realm of the gods. Perhaps it is fitting, then, that Cybill Shepherd rose to superstardom playing a television detective with a strong sixth sense. Actress Sybil Thorndike also brought this name fame in the dramatic arts.

Sigourney Her name sounds spirited, graceful, and tough: she could be all that *and* a talented actress. This name brings to mind actress Sigourney Weaver (*Alien, The Year of Living Dangerously, Gorillas in the Mist*).

Simone She may tend toward the mystical (Simone Weil), dramatic (Simone Signoret), or intellectual (Simone de Beauvoir), but whatever her talents, they could take her far. Simone is the French feminine form of SIMON.

Siobhan See SHIVAUN.

Sonia, Sonja, Sonya Sweet, clever, fascinating, hardworking: Sonia can be all these things. The world's most popular Sonia was Sonja Henie, a blonde Norwegian figure skater with a balletic style who in the 1930s became a worldwide sensation. She was called the "Pavlova of the Silver Blades." An artist of another type was Sonia Delaunay, an acclaimed graphic, textile, and fashion designer of the 1920s. Sonia is a diminutive of SOPHIA, often used as an independent name.

Sophia, Sofia, Sophie Her European name combines Old World elegance with Hollywood glamour. It is most often associated with actress Sophia Loren. The name comes from the Greek and means "wisdom." It originated in the Byzantine Empire as the name of Istanbul's great church Hagia Sophia ("divine wisdom") and thus became a favorite name in Greece and Russia.

Stevie A quirky charm surrounds a girl named Stevie. Although Stevie is a form of the masculine STEPHEN, it has seemed perfectly feminine as used by the witty English writer Stevie Smith, and by the rock singer Stevie Nicks.

Suzanne Her name combines grace and strength in an elegant way that is uniquely French. It is famous in ballet because of Suzanne Farrell, in movies and television because of Suzanne Somers and Suzanne Pleshette. Like SUSANNA and SUSAN, the name means "lily." Diminutives: Sue, Susie, Suzy.

Sybil See CYBILL.

Sylvia, Silvia Beautiful, popular, emotional, intelligent, she may be a wonderfully expressive actress, singer, designer, or poet. Sylvia means "of the woods" in Latin and recalls the popular "sylvan glades" of English poetry. Famous Sylvias include poet Sylvia Plath, English landscape architect Sylvia Crewe, teacher and novelist Sylvia Ashton-Warner, and the first publisher of James Joyce's novel *Ulysses*, Sylvia Beach.

Tallulah She could be flamboyant, opinionated, and all-around wonderful—like American stage actress Tallulah

Bankhead, a theatrical legend for her roles in plays of the 1930s and 1940s such as *The Little Foxes* and *The Skin of Our Teeth.* The name may come from Tallulah Falls in Georgia. It was also Tallulah Bankhead's grandmother's name.

Tama She could be a hot young artist or writer—like the popular chronicler of New York's "downtown" art scene, Tama Janowitz (*Slaves of New York*). This name could be used as a short form of Tamar or Tamara, which come from Hebrew and mean "palm tree."

Tammie, Tammy A down-home country feel permeates her name, which is often associated with country singer Tammy Wynette. The name may have originated as a diminutive of Tamsin or Thomasin (both feminine forms of THOMAS). It is also sometimes used as a diminutive of Tamar or Tamara.

Tanya Pretty, ambitious, talented, creative: Tanya can be all those things. The name is known to many because of country-and-western singer Tanya Tucker, who became a popular sensation at just age thirteen. Tanya is a Russian name, a diminutive of Tatiana. Alternative spelling: Tania.

Tatum When this name first appeared in screen credits, it sounded a bit odd. But your Tatum might be a hit in the movies, like Ryan O'Neal's daughter, Tatum O'Neal, whose talent and cheerful, wholesome personality now actually seem a part of this unusual name. A stylish alternative to Tatum might be Tate or Taite.

Tiffany If her name is Tiffany, she may be talented, popular, pretty—and worth a million. This name is known nowadays because of pop star Tiffany (full name Tiffany Renee Darwish), who by age sixteen had sold more than four million records and was a millionaire. The name has been traced to a medieval Latin word, *theophania*, meaning "manifestation of God." In medieval France, the form was Tifanie. Modern variations include: Tifani, Tiffani, and Tiffanie.

Tilda, Tillie, Tilly With this sweet, very old-fashioned name she may seem to wear her heart on her sleeve. She could be a good friend, or the author of good stories—like writer Tillie Olsen. Tilda and Tillie are short forms of MATILDA.

Tina She could be as wild as rock and roll's Tina Turner—or more low-key, like the bass player Tina Weymouth of the Talking Heads. Whatever she does, her name seems to promise that she'll have her own special style. The name originated as a short form of CHRISTINA.

Trudy See GERTRUDE.

Twyla With this name she could be a trendsetter. The name is often associated with the popular and original choreographer Twyla Tharp, who has created dances to a wide range of music, from classical pieces to Frank Sinatra songs. Twila is an alternate spelling. The precise origin of the name is not known.

Valerie Expressive, emotional, talented, she could become a singer, a composer, or perhaps a television star like Valerie Harper. Whatever her goals, she is apt to apply herself mightily, for the name comes from Latin and means "valorous" or "strong." Short form: Val.

Vanessa Her beautiful name comes from Greek and means "butterfly." It is known by association with such distinguished women as actress Vanessa Redgrave and artist Vanessa Bell, a member of the Bloomsbury group and a sister of Virginia Woolf.

Vanna The question is: what will Vanna wear? Something stunning, if she's true to her name. Vanna was a lucky name for Vanna White, who became a celebrity because of her role on TV's "Wheel of Fortune." Vanna could be a variation of VANESSA.

Virginia Famous in literature because of the groundbreaking writer Virginia Woolf (*To the Lighthouse*), this old-fashioned name is particularly feminine. Virginia means "virginal" or "pure."

Vita Vivid, lively, unique: that could be Vita. Her name comes from Latin and means simply "life." It may bring to mind English writer Vita Sackville-West, a member of the famous Bloomsbury group.

Vivien, Vivienne, Vivian While there is no guarantee she will be exquisite, Viviens tend to be *that* beautiful. She may also be a wonderful actress like Vivien Leigh (*Gone with the Wind, A Streetcar Named Desire*). Vivien comes from the Latin word for "lively."

Wanda Today her name is almost as rare as real magic wands, but it is famous in music history because of a Polish-French musician named Wanda Landowska, who almost single-handedly revived interest in the harpsichord in the twentieth century and founded France's École de Musique Ancienne. The meaning of this German name is uncertain.

Whitney Images of wealth, class, and popularity combine in her name. It may bring to mind heiress Gertrude Vanderbilt Whitney, who founded the Whitney Museum of American Art, or the gold-plated stardom of pop singer Whitney Houston. This is a last name that is sometimes used as a first name. Of Anglo-Saxon origin, it means "white island."

Willa Her name may bring to mind the wind on a vast prairie—and the great American author Willa Cather. Willa may be an Anglo-Saxon name, meaning "desired," or a short form of the Germanic name Wilhelmina.

Yoko A life of international fame and glamour could be in store for Yoko—like that of Yoko Ono, the widow of the Beatles's John Lennon, Yoko is a traditional and popular name in Japan.

Yolanda Saucy sambas, rowdy rhumbas, and all-American fun can be heard in her name. In the 1940s and 1950s, "Yolanda" was the female half of a popular ballroom dancing duo. She might still be a fabulous dancer, singer, waitress, comedienne, party-giver, or the world's best and friendliest telephone operator. The name may be related to VIOLA or Valentina.

Zelda Her dashing, jazzy, eccentric name is best known because of Zelda Fitzgerald, literary personality and wife of writer F. Scott Fitzgerald (*The Great Gatsby*). The name is a short form of the old Teutonic name Griselda.

Zora "The first will be last, and the last first" might be the motto for Zora, for though last in the alphabet, her name means "dawn." Zora Neale Hurston was a black American writer and anthropologist, acclaimed especially for her 1937 novel, *Their Eyes Were Watching God.* Zora is a Slavic form of Aurora, the name of the Roman goddess of the dawn.

BOYS' NAMES

Adrian This name has long had the cachet of culture, style, and sophistication. It brings to mind the great fashion designer of the 1930s and 1940s, Adrian (his full name was Gilbert Adrian Greenburgh), and in history it is associated with Roman Emperor Hadrian (Adrian), renowned for his love of beauty and the arts. The Pantheon in Rome was one of his many projects. From Latin, the name means "of Adria (Italy)" or "of the Adriatic coast."

Akira Bravery, brilliance, daring, violence, humor, pity, sacrifice, and entertainment are all part of this name, made famous by Japanese movie director Akira Kurosawa. This Japanese name is known around the world to film aficionados and associated with the humanity of Kurosawa's films such as *Rashomon* and *The Seven Samurai.*

Aldo See ALDOUS.

Aldous A seriously creative individual is what one might expect when meeting Aldous for the first time. This name is often connected with English writer Aldous Huxley (*Brave New World, Point Counter Point, Eyeless in Gaza*). Of Germanic origin, the name includes a word for "old" and is sometimes interpreted as meaning "from the old house." The variations Aldis and Aldus have a somewhat more sprightly feel, as does the Italian form, Aldo.

Alec Mild-mannered and creative Alec may achieve great things, like actor Sir Alec Guinness. Alternate spellings include Aleck, Alic, and Alick. This name originated as a short form of ALEXANDER.

Alistair Years of the "Masterpiece Theatre" series on television, introduced by Alistair Cooke, have shown to everyone what a select few knew all along: that this name bespeaks broad education, sophistication, and well-bred civility. This distinguished name is a Scottish Gaelic form of ALEX-

ANDER. The many forms include Alistair (the most common English spelling), Alasdair (the authentic Scottish spelling), Alastair, Allaster, Allistair, Allister, and Alisdair.

Alvar An Alvar is apt to have his own distinctive style—perhaps even to set the trends that others follow. This name is associated with modern Finnish architect and industrial designer Alvar Aalto. The meaning and origin are obscure; it may be from Old English like ALVIN.

Alvin He could be the most popular kid on the block, with equal measures of talent, friendliness, and creativity. One well-liked Alvin is the choreographer Alvin Ailey. The name is thought to come from Old English, and is interpreted as "elf friend" or "old friend." Variations include Alwin, Alwyn, Alvan, Elvin, Elwyn, and Elwin.

Ambrose His quirky name may indicate a highly creative, unusual person. In American literary history, the name is connected with journalist, satirist, and short-story writer Ambrose Bierce, who was widely acclaimed around the turn of the century. The name comes from a Greek word meaning "immortal."

Angus Kilts, lochs, and beautiful countryside come to mind with his name, which is far more common in Scotland than in the United States. This Gaelic name is also associated with British writer Angus Wilson, and was the name of a former county in Scotland.

Ansel American ingenuity and the rugged beauty of the American West are associated with his name, made famous by outdoor photographer Ansel Adams. This is a shortening of the Teutonic name Anselm.

Anthony, Antony Pride, energy, vitality: these are a few of the qualities commonly associated with Anthony. The name brings to mind a number of stars in the dramatic arts, including Anthony Quinn (*Zorba the Greek*), Anthony Perkins, and choreographer Antony Tudor. The name began as a Roman family name, as in Marc Antony. The original meaning is unknown. Diminutive: Tony.

Anton His name projects a vital energy, much like the name ANTHONY. The overall impression, however, is a shade more subdued. This Russian and German form of Anthony is often connected with Russian playwright and writer Anton Chekhov.

Archibald With this name he sounds destined for greatness: to inherit the ancestral manor, or to become a distinguished man of letters. Archibald MacLeish, a poet and a librarian of Congress, has contributed to recognition of this name in the United States. Of Germanic origin, meaning something like "noble and bold," this name has long been popular in Scotland. In other countries it may sound too affected for most tastes. For more on the diminutive, see ARCHIE.

Arlo This euphonic, plaintive name is perfect for a folk singer and composer—like Arlo Guthrie, the son of Woody Guthrie. The meaning of this name is obscure, but it could be a shortening of the Old English name Harlow.

Asher He may be the strong, silent type, as his name reveals little about him. The name is known in American art history because of Asher B. Durand, a painter of the Hudson River school. In Hebrew the name means "happy, blessed." Asher's euphonic similarity to currently popular names like ASHLEY and JOSHUA make it worth a second glance.

Athol Integrity and artistry seem to combine in Athol. The name is associated mainly with South African playwright Athol Fugard (*The Blood Knot*, *"Master Harold" and the Boys*), an Afrikaner known for his opposition to apartheid. The name is of Scottish origin, originally a place name.

Aubrey Wit, dash, and derring-do seem a natural part of

Aubrey. Best known for the stylish nineteenth-century British illustrator Aubrey Beardsley, this name has a rather English aristrocratic ring. Of Germanic and French origin, it means "elf rule."

Barnett With this name he might seem both stylish and distinguished. This English surname has been used as a first name from time to time, most notably by abstract artist Barnett Newman. Alternative spelling: Barnet.

Barton See BURTON.

Basil Interesting, inquisitive, and perhaps a bit stuffy is the popular image of Basil. The name's British feel can be partly explained by its association with Basil Rathbone, who played Sherlock Holmes in the movies.

Beau He has to be handsome, if his name is Beau. He could be a popular actor like Beau Bridges. Or, his inimitable sense of style could make him a legend in the highest circles—like Beau Brummell, the famous arbiter of style in the English court of George IV. In French, *beau* means "handsome." In English, it means "a boyfriend or sweetheart."

Ben Good humor and good will are indispensable traits in the typical Ben. The name is known for the wonderful seventeenth-century poet Ben Jonson, British actor Ben Kingsley, and entertainer Ben Vereen. Ben is sometimes used as an independent name, or it may be used as a short form of names like BENNETT, Benson, Benton, or especially BENJAMIN.

Bert Friendly and generous is the stereotype of Bert. He might even be an actor and comedian like Bert Lahr (the Cowardly Lion in *The Wizard of Oz*). The name is used on its own or as a short form of names like ALBERT and BERTRAM. For a variation with a different twist, see BURT.

Blake Likeable, creative, but perhaps something of a loner, is one common notion of Blake. Blake is an English surname brought into use as a first name. It is associated with poet William Blake and Hollywood director Blake Edwards. In Old English this name could mean either "pallid" or "black."

Bliss He might be highly emotional or artistic, possibly even a poet like Bliss Carman, a Canadian whose impressionistic poetry was popular around the turn of the century. Like the noun, the name means "serene happiness" or "spiritual joy." It could serve as a girl's name as well.

Booth His name has a rather old-fashioned, upper-crust, collegiate ring, partly because of author Booth Tarkington, whose popular novels (*The Magnificent Ambersons, Seventeen, Penrod*) were much read in the early part of this century.

Brandon See BRENDAN.

Brendan He is likely to be sociable, creative, and perhaps even brilliant if he fits his name. This old Celtic name is used particularly in Ireland, where it is associated with genius playwright and notorious drinker Brendan Behan. Variations include Brendon and Brandon; the latter may also be interpreted as an Old English place name. The literal meaning of the name is uncertain.

Bret, Brett A generous nature and sensitive insight will likely make him well liked and admired; an appreciation of nature and the arts may distinguish him as well. A century apart, authors Bret Harte and Bret Easton Ellis both wrote highly popular fiction on the wilder side of life in the West. The name means "Breton," that is, "one from Brittany."

Brian Clever and creative, but serious too, is the current American image of Brian. People tend to think of Brian as a kind and generous person as well. The name is connected with Brian Wilson, composer and most famous member of the Beach Boys; movie director Brian DePalma; and novelist

Brian Moore. This is a traditional name in Ireland, and there the first syllable is pronounced *bree* (rhyming with tree), or the name is pronounced as a single syllable, *breen* (rhyming with green). The spelling Brean is sometimes used to reflect the latter pronunciation. Other variations are Bryan and Bryon.

Brice His unique name has an appealing simplicity. In the arts the name is associated with abstract painter Brice Marden. The origin of this ancient Celtic name is uncertain. Bryce is an alternate spelling.

Brooks A natural vivacity and savoir faire seem part of the stereotypical Brooks, and a privileged background is implied as well. The name is associated with *New York Times* drama critic Brooks Atkinson, and for a Broadway theater, the Brooks Atkinson, named for him. Brooks is an English surname, meaning "dweller by the brook," that has come into use as a first name.

Bruce Bruce Springsteen and Bruce Willis have made this old Scottish name seem almost born in the U.S.A. Bruce's personality may be both manly and conflicted, macho and sensitive—at least according to the contemporary image. This name is also connected with the kung-fu actor Bruce Lee and the Civil War historian Bruce Catton. The name came from Normandy, where it was the name of a village, to Scotland, where it became the name of a great noble family. It is known there especially for Robert the Bruce, the first king of Scotland.

Bryan See BRIAN.

Bryce See BRICE.

Buddy His friendly, down-home name links him with the very origins of rock and roll. Buddy Holly made the name well known, along with his classic songs such as "Peggy Sue" and "That'll Be the Day." Jazzman Buddy Rich also made the name familiar. Linguists say the name comes from baby talk for "brother." In common speech it generally means "pal." Short form: Bud.

Burgess His name speaks of wealth, privilege, and the freedom to do what he pleases—perhaps as an artist, a writer, or an actor like Burgess Meredith. The name means "citizen" or "freeman," and in colonial Virginia and Maryland, a burgess was a member of the colonial legislature. The name also brings to mind writer Anthony Burgess (*A Clockwork Orange*).

Burt Handsome and manly is what he'll be if he's a typical Burt. He might even be a Hollywood star like Burt Lancaster or Burt Reynolds. The name may have originated as a short form of BURTON.

Burton He must be highly educated, dashing, and aristocratic if his name is Burton . . . or so it is supposed. The name is associated with actor Richard Burton (born Richard Jenkins) and the daring nineteenth-century English explorer Sir Richard Francis Burton. Of Old English origin, it is a surname brought into use as a first name for men, including Burton Cummings of the rock group the Guess Who. As an alternative, parents might consider Barton, which has a quite similar origin and connotation. For more on the short forms of these names, see BURT and BART.

Buster The silent film actor and director Buster Keaton (born Joseph Francis Keaton) may have taken his professional name from the slang term for a boy or man, as in "Hey, Buster." This name is also associated with the athlete/actor Buster Crabbe.

Byron Romantic, passionate, and highly intelligent is the popular image of Byron. The name may have originally been given in honor of the great English poet Lord Byron (full name George Gordon Noel Byron), who was also known for his dark, handsome appearance and many love affairs. The name comes from an Old English place name meaning "barn."

Carey, Cary He may be the hero of a romantic comedy—like the film characters played by Cary Grant (whose real name was Archibald Leach). With a suggestion of casual sophistication, androgyny, and friendliness, this name suggests an easy-going person. Cary and Carey came into use from the English surname, which may have originated with the Celtic name, Carew.

Cecil Artistic, clever, with a wonderful sense of style: that is one popular image of Cecil—fostered in part by Cecil Beaton, the English photographer, stage and costume designer, and by Hollywood director Cecil B. De Mille (*The Ten Commandments*). The name comes from an ancient Roman family name, derived from the Latin word for "blind."

Chet Dignified, unflappable, and always well groomed: that is the television image of Chet—learned by America through years of watching news anchor Chet Huntley (half of the Huntley-Brinkley news team). The name is a short form of CHESTER.

Clark Is he as seductive, earthy, and irresistible as Clark Gable? Most famous for his role as Rhett Butler in *Gone with the Wind*, Gable gave this first name a lasting appeal. It comes from the family name, which means "clerk."

Claud, Claude He might be a composer like Claude Debussy, a painter like Claude Monet, or a Nobel Prize-winning novelist like Claude Simon. Other famous bearers of this name include the anthropologist/structuralist Claude Lévi-Strauss and the pianist/composer Claude Bolling. In France, Claude has long been a name of distinction, and it has been used from time to time in the United States. The common American pronunciation, similar to the word "clod," may discourage some people from using it. The French pronunciation rhymes with "road." Claude comes from a Roman clan name, possibly meaning "lame."

Cliff, Clifford Clifford may seem highfalutin, but if he goes by Cliff he'll seem just a cut above the average guy. The name is known in the arts for the great playwright of the 1930s, Clifford Odets. Clifford was once the last name of a notable English aristocratic family, and the name still has a high-flown aura.

Clint, Clinton Good looks and daring combine in Clint's popular image, for this dashing short name is associated with actor Clint Eastwood. The name was first an English surname and place name, indicating a town on a hill or headland.

Clive Clever, worldly-wise, and perhaps British: this is the common notion of Clive. He could be a bestselling novelist like Clive Cussler (*Raise the Titanic!*) or Clive Barker (*Weaveworld*), or a drama critic like Clive Barnes. Clive is also the first name of the English author C. S. Lewis. The name comes from an English surname meaning "cliff."

Colman, Colum If he is called Colman, he might bring to mind Coleman Hawkins, the great, influential jazz saxophonist. Named Colum, his Irish heritage will shine through. These names recall the sixth-century Irish poet and preacher Saint Colman of Cloyne, and the writer Padraic Colum, who was active in the Irish literary renaissance. Both names mean "dove." Colm is a third variation.

Conrad, Konrad Conrad's good fortune is that when people hear his name they picture someone smart. They might be subconsciously recalling some of the world's brilliant Conrads, such as writer Joseph Conrad (born Jósef Teodor Konrad Walecz Korzeniowski), poet Conrad Aiken, or political cartoonist Conrad (Paul Francis Conrad). The name is of Germanic origin and means "bold or wise counsel." Konrad is the German spelling.

Curtis Pleasant is one image of Curtis, which makes sense because the name means "courteous." Originally a last name, it is often used as a first name as well, as for the musician Curtis Mayfield.

Dale Friendly, entertaining, and immensely likable is the typical Dale, as exemplified by writer and lecturer Dale Carnegie. The name is the Middle English word for "valley," still used in the phrase "over hill and dale." As a surname, it indicated a person who lived in a valley.

Dante Creativity, strength of character, and popularity all may combine in Dante. The name is world-famous because of one of the great creators of all time, Italian poet Dante Alighieri, author of *The Divine Comedy.* In the nineteenth century, the name also became well known because of English poet and Pre-Raphaelite painter Dante Gabriel Rossetti. The name comes from Latin and means "enduring."

Dashiell Tough, gutsy, and highly literate is the public image of Dashiell, from the literary career of Dashiell Hammett, originator of the hard-boiled detective novel (*The Maltese Falcon, The Thin Man*). The name seems to be a last name used as a first name.

Dean A straightforward sort of person is what one might expect Dean to be. Yet he might be an actor like Dean Stockwell, or have a silly side as well, like Dean Martin or Dean Jones. This first name comes from the surname Dean, which originally indicated a church officer. Today the word "dean" generally refers to a college administrator.

Derek, Derrick Daring, dashing, and successful is one common image of Derek. In the arts, famous Dereks include English actor Derek Jacobi and director John Derek (born Derek Harris). Derek and Derrick are forms of Theodoric, meaning "ruler of the people." Other forms include: Dereck, Derrek, and Derick. See also the related names DIETRICH, DIRK.

Dietrich With this interesting, unusual name, he may turn out to be an influential sort of person. The name brings to mind Dietrich Buxtehude, the Swedish composer and organist who was a great influence on J. S. Bach, and the German Protestant theologian Dietrich Bonhoeffer. Dietrich is a German form of Thoedoric and means "ruler of the people."

Dirk He is supposed to be athletic and good-looking—the strong, silent type—if he fits the current image of his name. It's often connected with actor Dirk Bogarde (whose name seems specifically designed to suggest a combination of Kirk Douglas and Humphrey Bogart). Dirk is a Dutch form of Theodoric, from the same root as DEREK and DIETRICH.

Dudley A genial bumbler is *one* stereotype of Dudley. But he could be a scion of an old, moneyed family—or a successful comedian like Dudley Moore. The name comes from the surname Dudley, which was a prominent family name in colonial Massachusetts.

Dustin With this name, he may be destined for stardom. Even if an acting career is not in his stars, his name will bring to mind one of the most talented and likable actors of recent times, Dustin Hoffman. Interestingly, Hoffman himself was named for a popular actor, silent film cowboy Dustin Farnum. Dustin is also an English last name.

Dylan A poetic nature is associated with Dylan. This name is linked to folk and rock singer/composer Bob Dylan, whose real name was Zimmerman before he named himself after poet Dylan Thomas. This Welsh name is said to mean "son of the waves."

Eddie If he is not a comedian at heart, he may not be a true Eddie. His popular predecessors include Eddie Cantor, Eddie Albert, and Eddie Murphy. Most Eddies are officially named EDWARD.

Edgar Suggestions of mystery and creativity accompany this name. It brings to mind three American writers: Edgar Allen Poe, Edgar Rice Burroughs (*Tarzan of the Apes*), and Edgar Lee Masters (*The Spoon River Anthology*). It also recalls former FBI director J. Edgar Hoover. The name comes from Old English, a combination of the words for "happiness," "riches," and "spear."

Elmore Toughness and intelligence go hand in hand in the popular image of Elmore. This name is connected with bestselling author Elmore Leonard.

Elvin, Elwyn, Elwin See ALVIN.

Elvis He who shares the name of the "king of rock and roll" will have a lot to live up to. The name will always bring to mind rock superstar Elvis Presley. For some, it will also recall new-wave rock star Elvis Costello (born Declan McManus). Considering how many Elvis Presley fans there are, it is surprising that more children have not been named for him. For Elvis admirers, other first-name alternatives are Presley and Aron (Elvis's middle name). The origin and meaning of the name Elvis are not known. One might say its de facto meaning is "the king."

Emerson Thoughtful and intelligent is the perception of this name. It recalls the American philosopher and poet Ralph Waldo Emerson of Concord, Massachusetts, and his beliefs in individualism and self-reliance. This surname comes from Old English and is sometimes used as a first name.

Emil, Émile Seriousness, creativity, and a European sophistication combine in the picture of Emil. The name is associated with French novelist and social reformer Émile Zola, and with German expressionist painter Emil Nolde. Émile is the French spelling; Emil is the German form. The name comes from an ancient Roman family name that is often said to mean "industrious."

Ephraim, Efrem He could be pleasant, sociable, but with a tough side—like the actor Efrem Zimbalist, Jr., in the role of the head G-man on the TV series "The FBI." His father, Efrem Zimbalist, Sr., was a famous violinist. Efrem seems to be a simplified spelling of Ephraim, a biblical name.

Ernest The earnest nature implied by his name is just one part of his interesting personality. He might become a great writer and sportsman like Ernest Hemingway; or a wonderful illustrator like Ernest H. Shepard, the original illustrator of *Winnie-the-Pooh*; or a successful actor like Ernest Borgnine. The name comes from an Old High German word for "struggle" and thus is interpreted as meaning "earnestness, vigor." The modern German spelling is Ernst.

Errol Swashbuckling courage and a devil-may-care charm are part of his name for those who associate it with the dashing movie star of the 1930s, Errol Flynn. The origin and meaning of the name are unknown.

Erskine His name speaks of literature, the American South, and a flair for language. It recalls especially the Georgia-born author Erskine Caldwell (*Tobacco Road, God's Little Acre*). To some people, Erskine might suggest a feminine name like Ernestine or Adeline. It is a last name and Scottish place name brought into use as a first name.

Eubie Style, flair, and fun are hallmarks of Eubie. This name is best known for Eubie Blake (born James Hubert Blake), the pianist and composer. (His most famous song was "I'm Just Wild About Harry.") Eubie might be derived from Blake's middle name, Hubert.

Eugene Dependability, seriousness, and creativity combine in his name. It may bring to mind a hard-working businessman—or a great artist, like Nobel Prize–winning playwright Eugene O'Neill, photographer Eugène Atget, or conductor Eugene Ormandy. The name is of Greek origin and means "well-born, noble." For more on the short form, see GENE.

Evelyn Eccentric, clever, and perhaps British is how one might picture a boy named Evelyn. As a masculine name, Evelyn is best known because of British writer Evelyn Waugh (*Brideshead Revisited, The Loved One*). It is more common as a feminine name. (See the entry under "Girls' Names" in "Athletes.") In Britain the first vowel is pronounced like the "e" sound in "meet," and in the United States it is pronounced like the "e" in "met." The name is of Germanic origin.

Farley An outgoing, likable guy is what one expects Farley to be. With the right surname, Farley can also sound quite accustomed to wealth and privilege. Usually a last name, Farley is known as a first name because of conservationist and writer Farley Mowat (*Never Cry Wolf*) and actor Farley Granger.

Ford His name is full of creative connotations—from actor Harrison Ford to industrialist Henry Ford to author Ford Madox Ford (*The Good Soldier*). Ford the writer (born Ford Madox Hueffer) was named for his grandfather, Ford Madox Brown, the Pre-Raphaelite painter.

Frank His name may sound a bit out of step and out of date, but he could become an astounding creative success like Frank (Francis) Sinatra, architect Frank Lloyd Wright, Frank L. Baum (author of the *Wizard of Oz* books), movie director Frank Capra, or artist Frank Stella. The Italian form is Franco, as in the name of another film director, Franco (Gianfranco) Zeffirelli. The name originated as a nickname for FRANCIS.

Fred A good old-fashioned man-to-man, pal-to-pal kind of guy is what one expects Fred to be. Creativity and humor are associated with the name too, which is known because of Fred Astaire, and old-time radio comedian Fred Allen. See FREDERICK for more on the name's origins and meaning.

Galway Irish mist and strains of poetry seem a natural part of Galway. As a personal name, Galway is best known because of the poet Galway Kinnell. Galway is also a city and county in the west of Ireland.

Garrison If his name is Garrison, he just might follow in the footsteps of humorist Garrison Keillor, creator of the tales of Lake Wobegon. This name seems to be a surname used as a first name, perhaps related to Garrett or Garrick (as in David Garrick, the eighteenth-century British actor, and one of the greatest in history).

Gary, Garry The typical Gary may be the strong and silent type—or the talkative and friendly type—but he is sure to have a creative side. This formerly obscure name became popular because of actor Gary Cooper. Outside of Hollywood, the real Gary may have Cooper's sensitivity and savoir faire—*and* a great sense of humor like Gary Larson (creator of *The Far Side* comics) or Garry Trudeau (creator of *Doonesbury*). The name is a fairly common one among men born from the 1940s through the 1960s, with a peak in popularity around 1950.

Gene Physical and social grace are linked with his name, which is known for actor/choreographer/dancer Gene Kelly (*An American in Paris*) and for Hollywood's most famous singing cowboy, Gene Autry. This name originated as a short form of EUGENE.

Geoffrey He may be an artist, photographer, fashion designer, or poet. As a poet he would be in good company with one of the best in the history of the English language, Geoffrey Chaucer (*The Canterbury Tales*). The modern American spelling of this name is JEFFREY. Some people may consider Geoffrey the "true" form of the name; others may consider it as quaint and affected as an Olde Shoppe. Short form: Geoff.

Gerard Gerard may have the kind of quiet strength that can carry him to great success. The name is known for the actor Gerard Depardieu, perhaps the most successful French film actor of all time, and for the influential English poet Gerard Manley Hopkins. In Old High German the name means "strong with a spear."

Graham, Grahame, Graeme Well-bred, artistic, and literary is America's impression of Graham. This Scottish name (originally a place name and a clan name) recalls novelist Graham Greene and writer Kenneth Grahame (*The Wind in the Willows*). In the United States it is more common as a last name than a first name (Billy Graham, Martha Graham, Katharine Graham), and may be best known as the middle name of Alexander Graham Bell.

Grant An all-American sort of aggressiveness and ingenuity are part of the typical Grant. The name is associated with painter Grant Wood (famed for his portrait of a farmer and his wife, *American Gothic*) and may also bring to mind actor Cary Grant. This is a case of a surname (meaning "great" or "tall") coming into use as a first name.

Gregory With the name that is associated with the masculine glamour of actor Gregory Peck, he could go far. Of Greek origin, this venerable name was used in the Roman Empire and in the Middle Ages and means "watchful." Short forms: Greg, Gregg.

Gustav, Gustave, Gustavus You may find Gustav at work in a loft in Soho, backstage in London, or in a garret in Paris . . . and if he opts for a more traditional career, he'll always have an artistic side. This name is shared by the novelist Gustave Flaubert, composer Gustav Mahler, and painter Gustave Klimt.

Hal A complex and creative personality may lurk behind his simple name, which is best known because of theater director Hal Prince and actor Hal Holbrook. Hal is a nickname for Harold, Henry, or Harry. In Shakespeare's *Henry V*, the young king Henry is referred to as "Prince Hal."

Harold This name can sound both dramatic and introspective, and thus is well suited to a creative person. The name is associated with playwright Harold Pinter. From Old English it can be traced to the Old Norse name Harald, meaning something like "army power." Diminutives: HAL, HARRY.

Harrison With this name he may have the versatility, talent, and rugged good looks of actor Harrison Ford (*Star Wars, Raiders of the Lost Ark*). This is a last name (known especially for George Harrison of the Beatles) that is occasionally used as a first name.

Hart His name suggests a person of great feeling and creativity, perhaps like poet Hart Crane. It also brings to mind lyricist Lorenz Hart (the musical *Pal Joey*) and Pulitzer Prize-winning dramatist Moss Hart (*You Can't Take It with You*). The noun "hart" comes from Old English and means "a male deer" or "a stag."

Hayden, Haydon, Haydn Music is in his name, if he's called Hayden. He might become a poet, like Hayden Carruth, or a great composer like Franz Joseph Haydn. All three names are related surnames, of Teutonic origin, which are sometimes used as first names. The composer's name is correctly pronounced HIGH-den.

Herman A child named Herman may have an enigmatic side. This old-fashioned Germanic name is most often connected in the United States with Herman Melville, nineteenth-century author of the classic *Moby Dick*. It means "man of the army."

Homer With this unusual name, famous for thousands of years, he is bound to be something special. It was the ancient Greek poet Homer who wrote the *Iliad* and the *Odyssey*. It might also bring to mind the American painter Winslow Homer.

Horace His name seems like a bracing blast from the past . . . blowing in with newspaper editor Horace Greeley proclaiming "Go west, young man," and the Roman poet Horace composing his *Odes*. These people may provide young Horace with inspiration for a literary career. The name comes from a Roman clan name, Horatius. (The poet Horace's Latin name was Quintus Horatius Flaccus.)

Humphrey, Humphry He mixes aristocracy with Hollywood, a tough-guy attitude with the illusion of a charmed life. And, of course, who can forget actor Humphrey Bogart, famous as the lovelorn, war-weary café owner in *Casablanca*. The son of a New York City doctor and an acclaimed magazine illustrator, he was born Humphrey De Forest Bogart; Humphrey was his mother's surname.

Hunter Whether he is born to privilege, or is beating a path to it, Hunter is the kind of person who is just naturally cool. The best-known Hunter is the gonzo journalist of life's wilder side, Hunter S. Thompson. This Old English name means "huntsman."

Ian Intelligence, inventiveness, geniality: these are a few of the qualities associated with Ian. The name is widely known because of Ian Fleming, author of the original James Bond novels. Ian McKellan, the Shakespearean actor, is another well-known Ian. The name is a Scottish form of JOHN.

Ingmar His name is linked with artistic inspiration and beauty, because of the acclaimed Swedish film director Ingmar Bergman. Though unusual in the United States, this name is a typical and common one in Sweden.

Inigo Innovative, imaginative, and on the go: that is how one might picture Inigo. This name is famous in art history because of Inigo Jones, the English architect who brought the styles of the Italian Renaissance to Britain. Inigo is a Basque form of IGNATIUS.

Irving Generous, sentimental, brilliant: one might picture Irving as being all these things. The name is associated with composer Irving Berlin, who wrote such immortal songs as "White Christmas" and "God Bless America." The name originated as a Scottish place name. Variations: Irvine, Irvin.

Jack Manly, streetwise, with an abiding dignity, he could also have a great deal of talent and creativity, like actor Jack Nicholson, author Jack London, or comedian Jack Benny. Jack is used as an independent name or as a nickname for JOHN.

Jackson A creative, forceful, trend-setting person is the popular image of Jackson. The name is famous in the history of modern art for the painter Jackson Pollock and his groundbreaking "dripped" paintings. In the annals of pop music it is connected with Jackson Browne. This is a last name that is sometimes used as a first name.

Jasper His attractive, unusual name is bound to intrigue and tantalize. Acclaimed artist Jasper Johns is the name's most famous bearer. It came into use as a "gem" name; in the Bible, jasper is one of the gemstones that decorates the high priest's breastplate.

Jay If his name is Jay, he is bound to breeze to success with stylish flair. The name brings to mind the 1980s novelist Jay McInerney (*Bright Lights, Big City*). Jay comes from the same Latin root as the bird name, jay. As a common noun, "jay" can also mean "a talkative person, a chatterbox."

Jeff, Jeffrey A trustworthy, all-American guy is the stereotype of Jeff. The name is associated with actor Jeff Bridges and country-and-western singer Jerry Jeff Walker. Jeff is usually considered a short form of Jeffrey, which is the modern spelling of GEOFFREY. See also JEFFERSON.

Jeremy Well-bred but not pretentious, traditional but not dull: that is one current image of Jeremy—which may come partly from the popular actor Jeremy Irons. The name is also known because of utilitarian philosopher Jeremy Bentham. It is a shortening of the biblical JEREMIAH, which means "the Lord is exalted."

Jerome The rather somber sound of his name is lightened by its association with two particularly lively American artists: choreographer Jerome Robbins (*West Side Story*, and numerous ballets) and composer Jerome Kern (*Show Boat*, "Smoke Gets in Your Eyes"). It is also associated with the Christian scholar Saint Jerome, whose Latin translation of the Bible became the Vulgate (official Catholic text). Jerome comes from the Greek name Hieronymus, meaning "holy name."

Jerry In entertainment this name is big—from Jerry Lewis to country-and-western star Jerry Jeff Walker to Jerry Garcia of the Grateful Dead. He may seem like an ordinary guy—but he is likely to have a special talent for finding fame, fortune, or simply a satisfying life. In other fields, a Jerry can succeed nicely too. This name originated as a diminutive of GERALD or JEREMIAH. It is still used that way, or as an independent name.

Joel One may think of Joel as extroverted and dramatic, an entertainer at heart. The name brings to mind actor Joel Grey (*Cabaret*) and the singer Billy Joel. Also connected with the biblical prophet Joel, author of one of the most poetic books of the Bible, the name is a common one in the Bible and means "Yahweh is God."

Julian Artistry and perhaps a hint of affectation are part of this elegant name. The name is associated with Julian Lennon (son of John Lennon) and post-expressionist artist Julian Schnabel. The name is a variation of JULIUS, a Roman clan name.

Keir Handsome, strong, and fearless is the popular image of Keir. In the twenty-first century, he could be an astronaut—or seem like one, like the actor Keir Dullea in *2001: A Space Odyssey*. This ancient Gaelic name means "swarthy" or "dusky."

Keith If his name is Keith, he may waste no time in distinguishing himself in the world. Like guitarist and composer Keith Richards of the Rolling Stones, he could be at the top before age thirty. The name may also bring to mind actors Brian Keith and Keith Carradine and pianist Keith Jarrett. It is from Scotland, of Celtic origin. The meaning is uncertain, possibly "wood" or "forest."

Kenneth Mild-mannered, jovial, serious, civilized: Kenneth can be all these things. This Scottish name has belonged to some distinguished creative achievers, including the poet Kenneth Rexroth, the economist John Kenneth Galbraith, and Kenneth Clark, host of television's "Civilization" series. The name comes from Scottish Gaelic and means "handsome." Short form: Ken.

Kingsley This jaunty, aristocratic (or kingly) sounding name seems sure to place him on top of one realm or another. The name has great literary associations because of famed English novelist Kingsley Amis (*Lucky Jim*) and, before him, clergyman and writer Charles Kingsley (*The Water Babies*). The name comes from Old English and means "king's wood or meadow."

Kirk Masculine good looks, toughness, and sensitivity are all part of the traditional image of Kirk—created mostly by the actor Kirk Douglas. The name comes from Old Norse and means "church." The word "kirk" is still used for "church" in Scotland.

Lanford His odd but distinguished-sounding name could take him far. He could even be a Pulitzer Prize–winning dramatist like Lanford Wilson (*Talley's Folly, Burn This*). Lanford may be a last name used as a first name.

Laurence, Lawrence A noble sort of sophistication is part of Laurence; if he is not born to money he can, in any case, seem born to class. Plus, he can always become one of the boys as Larry. Famous bearers of this name include actor Sir Laurence Olivier, author Lawrence Durrell, and bandleader Lawrence Welk. Notable and entertaining Larrys include actor Larry Hagman and talk-show host Larry King. The name comes from Latin and means "from Laurentium," a town in ancient Rome named for the laurel tree. In ancient times a wreath of laurel leaves was conferred as a symbol of honor or victory.

Lee A boy named Lee may have to try harder, but that could just mean he'll end up like actor Lee Majors, cast as the hero of a TV series like "The Six Million Dollar Man." Or, he might become the head of a giant automobile company, like Lee Iacocca, who is also a bestselling author. Lee is an Anglo-Saxon surname that means "meadow." It is sometimes given as a first name in honor of the Confederate general Robert E. Lee. For Lee as a girl's name, see the listing under "Girls' Names."

Lenny See LEONARD.

Leo He may be a lion of world literature, like Leo Tolstoy, or a lion of the bestseller lists, like Leo Buscaglia. This Latin name means "lion." It is also the fifth sign of the zodiac. Those born under this sign are said to be gregarious and fun loving, and they love to be the center of attention.

Leonard, Leonardo Expressive, expansive Leonard may

roar, growl, or purr, but he will always entertain. This name is often associated with composer and conductor Leonard Bernstein. The short forms of the name, Len and Lenny, have much the same character as Leonard. One well-known Lenny is comedian Lenny Bruce. The Italian form is famous for the titan of Renaissance art, Leonardo da Vinci. The name comes from Latin and means "bold as a lion."

Les Cool and casual is the typical Les. As a musician he might even rival the great guitarist Les Paul, whose name is also known for the type of electric guitar he invented. Les is usually a short form of Lester.

Lewis, Louis, Luis Wherever he's found, a man named Louis may have a special savoir faire. In Hollywood, Louis B. Mayer became the king of movie producers. In the world of jazz, Louis Armstrong (born Daniel Louis Armstrong) became perhaps its greatest improvisational genius. In Spain, the name is Luis, as in film director Luis Buñuel. Both the original French form (Louis) and the English form (Lewis) are used in the United States. Lewis has a more bookish connotation, perhaps from its association with the author of *Alice in Wonderland*, Lewis Carroll (born Charles Lutwidge Dodgson). The name originated with an Old High German name meaning "famous in war." For more on the short forms of Louis, see LOU, LEW.

Liam The graceful lyricism of his name may indicate a good storyteller, like the Irish novelist Liam O'Flaherty. Liam is an Irish diminutive of WILLIAM and is a traditional name there.

Lionel Clever and wise: that may be the typical Lionel. The name recalls pop musician Lionel Richie and social and literary critic Lionel Trilling. Of the same Latin origin as LEO and LEONARD, Lionel is a more peaceful name, one that does not seem to ask for so much attention. It means "little lion."

Lytton With this name he must be bound for a literary career. It recalls the Bloomsbury group and the eminent Lytton Strachey (biographer and critic). It also may bring to mind popular Victorian novelist Edward Bulwer-Lytton. Originally a surname, Lytton is used occasionally as a first name.

Man With this name he will no doubt be a fascinatingly creative individual—like the genius artist Man Ray (photographer, painter, and a founder of the Dada movement). Man could be a short form of Manfred, Manuel, or EMANUEL.

Marlon, Marlin Handsome, charismatic, perhaps a bit rebellious—this is the popular view of Marlon. The world's best known Marlon is actor Marlon Brando, from whom the name gets much of its appeal. These unusual names probably originated as surnames.

Marsden A genteel, creative type: that is how one pictures Marsden. The name is associated with American painter Marsden Hartley, whose abstract works and landscapes are known for their forceful simplicity. Marsden is an Old English place name and a surname, occasionally used as a first name.

Maurice Gallant is the word for Maurice. This name is best known for French actor, dancer, and singer Maurice Chevalier, but it is not a uniquely French name. In the United States it is also known for the singer Maurice White of Earth, Wind and Fire and for the singer/songwriter Maurice Gibb of the Bee Gees. The name comes from Latin and means "Moorish" or "dark-skinned." Morris is an alternative form of the name.

Mel Easygoing is the popular image of Mel. He's also likely to be handsome, like Mel Gibson (*Mad Max, The Road Warrior*); or funny, like Mel Brooks. This name is used on its own or as a short form of MELVIN, Melbourne, Meldon, Melville, or similar names.

Merce Highly coordinated, graceful, innovative: Merce could be all of these things, if he takes after famed modern choreographer Merce Cunningham. This name could possibly be related to the surname Mercer, which is sometimes used as a first name.

Mercer See MERCE.

Merle A casual, friendly, down-to-earth person is what one expects of a man named Merle. And if he sings, he might pull your heartstrings and make you smile, like the country-and-western star Merle Haggard. In French the name means "blackbird." It has also been used as a girl's name; see the listing under "Girls' Names."

Mervin, Merv Magically charming and entertaining is the popular image of Mervin. This Welsh name comes from the same root (a place name) as Merlin, the name of the magician in the legends of King Arthur. In the United States, the name is best known for talk-show host and financier Merv Griffin. The British spelling is Mervyn.

Michael Friendly, popular, and multitalented is the current image of Michael, and in recent years the Michaels of the world have been busy proving it right. In the world of entertainment there are Michael J. Fox, Michael Jackson, and Michael Douglas. Using the Russian form of the name there is dancer and choreographer Mikhail Baryshnikov. The name was quite rare in the United States and Britain until the 1930s or so. From that time it continued to rise in popularity through the early 1980s, so that by 1990 it could be the most common name for American males under the age of forty. The name comes from Hebrew and means "who is like God?" Another form of the name, used in the Bible, is MICAH. Michael's usual short form is Mike; more rare is MICK. For more on the diminutive, see MICKEY.

Michelangelo He may paint, sculpt, compose, or make movies like an angel. Whatever he does, he will be supported by the creative genius suggested by his name. The great artist of the High Renaissance, Michelangelo Buonarroti (the frescoes of the Sistine Chapel, *David*) is of course the "patron saint" of this name. It is also known for the Italian filmmaker Michelangelo Antonioni. This Italian name refers to Michael the Archangel.

Mick Raucous, rowdy, and fun-loving is the stereotype of Mick—largely from the hot-blooded Rolling Stones singer, Mick Jagger. In the world of popular music, the name is also connected with Mick Fleetwood of Fleetwood Mac. Mick is generally a nickname for MICHAEL. Be warned, though, that the word "mick" is also an old derogatory term for an Irishman.

Milan A European sophistication lingers around his name, which recalls the Italian city of Milan and acclaimed Czech writer Milan Kundera (*The Unbearable Lightness of Being*). The name may possibly come from a Greek word for "mill" or "millstone."

Miles Strength of character blends with a lively, fun-loving nature in the ideal Miles. He may soothe, entertain, and jazz up the world like trumpeter Miles Davis. The meaning of this name is unknown; it may come from Latin and mean "soldier." It has occasionally been used for women (see the listing in "Girls' Names"). Alternative spelling: Myles.

Milton The creative, hard-working Milton might become a poet, like the great John Milton (*Paradise Lost*); a comedian like Milton Berle; or a graphic designer like Milton Glaser (his 1966 poster of Bob Dylan may be his most famous). This name comes from Old English and means "mill town." Short form: Milt.

Montgomery Irresistible: that is Montgomery, at least the movie version played by Montgomery Clift in film classics such as *Red River* and *The Heiress*. Diminutive: Monty.

Morris See MAURICE.

Nat His simple name could indicate great things in store. He could be as popular and successful as the amazing singer Nat "King" Cole. It is a short form of NATHAN or NATHANIEL.

Nathanael, Nathaniel His old-fashioned name could signal a highly imaginative, successful individual. It is best known because of two of the best and most distinctively American writers, Nathaniel Hawthorne and Nathanael West. The name comes from Hebrew and means "gift of God." Short form: NATHAN.

Nigel On hearing the name Nigel one might picture a clever and unusual person—the name is very British. This rare name is best known for the actor Nigel Bruce (Dr. Watson in the Sherlock Holmes movies). The name has been traced to a Medieval Latin name meaning "little black one," which is said to have developed from the Old Norse name Njal (an early form of NEIL).

Noel Witty, sophisticated, and very bright is the stereotype of a man named Noel—created mostly by the English actor and playwright Noel Coward. This name comes from the French word for "Christmas" and is also used for women (see NOEL under "Girls' Names" in the chapter on Leaders). Noel was also one of the middle names of the romantic poet Lord Byron (George Gordon Noel Byron).

Omar Masculine, romantic, macho: that is the stereotype of Omar. The name is best known because of actor Omar Sharif and eleventh-century Persian poet Omar Khayyám (*Rubaiyat*). This ancient Semitic name appears once in the Bible (Genesis 36:11).

Orson Orson could be a dark, brooding personality . . . a friendly, cuddly fellow . . . or a genius director and actor like Orson Welles (*Citizen Kane, The Magnificent Ambersons*). The name is also associated with science fiction writer Orson

Scott Card and actor Orson Bean. Of Latin-French origin, Orson means "bear."

Oscar Creative, extroverted, a trendsetter: that could be Oscar. He could become an internationally famous fashion designer like Oscar de la Renta; a beloved lyricist like Oscar Hammerstein II (*South Pacific, Show Boat*); or a superb wit and literary stylist like Oscar Wilde (*The Picture of Dorian Gray, The Importance of Being Earnest*). Oscar is an ancient Anglo-Saxon name meaning "god spear."

Owen With this simple, gentle-sounding name, he projects both humility and strength. Owen is a traditional Welsh name, but it has a very American ring too, associated with Owen Wister, author of the classic first Western novel, *The Virginian.*

Pablo His name is linked in history to three great creative geniuses: artist Pablo Picasso, poet Pablo Neruda, and cellist Pablo Casals. Pablo is the Spanish form of PAUL.

Padraic Artistic, literary, and very Irish: that is the stereotype of Padraic. The name is an Irish form of Patrick, associated with Irish-American writer Padraic Colum, a well-known figure of the Irish literary renaissance.

Percy Talented and aristocratic is the common image of Percy—created in large part by English poet Percy Bysshe Shelley. The name originated as an aristocratic surname in England. It is also a surname in the United States, notably of author Walker Percy.

Phineas He is apt to be a showman at heart, if he fits his name. Phineas was the first name of P. T. Barnum, founder of the circus known as "The Greatest Show on Earth." The name is of Egyptian origin and means "the Nubian."

Randolph, Randolf, Randy Gallant, clever, creative, and distinguished, this grand-sounding old name comes from Old

English and means "shield wolf." The name is perhaps best known as the middle name of flamboyant newspaper magnate William Randolph Hearst. It is also associated with Randolph Caldecott, the acclaimed children's book illustrator, and actor Randolph Scott. The easy-going diminutive form is currently famous in country-and-western music because of Randy Travis, who burst on the scene in 1986 with his album *Storms of Life*. It is also known for actor Randy Quaid.

Raphael Harmony, health, and artistry are all traditionally associated with Raphael. The name is best known for the great Italian Renaissance painter Raphael Sanzio, whose compositions are some of the greatest in history. In Hebrew the name means "God has healed." The Spanish form of the name is Rafael.

Ray, Raymond Quiet determination and loads of talent seem to combine in the typical Ray or Raymond. In the ranks of artistic overachievers, they have everyone beat. This humble but seemingly magical pair of names is associated with authors Raymond Chandler, Raymond Carver, and Ray Bradbury; actors Ray Bolger, and Raymond Burr; and musician Ray Charles. Of Germanic origin, Raymond means "counsel protection." Ray is a short form of Raymond, sometimes used as a separate name.

Rex Suave and self-assured is one popular image of Rex. The name is often connected with actor Rex Harrison (*My Fair Lady*) and author and critic Rex Reed. In Latin, Rex means "king."

Reynold, Reynolds His name expresses strength and masculinity, combined with insight and imagination. It is best known because of novelist Reynolds Price. This name is of Germanic origin and means "counsel power."

Robin His bright, optimistic name might be the beginning of a dazzling personality—like that of actor and comedian Robin Williams. This name originated as a diminutive of ROBERT.

Rodney, Rod Stardom could be in store for the boy with this name, which comes from the Old High German word for "fame." Actor Rod Steiger and comedian Rodney Dangerfield have helped make the name well known.

Roman, Romanus The weight of antiquity combines with *la dolce vita* in the city of Rome—and in his name. The name Roman is known to some because of controversial film director Roman Polanski. Of Latin origin, it means "Roman" or "of Rome."

Ross A strong, masculine image is part of his name, which may be most often associated with the popular writer Ross D. MacDonald. The original meaning of this Scottish name is unknown.

Rudolf, Rudolph Grace, athleticism, and a magnetic appeal all combine in the classic Rudolph. This name has been made famous by dancer Rudolf Nureyev and actor Rudolph Valentino ("the Sheik" of silent films). Diminutive: Rudy.

Russ, Russell Intelligent and good-natured is the typical Russell or Russ. He could be bound for success in almost any area; he might be a novelist, like Russell Hoban or Russell Banks, or a newspaper columnist like Russell Baker. Russell originated as a last name, indicating a red-haired man. The short form, Russ, is sometimes used as an independent name. RUSTY is also used as a nickname.

Rust, Rusty Friendly and good-hearted is the popular image of Rusty. Rust may be similar, but with a harder edge. Rust Hills, a writer and fiction editor of *Esquire*, is one notable person known by this name. Rusty is used as a nickname for RUSSELL or as an independent name.

Ryan Masculine, attractive, successful: this was the image of Ryan in the 1980s, when Ryan became one of the most popular names for baby boys in the United States. The name became famous at least partly because of actor Ryan O'Neal (*Love Story*, *Paper Moon*). It originated as an Irish last name; the meaning is unknown.

Sandro Colorful, stylish, urbane: Sandro could be all that and more. This Italian name is associated with Sandro Botticelli, one of the great painters of the Italian Renaissance (*Birth of Venus*, *La Primavera*). It is the short form of Alessandro (ALEXANDER).

Scott Creative, extroverted, unique: that is the typical Scott. He could become a composer like Scott Joplin (*Maple Leaf Rag*), a novelist like F. Scott Fitzgerald (*The Great Gatsby*), or anything that takes artistry, ingenuity, and drive. Though Fitzgerald's first name was Francis, he went by Scott. The name comes from the surname Scott (meaning "a Scot" or "one from Scotland"). Scot is an alternative spelling.

Seamus His name evokes an artistic personality . . . and images of Ireland. Seamus Heaney, the Northern Irish poet, has helped make this name known in the United States. It is the Irish form of JAMES, pronounced SHAY-mus. Shamus is an alternative spelling.

Sean Good-looking, creative, and all male: that is the popular image of Sean—from actors Sean Penn and Sean Connery. The name is also known as that of Irish writers Sean O'Casey and Sean O'Faoláin. The name is an Irish form of JOHN and is also spelled Shawn or Shaun.

Sherwood Idealistic and imaginative: that is one picture of Sherwood. The name is immortal in American literature for Sherwood Anderson (*Winesburg, Ohio*).

Sidney He can make himself a smashing success if he is a typical Sidney. He might be a bestselling novelist like Sidney

Sheldon, an actor like Sidney Poitier, a poet and musician like Sidney Lanier, or a comedian like Sid Caesar. The name comes from an English aristocratic surname. Sydney is an alternative spelling. Short form: Sid.

Somerset His name gives him a distinctly literate, British air. It is associated with English author W. Somerset Maugham (*Of Human Bondage*, many short stories).

Sonny Disarming and endearing are the two main qualities of his name. As a casual form of address, it means "boy" or "young man." As a first name it was made famous by actor/singer Sonny Bono.

Stephen, Steven Eminently likable, creative, and successful Stephens seem to be the norm. Consider, for example, director Steven Spielberg (*E.T. the Extraterrestrial*), actor Steve McQueen, musician Stevie Wonder (given name Steveland Judkins Morris), and writer Stephen Crane (*The Red Badge of Courage*). First used in honor of Saint Stephen, an eloquent speaker and the first Christian martyr, the name comes from the Greek word for "crown." Short form: Steve. Diminutive: Stevie.

Sydney See SIDNEY.

Sylvester Rocky's strength and Rambo's bravado are associated with Sylvester—from Sylvester Stallone's long-running career as America's favorite he-man. Like the feminine name Sylvia, Sylvester comes from the Latin word for "forest." Alternative spelling: Silvester. Nickname: Sly.

Terence Urbane, witty, well-bred: that is the stereotype of Terence. The name recalls the Roman comic playwright Terence, and it comes from a Roman clan name. Alternative spelling: Terrence. Diminutive: Terry.

Thelonious Eccentric, innovative, important: he could be all those things *and* have music in his blood if his name is

Thelonious. This name is famous because of the great jazz pianist and composer Thelonious Sphere Monk.

Thornton A serious, noble-minded individual is what one might expect Thornton to be. The name is connected with the great American writer Thornton Wilder (*The Bridge of San Luis Rey, Our Town, The Skin of Our Teeth*). Thornton comes from an Old English place name meaning "settlement among the thorns."

Timothy Attractive, honest, and perhaps slightly shy or timid: this is the stereotype of Timothy. The name is well known because of actor Timothy Hutton and 1960s counter-culture guru Timothy Leary. The name comes from Greek and means "honoring God." For more on the short form, see TIM.

Treat Generous, popular, entertaining: that is one way to picture Treat. The name is associated with actor Treat Williams. It recalls the noun "treat," meaning "something freely given that is a special delight or pleasure."

Trevor Smart and skillful is one popular image of Trevor. This name is best known for English stage director Trevor Nunn (*Cats*) and actor Trevor Howard. It is of Celtic origin, perhaps meaning "great homestead."

Tyrone Gallant, masculine, and dynamic: that is the picture of the ideal Tyrone. The name is most often associated with actor Tyrone Power. Variation: Tyron.

Vasili, Vasily Exotic, powerful, and probably Russian: that is how one might describe Vasily. In art history, the name is known because of Vasily Kandinsky, an originator of modern abstract art. Vasili/Vasily is the Russian form of BASIL. Wassily is an alternative spelling.

Vaughan, Vaughn Music and poetry seem part of this old Welsh name. It is known because of composer Ralph Vaughan

Williams and metaphysical poet Henry Vaughan. In the 1960s, actor Robert Vaughn put the name in the public eye. Of Celtic origin, the name means "small."

Vincent He may have an innovative, invincible spirit if his name is Vincent. This name is famous for one of the world's great painters, Vincent van Gogh. In more recent times, it has been associated with actor Vincent Price. Of Latin origin, the name means "conquering." The Italian form is Vincente, best known for the Hollywood director Vincente Minnelli. Short form: Vince.

Virgil An old-fashioned, classic greatness is associated with his name, which comes from that of the immortal Roman poet Virgil (the *Aeneid*). In the twentieth century, the name is connected with composer Virgil Thomson (*Four Saints in Three Acts, The Mother of Us All*). It originated as a Roman clan name.

Wallace His forceful-sounding name could take him far in almost any field. In the arts, the name is associated with novelist Wallace Stegner, poet Wallace Stevens, and actor Wallace Beery. Wallace originated as a surname in Scotland.

Walter This name seems to combine creativity with an innate ability to inspire trust and confidence—like Walt Disney, Walter Cronkite, and Walter Matthau have done. In history the name is associated with Sir Walter Raleigh, a multitalented Englishman who was a poet, courtier, and sponsor of the first English colony in North America. Walter comes from an Old High German name meaning "army commander."

Washington Eloquence, wit, and integrity are all associated with Washington. As a first name Washington is best known because of writer Washington Irving, whose tales were acclaimed for their graceful style and sophistication.

Wayne A man of sincerity and a down-to-earth personality is what one expects of a typical Wayne. The name is associated with singer Wayne Newton and actor John Wayne. It originated as a surname, meaning "wainwright," in other words, "a builder or repairer of wagons."

Wilfred, Wilfrid Dignified, scholarly, and courageous, if necessary: that is how one might picture the typical Wilfred. The name is connected with World War I poet Wilfred Owen and author and critic Wilfred Sheed. This ancient Anglo-Saxon name means "resolute for peace." Short form: Will.

Willis Outgoing, popular, perhaps destined for a career as an actor: that is one way of picturing Willis. This name is best known nowadays because of actor Bruce Willis on the TV series "Moonlighting." More common as a surname than a first name, it means "son of Will." Nickname: Bill.

Winslow Like the American painter Winslow Homer (*The Fog Warning, Breaking Storm, Snap the Whip*), he may become one of America's great original artists. Whatever he does, people will always hear something of the wind and the sea in his name. The first part of this Old English name can be interpreted as an old Anglo-Saxon name, Wine, meaning "friend" or "friendly." Nickname: Win.

Wolfgang He may be artistic, outgoing, and perhaps even a genius—like the great composer Wolfgang Amadeus Mozart. In the 1980s the name also became known for the celebrated chef, Wolfgang Puck. This German name means "wolf strife."

Wynton Lyrical, elegant, hot, cool: Wynton can be all that and more, if he takes after the trumpeter Wynton Marsalis. This upscale-sounding name seems to be of Old English origin, like Wyndham or Winston.

Wystan A genteel, creative individual—perhaps born with a silver spoon in his mouth—is what one might expect Wystan to be. This unusual name was the first name of poet W. H. Auden (Wystan Hugh Auden).

Zane Sturdy, reliable, enterprising—the kind of man who was around when the West was won—is the image of Zane. This name is associated with the dean of Western novelists, Zane Grey.

Zubin Artistic, vibrant, flamboyant: that is the popular image of Zubin. The name is known in the United States because of Zubin Mehta, the Indian-American conductor and musical director of the New York Philharmonic.

4
LEADERS

A leader can be found in many places: at the head of a corporation, a nation, a political movement, or at the top of the social register. What most of the people *and* their names have in common is that they inspire confidence. Among these names are some of the oldest, most traditional American first names—names that came over on the *Mayflower* and have been American standbys ever since. Other names included in this chapter come from around the world, and because of their meanings, sounds, and connections with famous leaders they are strong leadership names. Naturally, not every child given one of these names will exercise the powers of a leader, but with one of the following names he or she will enjoy an association with a leading individual.

GIRLS' NAMES

Abby, Abigail The grace of tradition surrounds her name. Its most famous bearer was the spirited and intelligent Abigail Adams, one of the most distinguished women of the

American Revolution and wife of John Adams, the second president of the United States. The name came into use because of the biblical heroine Abigail, who is admired for her beauty, dignity, and wisdom (1 Samuel 25). Of Hebrew origin, the name means "my father is joy" or "father joy." The diminutive Abby is often used as an independent name.

Angela A unique aura of power surrounds Angela. The name comes from the Greek word for "angel," and true angels are powerful beings. The name has often been used in honor of Saint Angela Merici, an Italian nun who founded the Ursuline Order. Variations: Angelina, Angeline. Diminutive: Angie.

Ann, Anne One of the best-loved names in English for five hundred years, and in France and Russia for even longer, Anne bespeaks both capability and caring—a mixture not forgotten by today's woman, balancing a career and a family. Famous Annes of past and present include England's Queen Anne (whose name is remembered in Queen Anne–style furniture and the flower, Queen Anne's lace), today's Princess Anne, English Protestant martyr Anne Askew, publisher and society figure Ann Getty, and politicians Anne Armstrong and Ann Richards. The name, from Hebrew, means "grace." It came into use in honor of Saint Anne, mother of the Virgin Mary. For other forms of the name, see ANNA, HANNAH, ANNETTE, and ANNIE.

Antoinette Like the palace of Versailles, there's something grand, romantic, and even a bit intimidating about Antoinette, even if she goes by one of the name's variations, Toinette or Toni. In addition to France's incomparable queen Marie Antoinette, Antoinette Louisa Brown Blackwell, abolitionist and the first woman minister in the United States, has lent an aura of strength and grace to the name. This French name is a feminine form of Antoine (ANTHONY).

Augusta See AUGUSTUS.

Barbara Dependability, a quick wit, and a touch of sophistication: all these are qualities one expects to find in a Barbara. Leading Barbaras include diplomat Barbara Salt, who became the first British woman ambassador; economist Barbara Ward; and Congresswoman Barbara Jordan. This name originated in Greek and means "a stranger" or "foreigner." Short forms: Bab, Babs. The diminutive Babette is also used, though in France it is usually a diminutive of Elisabeth.

Bella, Bell, Belle Desperado or Democrat, she's nothing if not a flamboyant and attractive firebrand. The name is best known because of famed Western outlaw Belle Starr and lawyer and liberal politician Bella Abzug. It comes from Latin and means "beautiful." (As they say in Italy, "*Ciao, bella*"—"Hey, beautiful.") The name probably came into use as a short form of ISABEL or ISABELLA.

Berenice, Bernice In the third century B.C., two powerful queens named Berenice reigned over Egypt. This dignified, interesting name comes from Greek and means "bearer of victory." Bernice is a common variation. The diminutives Barrie and Berry have a cheerful, preppy sound.

Bess Kindness, quiet strength, and other old-fashioned qualities seem a natural part of Bess. This short form of Elizabeth is best known because of First Lady Bess Truman and Queen Elizabeth I, "Good Queen Bess." For more on origins and meaning, see ELIZABETH.

Beth See ELIZABETH.

Betsy, Betsey A simple, wholesome goodness seems to surround her name, which recalls Betsy Ross, the seamstress from Philadelphia who, according to legend, made the first American flag. Betsy is a diminutive of ELIZABETH.

Brooke, Brook Social status is Brooke's middle name. In terms of Old Money, one can't outclass the queen of philanthropists, Brooke Astor. Brooke is a last name that has come into use as a first name.

Carla In the very best sense of the word, Carla is a gentleman. The name is a feminine form of CHARLES, which means simply "a man." In business, law, government, or simply organizing a party for her many friends or associates, your Carla may be fair, efficient, and generous. Carla Anderson Hills, trial lawyer and politician, became Secretary of Housing and Urban Development under President Ford, and was the third woman to hold a cabinet post.

Caroline, Carolyn The name Caroline has a ring of privilege; Carolyn sounds a bit more ordinary, but both names have a regal air. In the twentieth century, Caroline is often thought of as a royal name, because of Princess Caroline of Monaco and Caroline Kennedy Schlossberg. CAROLINA is a more dramatic, romantic-sounding version. The names developed from CHARLES. For more on the diminutive, see CARRIE.

Carrie, Carry Her name has a pleasant, slightly old-fashioned sound that has never really gone out of style. In the nineteenth century, you could probably have found her as a pioneer woman crossing America in a covered wagon. Or she might have been destroying saloons with a hatchet like the temperance activist Carry Nation. This name originated as a diminutive of CAROLINE but has long been accepted as an independent name.

Catherine See KATHERINE.

Christine, Christina Sophisticated, charming, and, above all, good: who could ask for more? Queen Christina of Sweden set the standard, becoming one of the most admired women in Europe in the seventeenth century. Of similarly noble mind and character was the medieval lady and poet Christine de Pisan, and the nineteenth-century poet Christina Rossetti. Of Greek origin, the name means "Christian." For more on the short form, see CHRIS. Diminutives: Chrissy, Christy.

Clair, Claire See CLARE.

Clare Strength, idealism, femininity, drive: this is what the world expects to find in Clare. In the Middle Ages, Clare of Assisi founded the first order of nuns, and the name was often used later in her honor. The name is also known because of journalist and politician Clare Boothe Luce. Clare means "bright"; it is the English form of CLARA. The French spelling, Clair, can also be used. Claire is another variation.

Claudia Her somber-sounding name dates back to ancient Rome, recalling the Emperor Claudius and other leaders known by the masculine form of the name. One of the United States's first ladies was Claudia Johnson, but she preferred to use her more lively nickname, Lady Bird. Claudia comes from a Roman clan name. For the French version, see CLAUDETTE.

Constance Steeped in old-fashioned American dependability and faithfulness, the name has also been a popular one around the world, for leading women including the English suffragette Constance Lytton, the Irish nationalist Constance Markievicz, and the famous literary translator Constance Garnett. Constance has the expected meaning, "constant" or "firm of purpose." The name was used by the New England Puritans, along with names such as Patience and Charity. The diminutive Connie is sometimes used as a separate name.

Cora, Coretta Strength, courage, and femininity all combine in the typical Coretta. The origin of this name is the Greek word *cora*, meaning "daughter" or "maiden." It is most often associated today with Coretta Scott King, civil-rights leader and widow of Dr. Martin Luther King, Jr.

Damaris Friendly, popular Damaris may well know her own mind—and not be afraid to stand up for her beliefs. This rare name is associated with Damaris Masham, an English scholar in the seventeenth century who argued for the education of women, against the common beliefs of her time. The origin and meaning of the name are unknown; it is mentioned in the New Testament as the name of a woman converted by Paul in Athens (Acts 17:34).

Deborah, Debra Courage, daring, and a desire to be at the center of the action seem to be a part of this name. In the American Revolution, Deborah Sampson disguised herself in men's clothing in order to fight as a soldier for the cause of liberty. In the Bible, Deborah was one of the most powerful women—a judge, prophetess, and a poet (Judges 4–5). The name comes from Hebrew and means "bee." Short form: Deb. Diminutive: see Debbie.

Diana, Diane The pinnacle of beauty, taste, and style is none too high for Diana. The pantheon of leading Dianas includes the Princess of Wales (born Lady Diana Frances Spencer); Diana Vreeland, who as editor-in-chief of *Vogue* magazine became the world's high priestess of style; the leader of the Supremes, Diana Ross; and esteemed critic Diana Trilling. In Roman mythology, Diana was the virgin goddess of the hunt and of the moon. She was the Roman equivalent of the Greek goddess ARTEMIS.

Dorcas A woman of initiative and good works is the traditional image of Dorcas. The name came into use in honor of a woman whose charity is described in the New Testament (Acts 9:36–42). A Dorcas Society is a women's group that supplies clothes to the poor. The name comes from Greek and means "gazelle."

Dorothea To hear her name for the first time is to picture a woman of noble grandeur . . . and true grit. The world's famous Dorotheas include Dorothea Dix, the social reformer and chief of nurses for the Union Army in the Civil War; Dorothea Beale, English educator and feminist; and First Lady Dolley Madison (whose given name was Dorothea). The classic name means "gift of God" and is the original Greek/Latin form of DOROTHY. Diminutives: Dolley, DOLLY, Doll, Dot, Dottie.

Eleanor, Eleanora, Eleonora, Elinor A glimmer of royalty seems to surround her name, which is known for the French and English queen Eleanor of Aquitaine, a twelfth-century power broker, and for First Lady Eleanor Roosevelt. This name has been in use since the Middle Ages. Of French origin, it is believed to be a variant of HELEN. Diminutives: Ellie, Elly, NELL, NELLIE, NELLY.

Elizabeth, Elisabeth Regal, beautiful, powerful, and popular: Elizabeth may be all these things. Consider, for example, England's Queen Elizabeth II and her distant predecessor in history, Queen Elizabeth I, who gave her name to the whole Elizabethan Age. Or perhaps she will take after Elizabeth Blackwell, the first woman awarded an M.D. degree; Elizabeth Garrett Anderson, the first woman doctor and the first woman mayor in England; cosmetics entrepreneur Elizabeth Arden whose real name is Florence Nightingale Graham; American suffrage worker Elizabeth Cady Stanton; or Elizabeth Agassiz, a naturalist and the first president of Radcliffe College. The name comes from Hebrew, meaning "oath of God." In the Bible, it is the name of the mother of John the Baptist. The French spelling is with an "s." The diminutive Betty is known for two leaders of great vitality, First Lady Betty Ford and feminist writer and organizer Betty Friedan. Other diminutives and variations include: Beth, BESS, BETSY, BETTE, ELIZA, Elsie, Elise, LISE, Liz, LIZA, and Lizzie.

Ellen With a keen mind and forceful personality, she's got what it takes to carry the show. Ellen Spencer Mussy became one of the first women lawyers in the United States. Ellen

Wilkinson (called "Red Ellen," partly for her politics and partly for her flaming hair) was a powerful English trade unionist, politician, and feminist. Ellen is a form of HELEN, originally from Scotland.

Emmeline, Emeline Her old-fashioned name brings to mind lace handkerchiefs, Victorian parlors, and two of the most famous English suffragettes, Emmeline Pankhurst and Emmeline Pethick-Lawrence. It is said to mean "industrious," as it seems to come from a Germanic word meaning "work." Diminutives: Em, Emmy.

Frances Her name suggests a sophistication and determination that could make her a leader in business, government, or a rarefied social set. Frances Perkins was a U.S. secretary of labor and the first woman appointed to the cabinet; Frances Willard was a leader in the fight for women's suffrage. For more on the diminutives, see FRANNIE, FRANNY. The diminutives Fannie and Fanny, extremely popular in the nineteenth century, are now obsolete due to the slang meaning, "buttocks," that has developed in the twentieth century. Frances is the feminine form of FRANCIS. Short form: Fran.

Francesca Her name has an authoritative European elegance that simply cannot be denied. It might bring to mind Francesca Cabrini (Mother Cabrini), the Italian-American religious leader and the first canonized American saint. This is the Italian form of Frances. See FRANCES for more on the name's origins and meaning.

Genevieve, Geneviève Her name is linked with the romantic city of Paris and its patron saint, whose fearless leadership saved the city from attack by Attila the Hun. In English the name may be pronounced GEN-a-vive; in French it is pronounced gen-vee-EV, with a soft "g." The name is of Celtic or Germanic origin, the meaning uncertain, though perhaps having to do with "race" or "people."

Gloria Diligence, beauty, and success seem to come naturally to Glorias. The world's best-known Glorias include Gloria Steinem, the feminist, writer, and founder of *Ms.* magazine; and Gloria Vanderbilt-Cooper, the "poor little rich girl" who became a painter, actress, and finally head of a successful fashion business. The name comes from Latin and means "glory."

Harriet She may be a crusader; she may be simply an unquenchable personality. Harriet Beecher Stowe and Harriet Tubman both fought to abolish slavery in the United States; Harriet Stanton Blatch was a leader in the movement for women's suffrage; many other Harriets in the nineteenth century led the way for women in journalism, medicine, and other fields. The name is a feminine form of HENRY. Diminutives: Hattie, Hatty.

Helen, Hélène, Helena Ever since the days of Greek legend, when the beautiful Helen of Troy was "the face that launched a thousand ships," Helen has been linked to beauty and power. In more recent times, Helen Gurley Brown launched the image of the "Cosmo Girl" as editor-in-chief of *Cosmopolitan.* Another famous Helen is author and lecturer Helen Keller. The name comes from Greek, meaning "the bright one." Helena is the Latin form (as in Helena Rubinstein, the beautician/businesswoman whose cosmetics bear her name). Hélène is the French version.

Isabel, Isabella, Isobel A lovely, mysterious risk-taker, you could find Isabel trading millions in stocks and bonds—or flying on the Concorde to adventures unknown. Isabella might be much the same, but a bit more old-school and grand. In world history, women known by this name are an impressive group, including Queen Isabella of Castile, who financed Columbus's discovery of the New World; Isabella d'Este, Italian Renaissance princess and patron of the arts;

and Isabella Stewart Gardner, the famed Boston art collector. These forms of ELIZABETH are used particularly in Scotland, France, Italy, and Spain.

Jacqueline, Jacquelyn Her name has a special glamour and power all its own from its association with one exceptional woman: Jacqueline Kennedy Onassis. But its great associations do not stop there. Intriguing with its European/masculine origin, the name is also associated with civil-rights leader Jacqueline Jackson (wife of Jesse Jackson), and aviator Jacqueline Cochran, the first woman to break the sound barrier. Jacqueline comes from French, as the feminine form of Jacques (JAMES). See JACKIE for more on the diminutive.

Jane Forthright, just, resilient, and perhaps something of a reformer, she is the type of person that others feel they can depend on. Some typical Janes of outstanding achievement include Jane Addams, social worker, suffragist, and Nobel Peace Prize winner; Jane Fonda, actress and political activist; politician Jane Byrne; and zoologist Jane Goodall, famed for her research on chimpanzees. The novelist Jane Austen led a more sheltered life than these other Janes, but she showed a similarly keen perception of human nature. Jane is a feminine form of JOHN and means "gift of the Lord."

Jean, Jeanne Feminine but strong is the image created by her name. It combines a sense of moral rectitude with a dash of glamour as in the most famous bearer of this name, the French heroine, Jeanne d'Arc—Joan of Arc. Jean and Jeanne are both feminine forms of JOHN, which means "gift of the Lord." Jean is Scottish in origin, while Jeanne is French. Diminutives: Jeanie and Jeannie.

Jeanette, Jeannette Her name sounds a little more flowery than JEAN, JEANNE, or JANET, but like them she could be a strong-minded person who achieves a great deal—like the feminist and pacifist Jeannette Rankin, the first woman elected to the United States Congress (1917). This French diminutive of JEANNE is a traditional favorite in Scotland.

Josephine Idealistic, outspoken, kind, Josephine may do great good in the world. The nineteenth and twentieth centuries have a proud collection of Josephines, including Josephine Baker, doctor and public-health activist; Josephine Baker, the acclaimed revue dancer who worked for the French Resistance in World War II; Josephine Shaw Lowell and Josephine Goldmark, American social reformers; and Josephine Butler, English feminist. The name was popularized by the glamorous Empress Josephine, wife of Napoleon. It is a French feminine form of JOSEPH. Short form: Jo.

Julia, Juliana, Julie She could be a proud, interesting, and perhaps even aristocratic person if she is like the famous Julias of the past. In the third century A.D., three powerful Julias (Julia Domna, Julia Maesa, and Julia Mammaea) were among the most influential leaders in the Roman Empire. In the fourteenth century, a beautiful, noble Florentine woman named Juliana Falconari became a religious leader and a saint. Julia Ward Howe was a social reformer who wrote the words to "The Battle Hymn of the Republic." Julie is a milder version of the name. The name is based on a Roman clan name, Julius.

Katherine, Katharine, Catherine An elemental grandeur surrounds her name, which is associated with publisher Katharine Graham; Catherine the Great, Empress of Russia; Catherine of Aragon; and Catherine de Médicis. The name comes from Greek and means "pure." Catherine reflects the French spelling, while Katherine is true to the original Greek orthography. Variations and diminutives: Kathryn, KATHLEEN, Kathy, Cathy, Kay, Kate, Katie, Katy, Katrina, Kit, KITTY.

Livia Proud, elegant, and perhaps a bit overpowering is the classic Livia. In ancient Rome, Livia was the formidable wife of Caesar Augustus; she was known for her great dignity and powerful influence on affairs of state. The name is sometimes considered to be a short form of OLIVIA, but it is not related. It comes from the Roman clan name Livius.

Lucy She may have a bold, courageous nature if she is a typical Lucy. Like Lucy Stone, the American feminist and abolitionist leader, she could be an eloquent speaker. Or she may be more like Lucy Walker, the English mountaineer. The elegant-sounding Lucia is the Latin, Italian, and Spanish form of the name. Originally from Latin, it means "light."

Lydia She could be an all-American entrepreneur and marketing genius—like Lydia Pinkham, who in the nineteenth century created and marketed "Mrs. Lydia E. Pinkham's Vegetable Compound," one of the most successful patent medicines of all time. The Lydia of the Bible was a successful businesswoman, too (Acts 16:14–15). The name comes from Hebrew, and means "one from Lydia," a region of Asia Minor. Short form: Lyde.

Mamie Her name may sound very old-fashioned today, but it is precisely this gracious quality that could make it a fine candidate for revival. The name is associated with First Lady Mamie Eisenhower. It originated as a diminutive of MARY.

Margaret A no-nonsense leader is the typical Margaret. Prime Minister Margaret Thatcher of Great Britain, U.S. Senator Margaret Chase Smith, birth-control leader Margaret Sanger, and anthropologist Margaret Mead are just a few of the Margarets who have made their mark on the twentieth century. During the Renaissance, the queens Margaret of Anjou, Margaret of Navarre, and Margaret of Valois all wielded considerable power. The name comes from the Greek *margarites*, meaning "pearl." Diminutives include: Meg, Maggie, PEGGY, PEG.

Martha Wholesome, friendly, and attentive, Martha could be found serving a home-cooked meal—or presiding over a state dinner. The name comes from Aramaic and means "lady" or "mistress." It often brings to mind America's *first* first lady, Martha Washington. Diminutives: Marti, Martie, Marty, MATTIE, MATTY.

Matilda This name means "mighty in battle," and its fame dates back at least to the eleventh century, when Matilda was the most powerful woman in Normandy and England, as the wife of William the Conqueror. In the twelfth century, her granddaughter was the queen of England and elected "Lady of the English." Diminutives: MATTIE, MATTY, TILLY, TILDA.

Maxine Capable, popular, and a bit world-wise, she could be a political dynamo like Maxine Waters. The name implies leadership and creativity in almost any field. It is a feminine form of MAX. An attractive variation is Maxime.

Nancy Though this name does not have the long history of some in this chapter, it has a firm association with power and prestige. It is known because of Nancy Astor, the first woman to sit in England's Parliament, and First Lady Nancy Reagan. This name developed as a diminutive of HANNAH or ANNE and thus has the same meaning, "grace." The name's short form, Nan, is both brisk and gracious-sounding and is sometimes a nickname for Ann or Hannah as well.

Noel, Noelle, Nowell A name that rings like silver jingle bells, *Noël* is the French word for Christmas. In history the name brings to mind Lady Noel Byron, a famous English philanthropist. Nowell reflects the word's medieval spelling. The name is sometimes used for men as well (see "Boys' Names" in "Creators").

Patricia "Patrician" is the meaning of her name, and whether or not she really comes from a wealthy background, she is likely to have the social skills and savvy to go far. First

Lady Patricia Nixon is one famous bearer of this name. The name comes from Latin (PATRICK is the masculine form). Short forms and diminutives include Pat, Patti, Patty, and Tricia.

Phyllis Strong-willed but feminine is the popular image of Phyllis. The name is sometimes connected with Phyllis Schlafly, the anti-feminist campaigner. A Phyllis may have the graceful strength of a lovely tree, for in Greek mythology, Phyllis was a maiden who was transformed into a tree. In English poetry, Phyllis is often used as a name for a country maid. From Greek, the name means "leaf."

Rosalyn, Rosalynn Gracious, sociable, *and* intelligent: Rosalyn could be all this and more. The name is known because of First Lady Rosalynn Carter. Rosalyn is a form of ROSALIND.

Rose, Rosa Like a rose, she is beautiful, hardy, and perhaps a bit prickly. The name is associated with Rose Kennedy; Saint Rose of Viterbo and Saint Rose of Lima, the latter the first canonized saint in the New World; and Rose Schneiderman, American trade unionist. It was brought to England by the Normans in the eleventh century. The variant Rosemary combines Rose and MARY. Rosemarie is also used.

Sandra This relatively new name, first used in this century, is now heard in the halls of power, from Wall Street to Washington—to the U.S. Supreme Court. It is best known nowadays because of Supreme Court Justice Sandra Day O'Connor, the first woman appointed to the court. The name comes from Alessandra, which is the Italian feminine of ALEXANDER, meaning "defender of men." Sandra is also sometimes used as a short form of ALEXANDRA. For more on the diminutive, see SANDY.

Shirley Cheerful, bright, attractive, energetic, she could be a Congresswoman like Shirley Chisholm, the first black woman elected to the House of Representatives, or an ambassador like Shirley Temple Black. The name was particularly popular during the 1930s and 1940s. Shirley was originally an English family name which came into use as a girls' name. Many variations of this name—Sherley, Shirlee, Shirly, Shurly, Sherline, Shirleen, to name some—have been used, but they have not attained the general acceptance of the original form.

Susan Your Susan could be a woman with foresight and the ability to inspire others if she's anything like women's suffrage leader Susan B. Anthony, or educator Susan Blow, who started the United States's first public kindergarten. Susan is a short form of SUSANNAH, which in Hebrew means "lily" (a symbol of purity). Diminutives: Susie, Suzy.

Teresa See THERESA.

Theodora, Theodosia Grand, pretty, and perhaps a bit eccentric: that could be Theodora. The name is famous in history for Byzantine Empress Theodora, the beautiful and powerful wife of the Emperor Justinian. Theodora and Theodosia both mean "God's gift." Like the masculine form, THEODORE, they are of Greek origin. DOROTHEA is essentially the same name in reverse order.

Theresa, Thérèse, Teresa Her name has strong religious connotations, as it is associated with three Catholic heroines. Saint Teresa of Avila combined a life of contemplation with good works in the sixteenth century, and in the nineteenth century a young Carmelite nun was honored as Saint Thérèse of Lisieux. In 1979, Mother Teresa's work in the slums of Calcutta won her the Nobel Peace Prize. Theresa is the most common spelling in the United States; Thérèse is the French form. The origin and meaning of this name are obscure. It may come from Greek and mean something like "harvest." Diminutives: Teri, Terri, Terry, TESS, Tessa.

Toni See ANTOINETTE.

Ursula This name bespeaks a sympathetic yet courageous nature. It has often been used in commemoration of Saint Ursula who, according to legend, was a British Christian princess killed along with her eleven thousand handmaidens by Huns at Cologne in the fourth century. The Ursuline order of nuns was named for her. The name comes from the Latin *ursa*, meaning "she-bear."

Victoria Conscientious, diligent Victoria should not be underestimated. Queen Victoria reigned over Great Britain longer than any king or queen, presided over the expansion of the empire and the industrial revolution, and gave her name to the entire Victorian Age. The name, from Latin, means "victory." Diminutives: Vicki, Vickie, Vicky, Vikki.

Wallis A king could give up the throne for Wallis—like Edward VIII did to marry Wallis Warfield Simpson, who then became the Duchess of Windsor. Power and romance are entwined in this name, which is a surname brought into use as a first name.

Wilhelmina, Williamina If she is named Wilhelmina, she probably goes by one of the many nicknames associated with the name. The full name is most often associated with Queen Wilhelmina of the Netherlands, who was forced to flee her country when it was invaded in World War II. Wilhelmina is the feminine form of Wilhelm (William in German). Williamina is a Scottish variation. Diminutives of this name, often used on their own, include: Mina, MINNIE, WILLA, and WILMA.

Winifred Her Welsh name lends her a pleasant, unintimidating aura of sophistication. The name has two nice advantages: its meaning, "blessed reconciliation," and its preppy-sounding diminutive, Winnie. The diminutive is associated with the heroic South African political activist Winnie Mandela.

BOYS' NAMES

Abraham, Abram Greatness may be in store for Abraham, with this powerful and ancient name. Abraham of the Bible, the father of the Israelites, and United States president Abraham Lincoln, who held the union together and abolished slavery, are the two great heroes whose legacies echo in this name. A rare name in the twentieth century, two modern examples are Supreme Court Justice Abe Fortas and Abraham Saperstein, who became a lasting influence on basketball by founding the Harlem Globetrotters. Both Abram and Abraham are used as given names, but in the Bible, when God made his covenant with Abram (which probably meant "the father is exalted"), he changed his name to Abraham, meaning "father of a multitude." Short form: Abe.

Adlai Distinguished and thoughtful is Adlai's image, created by one impressive U.S. family. Adlai Ewing Stevenson was vice president under Grover Cleveland; his grandson, Adlai Stevenson, ran for president against Dwight Eisenhower; his great-grandson Adlai was a senator. The name comes from a list in the Bible (1 Chronicles 27:29).

Aidan This Irish name commemorates the humble and adventuresome Christian leader, Saint Aidan, a native of Ireland who traveled to the island of Lindisfarne off the coast of Northumberland to spread the gospel and found a monastery. The name comes from Gaelic and means "fire." Alternative spellings: Aden, Aiden.

Alexander, Alex An Alexander may not be easily satisfied with the status quo, and in the tradition of the Greek warrior Alexander the Great, some of them may set out to conquer the world. The name comes from Greek and means "defender of men." Short form: Alex.

Andrew He could be a leader by nature if his name is Andrew. Just a few of the world's top Andrews include industrialist and philanthropist Andrew Carnegie, U.S. president

Andrew Jackson, and Prince Andrew of England. The name came originally from Greek and means "manly." It is sometimes considered a Scottish name because Saint Andrew, one of the Twelve Apostles, is the patron saint of that country. The Scandinavian form is Anders, like the scientist Anders Jonas Angström. Andreas and Andrea, respectively, are the German and Italian forms. Short form: Andy.

August, Augustus Power and prestige of both worldly and unworldly sorts seem to be August's destiny. Augustus was the title conferred on the first Roman Emperor, meaning "exalted, sublime, and venerable." The name also brings to mind Saint Augustine, the most influential Christian theologian of all time. The various forms of this name are: August (German), Auguste (French), Augustus (Latin), and Augustin/Augustine (Latin diminutives).

Averil, Averill, Averell With this Old English name, he is apt to have a sixth sense for getting along in the world, bred in the bone as if from ages past. In recent times, the name's most famous bearer has been Averell Harriman, businessman, ambassador to the Soviet Union, and governor of New York. It means something like "wild boar" or "boar favor."

Barry Genial, likable, opinionated, smart—that is the popular image of Barry. The name is best known for the U.S. senator from Arizona, Barry Goldwater. Barry comes from the Old Irish names Berrach or Bearrach, of obscure meaning.

Benedict There may be an American prejudice against Benedict, based on the famous traitor of the American Revolution, Benedict Arnold. However, the name is connected with several admirable leaders. The name is used in honor of Saint Benedict of Nursia, the sixth-century founder of the Benedictine order of monks. It is also the name of several popes, and with its wonderful meaning one can see why. It comes from the Latin word *benedictus*, meaning "blessed."

Benjamin Friendly and innovative is the image of Benjamin, ever since Benjamin Franklin proved the existence of electricity in lightning with a kite and a key, founded America's first post office, wrote *Poor Richard's Almanack*, became a diplomat to France and America's favorite bespectacled hero. Other leading Benjamins include Benjamin Disraeli (a political essayist and novelist before he became England's prime minister), and Benjamin Cardozo (a U.S. Supreme Court justice and legal scholar known for his eloquence). Of Hebrew origin, the name means "son of the right hand," thus, "lucky." See BEN for more on the short form.

Bennet, Bennett Success in business could be in store for charming, ingenious Bennett. This name brings to mind Bennett Cerf, cofounder of the famous publishing company Random House. This variation of BENEDICT is also familiar as a last name.

Brigham A stern and brilliant leader is the popular conception of Brigham. The name is often connected with Mormon leader Brigham Young, who led the settlement of Salt Lake City. The name comes from an Old English family name meaning "settler at the bridge."

Calvin From predestination to the presidency—Calvin is apt to be leading the way. This family name came into use as a first name in honor of the great Protestant reformer, John Calvin. In the United States the name is also famous because of president Calvin Coolidge (born John Calvin Coolidge). Short form: Cal.

Carter Particularly in matters of taste, Carter is one to follow. The name is associated with art critic Carter Ratcliff and museum director J. Carter Brown. Of course it is also known because of U.S. president Jimmy Carter. The name comes from Old English and means "cart driver."

Charles A real Charles is a true man, in the very best

sense. The name comes from the Old High German word *karl*, meaning "man." The powerful king Charlemagne (also called Charles the Great and, in Latin, Carolus Magnus) was one of the first and greatest bearers of this name. Since the Middle Ages, the name has been used by royalty, including the contemporary heir to the British throne, Prince Charles. It is also associated with Charles de Gaulle, the French general and statesman. See CHUCK for more on the nickname. For more on the German form see CARL, KARL.

Chester His name may sound a bit old-fashioned, but it is still hearty. Chester Alan Arthur took the name to the White House as president in the nineteenth century, and Chester William Nimitz took it to war as commander of the Pacific fleet in World War II. This English name can be traced back to the Latin word for "camp." See CHET for more on the short form.

Claiborne, Clay, Clayborn, Clayborne, Clayton He could be a fighter by nature, but one with a nose for politics and compromise, like the famous American statesman Henry Clay. The name is also associated with boxer Cassius Clay (later known as Muhammad Ali). Clay is a last name that is sometimes used as a first name, as are Clayborn, Clayborne, Claiborne (associated with Rhode Island senator Claiborne Pell), and Clayton (associated with politician Adam Clayton Powell).

Constantine His unusual name suggests that he might be a highly successful maverick. Constantine I was the first Roman emperor to convert to Christianity, and was also known as a powerful and effective ruler. The name, from Latin, means "constant" or "steadfast."

Cotton With this distinctive name, he could be of very old New England stock—or perhaps just his name is. In the early 1700s, Cotton Mather was one of New England's most influential Puritan ministers. The name comes from an Anglo-Saxon last name, meaning "at the cottages."

Cyrus He will be powerful *and* diplomatic, if he is true to the traditional image of Cyrus. Cyrus Vance brought this name into prominence in recent years when he was U.S. secretary of state. Cyrus the Great, king of Persia in the sixth century B.C., was known for his just and diplomatic treatment of the diverse cultures within his empire. The name comes from Persian, possibly meaning "throne" or "sun." See CY.

Darius Daring and dynamic, this name is associated with the ancient Persian king Darius the Great, who met one of his few defeats at the Battle of Marathon in 490 B.C. The original meaning of the name is unknown; "the king" and "wealthy" have been suggested.

David The handsome boy who killed the giant Goliath with a sling and went on to become king of Israel—that's the ideal image of David. In the United States, David is a common name among business leaders, including David Packard, cofounder of the giant computer company Hewlett-Packard. In Israel's modern history, the name is known for statesman David Ben-Gurion. The name was favored in early America, along with many other Old Testament names, and rose to new heights of popularity in the mid-twentieth century. This ancient Hebrew name may mean "beloved." Short form: Dave. For more on the diminutives, see DAVY, DAVI.

De Witt Confidence, intelligence, and perhaps even a touch of arrogance are suggested by this name. It is best known for De Witt Clinton, a mayor of New York City and governor of New York in the early 1800s, famed as an early supporter of public education and city planning. The name is of Dutch origin.

Donald Strong, aggressive, but fun-loving is the popular image of Donald. It is the ninth most popular name among America's top one thousand CEOs, but it hit the publicity jackpot with megamogul Donald Trump. This Gaelic name, from the Highlands of Scotland, means "world-mighty." For more on the short form, see DON.

Douglas He could have a proud fighting streak, for this Scottish name is associated with five-star general Douglas MacArthur. It is a Scottish family name that came into use as a first name. Of obscure Gaelic origin, it may mean "dark" or "gray." Short form: Doug.

Dunstan His old Anglo-Saxon name can give him a distinct aura of privilege. Saint Dunstan is the most famous Anglo-Saxon saint, a tenth-century man of noble background who, in addition to his religious deeds, was a counsellor to kings and has been called "one of the makers of England."

Dwight His name suggests someone tough, friendly, and fair. It became well-known because of Dwight David Eisenhower (nicknamed "Ike"), who rose meteorically through the military to the rank of general, and was elected president of the United States. Dwight is an old New England family name; Timothy Dwight was a president of Yale (1795–1817).

Earl, Erle He is a man who can command respect, while seeming a bit creative and out-of-the-ordinary at the same time. His name does not have the centuries-long history of William, Charles, or John, but it has a long legacy as a surname and, more importantly, as a noble title. As a given name, it is connected with Supreme Court Chief Justice Earl Warren and former president James Earl ("Jimmy") Carter, Jr. The name's origin is Old English, meaning "warrior," "nobleman," or "chief." For a possible nickname, see EARLY.

Edward He might be ebullient or gloomy, impetuous or thoughtful—and, if he takes up the tradition of this century's famous Edwards, he'll be a newsmaker. The name brings to mind Senator Edward Kennedy; New York City mayor Edward Koch; newscaster Edward R. Murrow; and King Edward VIII of England, who gave up the throne to marry Wallis Simpson. This Old English name is interpreted variously as "guardian of family possessions," "prosperous guardian," or "happy guardian." Short form: Ed. For more on the diminutive, see EDDIE.

Ethan His name has an old New England gusto because of hero Ethan Allen, who led the Green Mountain Boys of Vermont in the American Revolution. In the Old Testament, Ethan was a wise man who lived at the time of Solomon (1 Kings 4:31). The Hebrew name means "ancient."

Felix His name means "happy," and happiness may indeed be one of his gifts. Two prominent Felixes have worked for the happiness of others: Felix Frankfurter, a Supreme Court justice, and Felix Adler, founder of the Ethical Culture Movement.

Franklin A keen mind and a jovial personality are qualities associated with Franklin. Two U.S. presidents had the name, Franklin Pierce and Franklin Delano Roosevelt. It also belonged to one of the most famous Americans of all time: the statesman and inventor Benjamin Franklin. Franklin seems to have been originally used as a first name in his honor. In medieval England, a franklin was a freeholder of nonnoble birth who held extensive property, thus, a "country gentleman." Short form: FRANK.

Frederick His name can sound imposing or casual, depending on whether he goes by Frederick, Fred, Ricky, or Rick. Famous Fredericks include abolitionist leader Frederick Douglass, communist philosopher and revolutionary Friedrich Engels, and a succession of Danish kings and Holy Roman Emperors such as Frederick the Great and Frederick Barbarossa. The name comes originally from Old High German and means "peaceful ruler." For more on short forms of the name, see FRED and RICKY.

George His name has a long, proud history, beginning with Saint George's slaying of a dragon. In England the Order of the Garter was awarded in honor of Saint George. Every American knows the name because of George Washington, and it is also associated with General George S. Patton and President George Bush. The name's original meaning, from Greek, is "farmer."

Hamilton A man of keen mind, appealing manners, and upper-crust background is the popular image of Hamilton. Hamilton is a surname that came into use as a first name, probably in honor of the early American statesman Alexander Hamilton. Hamilton Fish (possibly named for Alexander Hamilton) served as U.S. secretary of state in the late nineteenth century.

Hannibal Proud, brilliant, and strong, in a larger-than-life way: this is the traditional view of Hannibal. In ancient history, Hannibal was a general of Carthage, one of the great military geniuses of all time.

Harlan, Harland Serious, highly educated, with a keen mind and perhaps an elite background, this evocative name could take him as far as the Supreme Court, like Harlan Fiske Stone, Chief Justice from 1941–46. The name returned to the court in 1955 with Associate Justice John M. Harlan. This Teutonic name is said to mean "land of warriors."

Harry Friendly, dependable, traditional, this name is best known for the U.S. president Harry S. Truman. Today it is also known for Charles and Di's son, Great Britain's Prince Harry. It was a very popular name in the late 1800s, continued to be fairly popular through the 1940s, and was also known because of people like publishing magnate Harry Chandler. Harry is sometimes considered a diminutive of HENRY, but actually the reverse is true. When the Normans brought the name to England (in the French form, Henri), it was first Anglicized as Harry. Later it developed into Henry. It means "ruler of the house."

Henry Influence and power could be on Henry's agenda. The world's great Henrys include a long line of English kings ending with Henry VIII; explorer Henry Hudson; and industrialist Henry Ford. In the late nineteenth century, railroad heir Henry Huntington and steel magnate Henry Clay Frick were kings of American business. Like HARRY, Henry comes from the Old French name Henri, which came from an Old High German name meaning "ruler of the house." For more on its diminutives, see HAL and HANK.

Herbert This name is best known in history because of President Herbert Hoover. Not currently in fashion, it has a rather middle-aged, trustworthy sound. Herbert comes from an Old High German name meaning "bright army." Diminutives: Herb, Herbie, and BERT.

Horatio Forceful, intrepid, talented, and a bit romantic is the popular image of Horatio. The name brings to mind the great English naval hero Horatio Nelson, victor at the Battle of Trafalgar. Horatio comes from a Roman clan name.

Hubert Idealism and intelligence combine in the popular image of Hubert, created mostly by Hubert H. Humphrey. Of Germanic origin, Hubert means something like "bright heart/mind." The name was well known in the Middle Ages because of Saint Hubert, the patron saint of hunters.

Hugh Valiant Hugh may reign over his domain like a kind but powerful feudal lord. Now unusual, his name was a common one in medieval times. Hugh Capet, king of France in the tenth century, was the first of the Capetians. Hugh of Grenoble, Hugh of Lincoln, and Hugh the Great were all powerful figures in medieval England and France (and saints as well). This name is of Germanic origin, meaning "heart, mind." Diminutive: Hughie.

James A calm, sensible, yet courageous personality is the popular image of James. Among the leaders of corporate America in the 1980s, the name ranks among the most popular. The name's dozens of positive associations include U.S. presidents James Madison, James Monroe, and James Buchanan; and the King James Bible. In Hebrew, James and JACOB are the same name; they were later differentiated in English, French, and Spanish. The actual Hebrew meaning is unclear, though it is sometimes said to mean "the supplanter" because of the biblical Jacob's role in taking his brother's birthright. For more on the diminutives, see JIM and JIMMY.

Jefferson Courageous, dashing, persuasive, his name is sometimes associated with Southern hero Jefferson Davis, president of the Confederacy. This all-American name may also bring to mind the author of the Declaration of Independence, Thomas Jefferson, for whom Jefferson Davis was probably named. Short form: JEFF.

Jesse Destiny may knock on the door if his name is Jesse. The Rev. Jesse Jackson became one of the most influential leaders of his generation. In the Bible, Jesse was the father of King David. Of Hebrew origin, the name means "God is."

John If his name is John, he has what is perhaps the most beloved and popular name in the history of the English language. Forms of his name exist in many other languages as well. The name initially came into use in honor of John the Evangelist (called "the beloved" disciple) and John the Baptist. From the time of the first colonial settlements in America until 1950, John was continuously among the top three boys' names. Since about 1950 it has had a surprising slide, down to fifth place in 1970, and not even in the top ten in 1986. Now, for the first time in centuries, a child named John may not encounter many other children with the same name! At the same time, he will have the distinguished history of the name behind him. The world's famous Johns include John Adams, Pope John XXIII, John F. Kennedy, John Wesley, John Calvin, John Glenn, John Muir, John Marshall, John Jacob Astor, and John D. Rockefeller. In the United States, John is currently the number one name among CEOs of the top one thousand corporations. Forms of John listed elsewhere in this book include IAN (Scottish), SEAN (Irish), IVAN (Russian), Johannes, HANS (German), Jean (French), and Giovanni (Italian). (See also JONATHAN.) The name comes originally from Hebrew, meaning "the Lord is gracious." For more on the diminutive, see JOHNNY.

Joseph This name was a common one in the United States for many years and bespeaks a hard-working and capable person. Government and business leader, Joseph Kennedy, father of John, Robert, and Edward Kennedy, was one well-known bearer of this name. In the Bible, Joseph (of the "coat of many colors") was sold into slavery in Egypt and went on to become a powerful high official there. From the New Testament are Joseph of Arimathea and Joseph the husband of Mary. Diminutive: Joey. For more on the short form, see JOE.

Justin, Justinian, Justus He is fair and reliable in his dealings, if he lives up to the Latin meaning of his name, "just." It is known in history because of Emperor Justinian I, who codified Roman law in the sixth century.

Knox Brisk and assertive: that is the image of Knox. The name recalls Protestant reformer John Knox, the founder of Scottish Presbyterianism.

Leland Smooth, intelligent Leland could come from wealth—or mean to come into it. The name is sometimes connected with Leland Stanford, the railroad baron who founded Stanford University. (His given name was Amasa Leland Stanford, but he never used Amasa.) Leland comes from Old English, meaning "meadow land." Leland has fallen off in popularity in recent years.

Lincoln He could be a great leader, like Abraham Lincoln, with this name that is traditionally given in honor of the great U.S. president. The name originally comes from an English place name.

Lloyd He could be on his way up in business, government, or the arts with this name. The name's connections in high places are mostly British, such as David Lloyd George, the powerful politician and prime minister during World War I. Of Welsh origin, it means "gray."

Lyndon Hard work, intelligence, and friendliness seem to combine in this pleasant-sounding name. President Lyndon Baines Johnson became the most prominent American to bear this name. It seems to have originated as a surname, meaning "linden tree hill."

Madison Good-natured, well-mannered, and well-to-do is how one might picture Madison. In almost any field he could do well. The name recalls James Madison, the United States's fourth president and one of the framers of the Constitution.

Malcolm His name suggests a man who knows the ways of power, in the tradition of publisher and *bon vivant* Malcolm Forbes, or civil-rights activist Malcolm X (born Malcolm Little). In Scottish history, Malcolm III was a powerful ruler who killed the infamous Macbeth (thus avenging his father Duncan's murder). Of Scottish origin, the name comes from Gaelic.

Marcus A classic name for inspiring confidence, it is connected with the great Roman emperor Marcus Aurelius. It may also bring to mind the black nationalist leader Marcus Garvey. The name is the Latin form of MARK and is associated with the name of the Roman god of war, Mars.

Marshall In business, government, or academia he could go far. The name is known because of media guru Marshall McLuhan and nineteenth-century merchant mogul Marshall Field, whose name is carried on by the Chicago department store. Part of its power and prestige come from its use as a last name, notably for general and statesman George C. Marshall, Supreme Court Chief Justice John Marshall, and Supreme Court Associate Justice Thurgood Marshall. The name comes from an Old High German word meaning "keeper of the horses." In many countries, a marshal is the highest-ranking military officer.

Martin Martin's greatest power may be that of persuasion—like that of the young monk Martin Luther who began the Reformation, and the young minister Martin Luther King, Jr., who led the civil-rights movement in America. Martin Van Buren was the eighth president of the United States. Like MARCUS, MARK, and MARIO, this name derived from that of the Roman god of war, Mars. Diminutive: Marty.

Medgar A vision for the future and courage for the present: this could be the definition of his name. It is famous because of Mississippi civil-rights leader Medgar Evers.

Nelson He could be a popular leader if his name is Nelson. In the United States it is associated with the wealthy Nelson Aldrich Rockefeller, a four-term governor of New York and vice president. In England the name is sometimes given in honor of the great hero of the Battle of Trafalgar, Horatio Nelson. The name means "son of Neil" or "son of Nell."

Patrick Since he has the most famous of all the Irish names, it is best if he likes being Irish. In an amazing career, filled with courage and determination, Saint Patrick brought Christianity to Ireland in the fifth century, and he has been venerated there ever since. The American Revolution has a heroic Patrick too—Patrick Henry, who proclaimed, "Give me liberty or give me death." Patrick means "patrician." Short form: Pat.

Richard This name came to England with the Norman Conquest, and it has been used in English since. The world's leading Richards range from King Richard the Lion-Hearted to U.S. president Richard Nixon. Its original meaning is believed to be "powerful and bold" or "powerful ruler." For more on the short form, see DICK.

Robert This name means "fame bright," and its fame is now going on one thousand years. Past and present, the name's picture is bright with Roberts such as the heroic senator and presidential candidate, Robert Kennedy; the father of modern chemistry, Robert Boyle; and Confederate general Robert E. Lee. This distinguished and intelligent-sounding name is one of the most common for top CEOs in corporate America. The name is of Germanic origin, and its arrival in England dates from the Norman Conquest in 1066. Nicknames: Rob, Robbie, ROBIN, Bobby, Bob.

Ronald Powerful personal appeal is part of this name, which comes from Scotland and means "decreeing powers" or "mighty power." The world's most famous Ronald is the United States's fortieth president, Ronald Wilson Reagan. Nickname: Ron.

Rufus He is apt to be a capable and fiery individual if his name is Rufus. The name is associated in early U.S. history with politician Rufus King, who was a governor of New York and ran against James Monroe for president. In European history it is associated with William Rufus, the son of William the Conqueror who became king of England. Of Latin origin, the name means "red-haired."

Salmon A blast from America's high-flown past, this obscure biblical name was not unheard of when the abolitionist Salmon Portland Chase (1808–73) enjoyed an extremely distinguished career as a U.S. senator, governor, chief justice of the Supreme Court, and secretary of the treasury. In the Bible, Salmon was the great-grandfather of King David. This Hebrew name may mean "peace" or "strength."

Samuel, Sam A good man to have around in a crisis: that is the popular stereotype of Samuel and Sam. Famous Samuels include Texas statesman Sam Houston; revolutionary patriot Samuel Adams; labor leader and AFL founder Samuel Gompers; and movie mogul Samuel Goldwyn. This biblical name means "heard by God" or "name of God." Short forms: Sam, Sammy.

Standish An old-school, blue-blooded American is the

image of Standish. The name came to America on the *Mayflower* with the redoubtable leader of the Plymouth colony, Miles Standish.

Ted Popularity, good looks, and high achievement are all part of Ted's image. This name is associated with broadcasting's Ted Turner and the Senate's Ted Kennedy. The diminutive Teddy is best known for U.S. president Teddy Roosevelt. Ted is a nickname for both EDWARD and THEODORE, sometimes used as an independent name. Many Edwards and Theodores come to be known almost exclusively as Ted.

Theodore Your Theodore could be much loved and highly esteemed, for his name comes from Greek and means "God's gift." One of the world's best-known Theodores is America's "Rough Rider" president, Theodore Roosevelt (the first teddy bears were named for him).

Thomas Dreams and ideals that could change the world are part of this name—along with two great men of the American Revolution, Thomas Jefferson (author of the Declaration of Independence) and the pamphleteer Thomas Paine. The name Thomas came to the Americas with the *Mayflower* and was one of the most popular names in the colonies. Other famous Thomases from around the world include bishop and martyr Thomas à Becket, Catholic theologian Thomas Aquinas, and connoisseur Thomas Hoving. This Aramaic name came into use through the Apostle Thomas and means "twin." Short forms: Tom, Tommy.

Thurgood Good will, good humor, and many other thoroughly good things can be heard in this name. It is famous for jurist Thurgood Marshall, the first black appointed to the U.S. Supreme Court. This seems to be a surname brought into use as a first name.

Truman "A faithful, loyal man" is the meaning of this Old English name, and that is the character it implies. Usually considered a surname, Truman recalls the U.S. president Harry S. Truman.

Warren Part manager and part artist, part creative spirit and part analytical advisor, Warren could be a successful actor *and* director/producer, like Warren Beatty. If he is of a more intellectual bent, he could take after Warren Earl Burger, Supreme Court chief justice. Of a political bent, he could be the second U.S. president named Warren, after Warren G. Harding. Warren originated as a last name—as in Earl Warren, who was Burger's predecessor as chief justice.

William Strong and successful: that is the image that has kept William going for one thousand years. This Norman name landed on British shores in 1066 with no less a personage than William the Conqueror himself. Other famous Williams of the past include William Shakespeare; William Tell (the Swiss hero remembered in the famous William Tell Overture); William Penn, the founder of Pennsylvania; and three U.S. presidents (Harrison, McKinley, and Taft). Other famous Williams include newspaper baron William Randolph Hearst, chewing-gum magnate William Wrigley, and CBS chairman William S. Paley. Among names of heads of the United States's top one thousand corporations, William ranks second only to John in popularity. Of Germanic origin, the name combines words for "will" and "helmet," and thus is often interpreted as "resolute protector." Short forms: Bill, Will. Diminutives: Billy, WILLIE.

Wilson This familiar last name has two claims on the United States presidency: Woodrow Wilson and Ronald Wilson Reagan. As an authoritative first name, it is known because of educator Wilson Riles, the first black superintendent of schools of California. Short form: Bill.

Winston Winston creates a distinctly aristocratic impression. The name is best known for Winston Churchill (full name: Sir Winston Leonard Spencer Churchill), the British statesman, soldier, orator, author, and twentieth-century Renaissance man. The name, from Old English, is mainly used as a surname.

Winthrop A true blue-blooded New England pedigree seems to come with this name. As a surname, it is famous in colonial history because of the Winthrop family of Massachusetts, starting with John Winthrop, who became governor of the Massachusetts Bay colony in 1629. In the twentieth century, the name has been used as a first name, most notably by Winthrop Rockefeller, a governor of Arkansas and a member of the wealthy Rockefeller family.

Woodrow A thoughtful, intellectual aura is part of Woodrow. The name is famous because of U.S. president Woodrow Wilson. It comes from Old English and means something like "from the hedgerow by the woods."

Zachary Action and zeal can almost be heard in this name, famous because of President Zachary Taylor, who was called "Old Rough and Ready." Zachary is a short form of ZACHARIAS, ZACHARIAH, or ZECHARIAH. Short form: Zach, Zack.

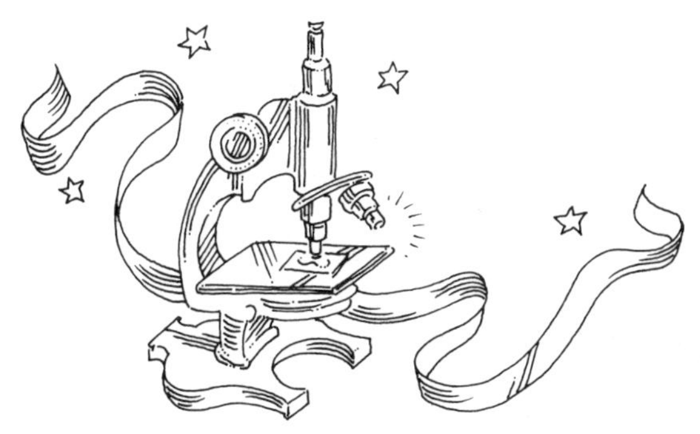

5
DISCOVERERS

The names that follow are associated with discovery of all kinds—in science, mathematics, law, religion, the arts, languages, geography, and more. They are names of people not afraid to push the outer limits of knowledge or experience, whether that means designing a computer or scaling a mountain. The famous people known by these names had guts, determination, creativity, and vision, and those are the traits these names imply. In English-speaking countries these names tend not to have strong associations with any one particular sector of society. They generally do not send an easily readable message like "artsy," "privileged," "educated," "popular," or "powerful." (Some of them, however, are common names in non-English speaking countries; their significance in those countries is beyond the scope of this book.) These are the most democratic names, ones that promise not beauty or highbrow family connections (though they can be part of the package too) but achievement.

GIRLS' NAMES

Ada Friendly, reliable, and smart is the current image of this old-fashioned name. It is associated with English mathematician (and daughter of Lord Byron) Ada Lovelace—and the high-level computer programming language, ADA, named in her honor. Ada is a short version of Adelaide or ADELINE that became popular in the late nineteenth century.

Adela, Adele No Twinkies, please, for Adele! This good-hearted, trustworthy-sounding name is known because of Adele Davis, a pioneer in the field of nutrition and health. Adela is another version of the name, with a slightly more elegant, flowery sound. This name is of Germanic origin and has been in use since the Middle Ages. It means "noble."

Agnes Righteousness and purity have long been associated with her name, which is often given in honor of the fourth-century virgin and martyr, Saint Agnes, who discovered new depths of faith in declaring Christ her bridegroom, in what is now the practice of all nuns. The name was used in medieval and Renaissance Europe. The variations Annice and Annis reflect the Pre-Renaissance spelling, Annes, and do not have the strong Catholic associations of Agnes. Originally from Greek, the name means "pure." Diminutives: Aggie, Nessie.

Aileen See EILEEN.

Alexandra A proud, fascinating, perhaps even aristocratic individualist: that could be Alexandra. She might indeed be like Alexandra David-Neal, who traveled in disguise to explore Tibet and become the first European woman to visit the forbidden city of Lhasa. Alexandra is considered an upper-crust name in England, but it has long been widely used in Scotland. Originally from Greek, Alexandra is the feminine form of ALEXANDER, and means "defender of men." Variations and short forms: Alexandria, Alexandrina, Alexa, ALEXIS, Alix, SANDRA, SANDY.

Amelia Amelia could be a dreamer and an individualist who has the determination to make her dreams come true. The name is most often associated with Amelia Earhart, the first woman to fly solo across the Atlantic (1932). (She later disappeared in the South Pacific while trying to fly around the world.) Like EMILY, Amelia comes from a Roman clan name, Aemilius.

Annice, Annis See AGNES.

Annie A lively, indomitable spirit is the mark of a typical Annie. The name is known for astronomer Annie Jump Cannon; mountaineer Annie Peck; and Western sharpshooter Annie Oakley, who challenged the limits imposed on women of her day. This diminutive of ANNE was often used as an independent name in the nineteenth century. Naturally, it has the same meaning, "grace."

Arlene Steadiness, endurance, and energy are all part of the popular picture of Arlene. The name has a distinctly twentieth-century flavor, having come into popular use in the 1930s. One notable Arlene was American mountaineer Arlene Blum. The origin and meaning of this name are unknown; it may come from Gaelic, meaning "pledge." Alternate spellings: Arline, Arleen.

Bernadette Her old-fashioned French Catholic name brings to mind striking images, new and old. Most famous is Bernadette of Lourdes, the young French girl whose visions of the Virgin Mary in 1858 made her name known around the world. This name is a feminine diminutive of BERNARD.

Eileen Precise: that is one popular stereotype of Eileen. She could excel as a scholar, like Eileen Power, the English historian who was a pioneer in the field of women's history. The name originated as an Irish form of HELEN. Variations include Aileen, Ayleen, and Ilene.

Germaine This name may herald an intelligent, sophisticated, and fearless challenger of ideas and beliefs. It brings to mind feminist author Germaine Greer. Of Latin origin, this French name means "German."

Honor, Honour, Honora A woman of grace, dignity, and intelligence: that is how one pictures Honor. In science, the name is associated with British cell biologist Dame Honor Fell. The name carries the obvious meaning. It was used by the Puritan colonists in New England, but generally it has been more common in Britain than in the Americas.

Irene The name is associated with brilliance in science because of Irène Joliot-Curie (daughter of Marie Curie), who with her husband won the 1935 Nobel Prize in chemistry. It comes from Greek and means "peace."

Joy What can one expect from Joy but a happy, generous nature? The name is fitting for Joy Adamson, the conservationist who returned Elsa the lion cub to the wild and described it in her book *Born Free.* The name comes from the familiar English word. Variations include: Joie (French), Joi, and Joya.

Judith A woman of strong character is the popular perception of Judith. The name is associated with astronaut Judith Resnick, who died in the *Challenger* disaster. Of Hebrew origin, the name means "Jewish woman." For more on the diminutive, see JUDY.

Lise Attractive and likable is the image of Lise. She might be brilliant as well, like Lise Meitner, the acclaimed Austrian physicist. Lise is a short form of ELIZABETH, used particularly in Continental Europe.

Marie Gentle and kind is a popular notion of Marie. This French form of MARY is known for many notable women, including French chemist Marie Lavoisier and scientist Marie Curie, the winner of *two* Nobel Prizes—one in physics and one in chemistry—for her discovery of radium and research on radioactivity.

Rosalind Her name suggests strength of character, femininity, and an inquiring spirit. She might be a great scientist, like Rosalind Franklin, the English molecular biologist who helped discover the structure of DNA. This name is generally described as being of Germanic origin, combining words for "horse" and "serpent." It is also sometimes interpreted as a combination of the Spanish words for "rose" and "pretty."

Sally Outgoing, sensible, and successful, she may come from a leading family—or rocket to new heights on her own, like the astronaut Sally Ride. Sally originated in England as a diminutive of SARAH; it later became well accepted as an independent name. Alternative spelling: Sallie.

Sheila She might break records—like English aviator Sheila Scott—or break the molds of history, like historian, feminist, and socialist Sheila Rowbotham. In Australia, "sheila" is slang for "girl," but that term is not related to the name Sheila. Sheila is an Irish form of Celia.

BOYS' NAMES

Alan, Allan, Allen, Alain With calmness and perseverance, Alan may set out to redefine the possible—and succeed! Alan Bartlett Shephard, Jr., became the first American to be launched into space. Alan M. Turing's theories on "thinking machines" foresaw the computer. Alain Robbe-Grillet set out to redefine the novel and set a new literary standard. This name may have originated with the Celts, perhaps as Alun, meaning "harmony." The French spelling is Alain.

Albert Idealism, honesty, dedication, and perhaps even brilliance are all qualities one expects from an Albert. The world's greatest Albert is, of course, Albert Einstein. The original German name is Albrecht, as in artist Albrecht Dürer. It means "noble-bright." The diminutives are BERT and Bertie in England and AL in the United States.

Alexis He may excel in medicine like Alexis Carrel, the winner of the 1912 Nobel Prize in medicine, or alter the way others look at the world, like social philosopher Alexis de Tocqueville. Alexis is sometimes used as a women's name, though it is traditionally used for men. Of Greek origin, it means "defender."

Alfred Curiosity combined with ingenuity and insight could take Alfred far. One Alfred invented dynamite and instituted the Nobel Prizes (Alfred Nobel). This Old English name derives from the words "elf counsel," signifying that elves (or some other supernatural power) give the bearer advice.

Amerigo He's bound to have exploration in his blood, if he is anything like Amerigo Vespucci. The Italian navigator explored the New World after Columbus, and it is for him that America is named. Perhaps another person named Amerigo will one day explore the frontiers of space.

Aristotle Fame and wisdom seem to be the birthright of an Aristotle. The Greek philosopher Aristotle is held in such esteem that the name may seem too potent to give an ordinary mortal, though it is used from time to time, particularly in Greece.

Asa This old-fashioned name harks back to the integrity and ingenuity of earlier days. Asa Gray was America's greatest early botanist. In Hebrew the name means "physician."

Bartholomew For five hundred years, ever since the Portuguese navigator Bartholomew Dias discovered the Cape of Good Hope, this name has been linked with discovery. Dias's name reflects the Portuguese spelling. See BART for more on the short form.

Bernard, Barnard This serious and intellectual-sounding name may herald a *re*-discoverer—like art critic and connoisseur Bernard Berenson, who brought to light many forgotten masterpieces of European art. The name comes from Old High German and means "bear bold" or "bear stern." Diminutives: Barney, Bernie.

Bertram, Bertrand This name may sound opinionated and a bit aristocratic, for it is known especially because of Bertrand Russell, the mathematician, philosopher, and liberal social reformer. (He was also an English earl.) This Teutonic name came to Britain with the Normans and means "bright raven." The form Bertrand is also a familiar name in France.

Blaise His name sounds like he will be blazing trails, but he could be a highly sophisticated pathfinder. This name is associated with seventeenth-century scientist and philosopher Blaise Pascal, whose discoveries contributed to physics, calculus, and the theory of probability.

Bronson Manliness and brawn are inherent in this Anglo-Saxon name. Yet an intellectual career might be in store for Bronson as well. Amos Bronson Alcott was an American educator, transcendentalist philosopher, and the father of the writer Louisa May Alcott (*Little Women*).

Bruno His name sounds earthy, but he may have a mind attuned to the mysteries of loftier spheres. Bruno Bettelheim, the famous psychologist, wrote on human behavior and the meaning of fairy tales; and Saint Bruno founded the Carthusian order of monks. This Teutonic name means "brown."

Buckminster With the name Buckminster, scientific innovation and creativity may come naturally to him. Buckminster Fuller, whose revolutionary designs include the geodesic dome, was one of the most innovative architects and engineers of modern times. He was born Richard Buckminster Fuller but went by Buckminster. Diminutive: Bucky.

Buzz He's likable and adventuresome, with a scientific bent, if he fits the popular image of Buzz. Buzz was the nickname of astronaut Edwin Eugene Aldrin, Jr., who followed Neil Armstrong out the hatch of Apollo 11 to become the second person to walk on the moon.

Carl, Karl This name suggests someone full of new ideas. Carl Sagan, Carl Jung, Karl Marx, the English philosopher Sir Karl Popper, and three Nobel Prize winners in science were named Carl or Karl. Carl is a form of CHARLES; Karl is the German spelling.

Christian, Christiaan Whatever his talents, he will likely use them well, so that his good name may rest lightly on his shoulders. The name's meaning, "follower of Christ," may inspire a life like that of Christiaan Barnard, who performed the first successful heart transplant. Several Nobel Prize winners also have this name, which is much more common in Europe than in the United States.

Christopher Like Christopher Columbus, he may be destined for great discoveries. The name comes from the Greek word *Kristophoros*, meaning "Christ bearer." In Italian it is Cristoforo; in Spanish it is Cristóbal. According to legend, Saint Christopher carried the Christ child across a river. Saint Christopher is also the patron saint of travelers.

Chuck Men who go by this unassuming, informal name can do some surprising things! In fact, breaking down barriers may be a specialty for some Chucks, such as Chuck Yeager, who became the first pilot to break the sound barrier. Chuck is usually a nickname for CHARLES.

Clarence His name may sound vaguely aristocratic, but if he's like Clarence Seward Darrow or Clarence Birdseye, he won't sit on his laurels. As a lawyer, Darrow used his ingenuity to defend the underdog. As an inventor, Birdseye's experiments created the frozen food industry. Clarence is sometimes said to mean "illustrious" or "bright," as it seems to come from the Latin word *clarus*.

Columbus For the adventurous Columbus, anything is possible. Columbus has occasionally been given as a first name in honor of Christopher Columbus, and with the five hundredth anniversary of his discovery of America to be celebrated in 1992, that's all the more reason to consider it.

Dana, Dane One expects a straightforward, upbeat person to go with this simple, attractive name. Originally a family name, Dana has been used as a name for boys and, more recently, for girls. The adventurous Richard Henry Dana, who set out on a sea voyage that became the subject of his famous book *Two Years Before the Mast*, may have inspired some use of the name. Dana and Dane are sometimes said to mean "Danish" or "a Dane." In Scandinavian countries, Dana is a feminine name derived from Daniela.

Darwin Like Charles Darwin, he may devise a scientific theory that rocks the world. Whatever he does, he is likely to be an interesting and original character. This family name has occasionally served as a first name.

Davy, Davi Davy could be described as a diamond in the rough, or a backwoods hero like Davy Crockett. In addition to being "king of the wild frontier," Crockett was a congressman and one of the valiant men who died at the Alamo. The name is a diminutive of DAVID.

Dennis, Denis Dennis may be happiest when his work and pleasure are one. The French philosopher Denis Diderot's curiosity about the world served his life's work, the revolutionary *Encyclopédie*, a foundation of the Enlightenment. The name comes from that of the Greek god Dionysius, the god of wine.

Edison He won't be able to take credit for the light bulb or the phonograph, but with this name he's likely to have an inventive spirit. This name recalls the great inventor Thomas Alva Edison.

Edwin He's talented, athletic, ingenious, and lucky, if he's a typical Edwin. The astronaut Edwin Eugene Aldrin, Jr., is famous as the second man to step on the moon. Edwin is an Old English name meaning "rich friend" or "friend of (family) possessions." Short form: Ed.

Eli His old-fashioned name suggests intelligence and ingenuity. It is most famous in history because of Eli Whitney, inventor of the cotton gin. This Hebrew name means "high."

Elias Like ELI, Elias could turn out to be a very inventive person. In the nineteenth century, Elias Howe was one of the inventors of the sewing machine. Elias is the form of the name Elijah that is used in the New Testament. It means "Yahweh is God."

Eliot, Elliot, Elliott He may seem mild-mannered, but he could turn out to be an American hero like Eliot Ness, uncovering crime and corruption as the young U.S. treasury agent who led "The Untouchables" in the famous crackdown on Chicago's gangsters and the notorious Al Capone. This is a last name, which is used as a first name.

Elmo See ERASMUS.

Erasmus With this name he could be a discoverer of new ideas, in the tradition of Desiderius Erasmus (born Geert Geerts), one of the most learned humanists and Christians of the Renaissance. If he takes to the sea, you might keep in mind that Saint Erasmus (also called Saint Elmo) is the patron of sailors.

Eric, Erik This proud Norse name has a heroic history. Of the many Scandinavian kings and heroes named Eric, the most famous was Erik the Red, the Norse chieftain who discovered Greenland circa A.D. 982. Eric means something like "honored ruler" or "powerful government."

Erwin Underneath this unassuming name could hide a genius, perhaps like Nobel Prize–winning quantum physicist Erwin Schrödinger. The name is of Germanic origin and may mean "boar friend." Irwin is a common variation. Irwyn is also sometimes used.

Euclid *Geometry Without Tears* could be Euclid's best-seller. He is bound to be associated with mathematics, for his name is the same as that of the third-century B.C. Greek mathematician, Euclid, whose theories provide the basis for geometry.

Ferdinand, Fernand A whole new worldview is not too much to expect of Ferdinand. The Portuguese navigator Ferdinand Magellan led the expedition that made the first voyage around the world. The French historian Fernand Braudel pioneered a new way of interpreting world history. This Germanic name means "adventurer."

Francis English explorer Sir Francis Drake and scientist Francis Crick (who with James Watson discovered the structure of DNA and won the Nobel Prize) are two famed discoverers to bear this name. Among early American colonists the name was popular, but in the nineteenth century it began to be used as a woman's name (see FRANCES), and it has declined in use for men ever since. This name has two sources. It began in France as François, from the same Latin root as the word "France." It got started in Italy with Saint Francis of Assisi, who was actually named Giovanni (John), but was always known by his nickname Francesco, "the Frenchman." The saint's popularity helped spread the name throughout the Western world as Francesco (Italian), FRANCISCO (Spanish), FRANZ (German), and Francis (English).

Francisco Power and adventure are associated with this name, which is known in history because of Spanish conquistador Francisco Pizarro. This is the Spanish form of FRANCIS.

Franz His name sounds both friendly and smart, a great combination for success. It is known in the sciences because of Franz Boas, the most influential anthropologist of all time. The name is a Germanic form of FRANCIS.

Galileo With the musical ring of his Italian name and its connection with one of the most brilliant scientific minds in history, there's no telling what he might do. Galileo Galilei's experiments with physics, his invention of the telescope, and his theory of planetary motion all transformed common notions about the universe.

Gerald His name may not seem dazzlingly exciting, but that will not prevent him from becoming a solid, even dazzling, success. Gerald Edelman won the Nobel Prize for unraveling the structure of the antibody molecule; Gerald Durrell turned his experiences as a zoologist into highly amusing books. The name seems to be a peaceable one, despite its meaning of "spear wielder" in Old High German. See JERRY for more on its nickname.

Hans This cheerful, pleasant name may herald a person of a similar nature. Hans is a short form of Johannes (the German form of John), meaning "the Lord is gracious." The name is also associated with Hans Küng, the Swiss Roman Catholic theologian, and several Nobel Prize winners in science.

Howard This name suggests an imaginative guy whose quests could possibly even make him as rich as Howard Hughes. In addition to Hughes, the name is that of Howard Carter, who, along with Lord Carnarvon discovered the tomb of King Tut. This noble English surname was brought into use as a first name in the past two hundred years. The original meaning in Old German may be "heart brave" or "high warden." Nickname: Howie.

Hugo A keen mind and diligent hard work are qualities

associated with Hugo. This name has a great legal tradition, starting with Hugo Grotius, the founder of modern international law. On the U.S. Supreme Court, Hugo Black worked to define new legal territory in the court's important rulings on civil rights. This Germanic name comes from roots meaning "heart" and "mind" and is thus sometimes said to mean "intelligent."

Ignatius, Ignace With the name Ignatius, he will be associated with both Catholicism and learning. Saint Ignatius of Loyola was the founder of the Society of Jesus (Jesuit order). The Latin name means "fervent" or "fiery."

Irwin See ERWIN.

Jedidiah For inspiring good old-fashioned trust, there is no one better than Jedidiah. Mountain man Jedidiah Strong Smith was one of the great explorers of the American West. In the Bible, Jedidiah was not a character but an epithet applied to Solomon, meaning "beloved of the Lord" (2 Samuel 12:24–25). Short form: Jed.

Jim Willing to strike out on new trails, he could take after Jim Bridger, the celebrated mountain man and Rocky Mountains explorer; or he may be more like Jim Henson, the inventive genius behind the Muppets. Usually, Jim is a diminutive of JAMES. Diminutives: JIMMY and Jimi.

Karl See CARL.

Kit Luck, ingenuity, and a love of life are the traits that go along with Kit. This name is best known because of famed frontiersman Kit Carson. Kit is a nickname for CHRISTOPHER.

Kurt Like Conrad, Kurt is a name that sounds very smart. It may bring to mind one of mathematics' geniuses, Kurt Gödel. This name developed as a diminutive of Conrad and Konrad. For more on origins and meaning, see CONRAD.

Learned His name could be his motto, but if he is like the famous jurist Learned Hand, he will do more than simply acquire knowledge. Learned Hand defended and helped expand the rights of free speech during more than forty years as a federal judge.

Leif His name speaks of physical prowess, adventure—and Leif Eriksson, the Norwegian navigator who discovered America around A.D. 1000. This ancient and pleasant-sounding Scandinavian name is said to mean "beloved" or "descendant."

Linus Linus is thought to be wise, intelligent, and peace-loving—and with good reason. Linus Carl Pauling won *two* Nobel Prizes, one for his discoveries in chemistry, the other for his work for peace. The name comes from Greek and means "flax."

Luther His name may suggest revolutionary ideas and strength of purpose. One notable bearer of this name was Luther Burbank, the famous agriculturist who developed many new varieties of fruits and flowers. It came into use in honor of Martin Luther.

Marco He's popular, lively, carefree, and adventurous if he lives up to the promise of his name. With such a name he could go far, like Marco Polo, who left Venice in the thirteenth century to become the first European to visit China. See MARK.

Max Maximum success in science, business, or the arts is Max's way. Five Nobel Prize winners share the name, including Max Planck, whose work led to the development of the quantum theory. Although used as a whole name, Max is actually a short form of Maxmilian or Maximilian, coined by German emperor Frederick III from the Latin.

Meriwether Happy trails seem in store for the person named Meriwether. The "Lewis" half of the famous Lewis and

Clark expedition that explored the uncharted American West was Meriwether Lewis. This name might also be used for a daughter.

Neil, Neal, Niels, Niall His ancient Celtic name will be forever famous because of Neil Armstrong, who on July 20, 1969, became the first man to walk on the moon. The name is used in various forms throughout Scandinavia and in England, Ireland, and Scotland. The form Niels is best known for the great Danish physicist Niels Bohr. Niall is the Old Irish form of the name. It means "champion."

Nicholas, Nicolas, Nicolaus He may be a kind and generous "jolly old Saint Nicholas," or a brilliant star of science, like the astronomer Nicolaus Copernicus. The name combines the Greek words for "victory" and "the people." For more on the short form of the name, see NICK.

Noam An astute individual is expected if his name is Noam. If he is anything like the famous linguist Noam Chomsky, who revolutionized his field, he will fill the bill. He may be very likable too, for the name in Hebrew means "delight."

Norbert He is bound to be smart, and he could be a genius, if he fits the image of Norbert. This name is associated with mathematician Norbert Wiener, who invented cybernetics. In Old German it means "famous in the North."

Norman No, the Norman Conquest wasn't his doing! But the world's Normans have done some important things. The agronomist Norman Ernest Borlaug won the Nobel Peace Prize for his work toward eliminating world hunger. Norman Cousins discovered that laughter and a positive attitude can promote good health. The name means "North man," thus "one from the North."

Plato This classical name seems to herald someone of great natural curiosity and wisdom, like the Greek philosopher Plato. The Greek form of the name is Platon.

René His French name is known all over the world thanks to René Descartes, the father of modern philosophy, the founder of analytic geometry, and more. It is given to girls as well (spelled Renée).

Roald He is bound for adventure and discovery, if he is like Roald Amundsen, the first man to reach the South Pole. This Scandinavian name means "famous power."

Sigmund, Siegmund Intellectual brilliance is associated with Sigmund, due to the fame of psychiatrist Sigmund Freud. In Norse mythology, Sigmund was a famous warrior. The name means "victorious protection."

Stanislaw, Stanislaus He will have a bold and intrepid spirit if he lives up to his name. He might explore the universe as an astronaut—or as a science-fiction writer and philosopher like Stanislaw Lem. This Slavic name means "glory of the camp." Stan could be used as a short form.

Tycho At an international astronomy conference, Tycho could be the envy of all for his jaunty, sophisticated, and appropriate name. Tycho Brahe was a famous Danish astronomer of the sixteenth century. The name is pronounced TIE-co.

Vasco A gallant and intrepid spirit is suggested by this name, famed for two great seafaring explorers. Vasco Núñez de Balboa discovered the Pacific Ocean in 1513, and the Portuguese navigator Vasco da Gama was the first European to travel by sea to India.

Werner, Wernher His name expresses power mingled with a sense of mystery and the unknown. It is familiar in America because of Wernher von Braun, the German-American rocket engineer. It means "warrior protector" or "guard."

Yuri In most of the world, this name brings to mind one man: Yuri Gagarin, the Soviet astronaut who became the first man in space in 1961. Yuri is a Russian form of GEORGE.

Zebulon, Zebulun His unusual name may suggest an idiosyncratic person, bound for discoveries and adventure, like the American explorer Zebulon Pike, who discovered Pike's Peak in Colorado. This Hebrew name means "to honor" or "to endow."

Zeno His name may puzzle some people, but that may suit him fine if he is like the Greek philosopher Zeno. Zeno's paradoxes, devised in the fifth century B.C., continue to confound scientists and philosophers today.

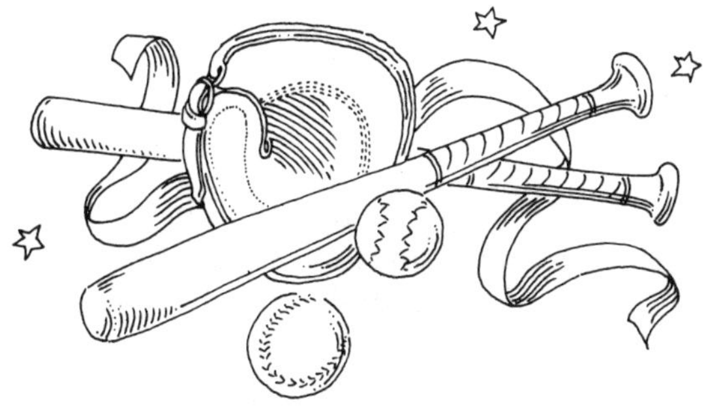

6
ATHLETES

The following names are famous because of their connections with some of the world's greatest sports heroes and heroines. They are names that hint that the bearer just *might* be Olympics or World Series material. More than that, they imply qualities of health, power, control, determination, sportsmanship, friendliness, and fair play. They are names that could serve well in many fields, but particularly in business, where the drive and competitiveness learned in sports may be an integral part of corporate life.

Many famous sports figures are best known by their nicknames, or by a short form of their full name. Some of these nicknames and short forms are given here.

GIRLS' NAMES

Althea, Althaea An aura of classical greatness surrounds Althea, for in the tennis pantheon of immortals reigns Althea Gibson. She was not only one of the sport's great champions, but the first black to play in the U.S. championships and at

Wimbledon. Althea comes from a Greek word that means "healer." It is also the name of a shrub known as "rose of Sharon."

Babe Anyone named Babe is simply the best! So this is a name that usually takes some living before it really fits. Babe Didrikson Zaharias (born Mildred Didrikson) is generally considered the United States's greatest woman athlete ever. Among many other feats, she won Olympic gold medals in track and field and was a dominant figure in women's golf for almost two decades. For baseball's legendary Babe Ruth, see the listing under "Boys' Names."

Billie Jean Vivacity, toughness, and determination are linked with Billie Jean. And if she's like tennis star Billie Jean King, she's a winner and just the type to beat someone like Bobby Riggs in a "Battle of the Sexes."

Chris A keen competitor and courteous colleague is the vision Chris brings to mind. She may be a champion too, in the tradition of tennis star Chris Evert Lloyd. Chris is a short form of CHRISTINE or CHRISTINA. The diminutive is Chrissie.

Dawn "One who brings sunshine" is an apt definition of Dawn. With its cheerful meaning and brevity, Dawn makes a fine name for an athlete such as Dawn Fraser, the Australian swimmer and Olympic gold medalist in 1956, 1960, and 1964.

Evelyn This name has belonged to medieval ladies *and* modern track stars, and it has a time-honored connotation of both grace and grit. The track champion Evelyn Ashford is one of many women who have done the name honor. Other, older forms of the name are Avelyn (Middle English), Aveline (Norman French), and Avelina (Old High German). In the past it has sometimes been used as a man's name as well (see "Boys' Names" in "Creators").

Evonne See Yvonne.

Florence This name may be breaking out of its old-fashioned image, thanks to the glamorous, record-breaking track star Florence Griffith Joyner. This name dates from ancient Rome and was later used in Britain primarily for men. In the nineteenth century, it was popularized by Florence Nightingale, whose parents gave her the name because she was born in Florence, Italy. From Latin, the name means "flowering." Diminutives: Flo, Florie, Florrie, Flory, Floss, Flossie, Floy.

Hana In the world of international tennis, her name brings to mind Hana Mandlikova, the cute, successful Czechoslovakian star known for her elegant style on the court. But this is a truly international name, for in Europe it could be taken as a short form of JOANNA or HANNAH, while in Arabic the same name means "joy," and in Japanese it means "blossom."

Irina Her name suggests a special calm beneath her strength, as befits its meaning: "peace." To Americans, this Russian name also signifies athletic power and prowess, exemplified by Irina Press, the great Russian track and field champion, and Irina Rodnina, the great Russian ice skater. This is a Russian form of IRENE.

Jackie Bright, vivacious, energetic, attractive—that is just the *average* Jackie. The *super* Jackie could become one of the fastest women in the world, like track star Jackie Joyner-Kersee. Jackie is used as an independent name, or as a diminutive of JACQUELINE.

Janet Steady, confident, and cheerful: this is the popular image of Janet. In Olympic sports it is connected with the petite and spritely gold medal swimmer Janet Evans. This form of JANE originated in France but became especially popular in Scotland.

Larissa Her name sounds like a combination of Laura and

Lisa, but it actually comes from a Latin word meaning "cheerful." With this happy yet dignified name she might follow in the steps of Larissa Latynina, a Russian athlete and one of the most successful gymnasts of all time.

Lottie Old-fashioned friendliness, gumption, and a good dash of originality are what one might expect of a Lottie. When Lottie Dod was a famous British tennis prodigy in the nineteenth century, the name was much more common than it is today. Lottie originated as a diminutive of CHARLOTTE.

Martina, Martine She could be a tough competitor, for her name comes from the Roman god of war, Mars. Martina Navratilova has won the Wimbledon singles title eight times through 1988 (only Helen Wills Moody won more) and holds the record for winning Wimbledon six times in succession. The name's masculine form is MARTIN.

Maureen A kind and friendly—and winning—nature are what one expects of her. Maureen Connolly ("Little Mo"), one of the top tennis players of all time, helped make this name well known. This Irish name is a diminutive of Mary. The Irish spelling, Mairin, is not usually used in the United States but might appeal to parents in search of a very unusual name.

Nadia She could be a romantic, elegant, enigmatic figure, who may seem on a higher, more exotic plane than the rest of the world. The name's most famous bearer is Nadia Comaneci, the first gymnast to achieve a perfect score of 10 in an Olympic event. This Russian name means "hope." NADINE is the French form.

Olga Proud and serious is the traditional image of Olga, but ever since the effervescent gymnast Olga Korbut bounded straight to fame and victory in the 1972 Olympic Games, the name has had a new kind of recognition. This Russian name comes from an Old Norse word meaning "holy." Helga is the form used in Scandinavia.

Stephanie, Stephie, Stefanie, Steffi Attractive, energetic, and determined are adjectives that come to mind when one thinks of Stephanie. She may even turn out to be a Grand Slam tennis champion like Steffi Graf (full name, Stefanie Maria Graf). Like STEPHEN, the name originates from the Greek word for "crown." It was originally a French name.

Tracy Lively, gritty, feminine: that is the public image of Tracy. In sports the name has a winning edge because of its association with Tracy Austin, the blonde Californian who became a tennis sensation when she was still in braces. In the 1984 Olympics it became known for swimmer Tracy Caulkins. Other forms of the name include Tracey, Traci, and Tracie.

Willye If her name is Willye, she's got a great sports heritage behind her, with men like Willie Mays (see "Boys' Names") and a great woman's long jump champion like Willye White. Like WILMA, this name may come from WILHELMINA.

Wilma There is something heroic about this simple, unusual name, as if it's saying "we try harder." For Wilma Rudolph that meant overcoming not only poverty but a crippling childhood disease to become an Olympic gold medalist in track. This heroine was dubbed "the black gazelle." Wilma may come from WILHELMINA.

Yvonne, Evonne Two traits associated with Yvonne are grace and strength—which the French might ascribe to her French name. Those in the know would credit the influence of Evonne Goolagong Cawley, famous for her happy personality and balletic form on the tennis court. Yvonne is the name's traditional spelling; it is the feminine form of the French name Yvon, which may mean "archer." Other forms of the name include Ivonne, Yvonna, and Yvette.

BOYS' NAMES

Al He's a competitor with class and drive, especially if he's behind the wheel of a race car, like Al Unser and Al Unser, Jr. Al is usually a short form of ALBERT, ALEXANDER, or Alphonse, but many men with these names go by Al on all but the most formal occasions.

Babe This great sports nickname belongs of course to baseball's one and only Babe Ruth (George Herman Ruth). Ruth's other nickname, "The Bambino," means "the baby" or "the kid" in Italian, so you might want to try that one out on your infant. (See also the listing under "Girls' Names.")

Bancroft, Ban Tough but pleasant is the impression given by this name. Ban was the form used by Byron Bancroft "Ban" Johnson, who as president of the American League from 1894-1927 turned it into a major league.

Bart, Bartlett Power, speed, and style are all expected of Bart. This name is best known for the great football quarterback Bart Starr (born Bryan Bartlett Starr). More recently, it has become known because of Bart Giamatti (full name: A. Bartlett Giamatti), president of baseball's National League. Bart is also used as a short form of names like BARTHOLOMEW and Barton.

Bjorn The boy named Bjorn is apt to have bounce, and the man is likely to have a definite international sophistication. The tennis star Bjorn Borg made this Swedish name famous when as a teenager he led the first Davis Cup victory in Sweden's history, and he went on to win Wimbledon five times. Parents with a Scandinavian background or surname might especially consider the name.

Boris Boris could have drive, power, charm, sophistication, and a touch of arrogance—like German tennis star Boris Becker. The name is of Russian origin, meaning "battle."

Brad There's probably not a girl in the world who would refuse a blind date with a Brad, unless she suffered from an incurable case of low self-confidence. Most people think of Brad as a manly sort of guy: handsome, athletic, perhaps like tennis star Brad Gilbert. The word "brad" means "broad" in Old English. Other variations of the name are Bradford (broad ford), Bradley (broad meadow), and Bradwell (wide spring).

Bronko He's a powerhouse of strength and endurance, if he's anything like the legendary Chicago Bears football player Bronko Nagurski. Nagurski's given name was Bronislau, but from childhood he was called Bronko.

Cap His name suggests someone smart, fast, and an all-around great kid . . . maybe a bit old-fashioned, since his name has not been used much lately. Cap is sometimes short for CASPAR, but in the early days of baseball, first baseman-manager Cap Anson was known to everyone as Cap, though his given name was Adrian.

Casey He is capable of bravery and bravado, sacrifice and swagger if he lives up to the traditional meaning of his name. As a sports name it means Casey Stengel (born Charles Dillon Stengel), the colorful manager who took the New York Yankees to seven world championships. In history and song, it means Casey Jones (born John Luther Jones), the locomotive engineer who gave his life but saved his passengers in the famous wreck of the Cannonball Express. Jones's nickname came from the town of Cayce, Kentucky.

Cassius He could be proud and cunning as a Roman senator—or one of history's great boxers. The name first belonged to an ancient Roman family, the most famous member of which led the conspiracy to assassinate Julius Caesar on the Ides of March. The most famous American Cassius is the great boxer Cassius Marcellus Clay, Jr. He changed his name to Muhammad Ali when he became a Black Muslim.

Cy An old-fashioned aura surrounds this jaunty, casual name. Some of that doubtless comes from Cy Young (born Denton True Young), who at the turn of the century was one of baseball's great pitchers. Cy is usually a short form of CYRUS.

Darryl, Daryl, Darrell He's likely to be popular and talented, and if he's like Mets right fielder Darryl Strawberry he's also a home-run hitter. Of unknown origin, this name may come from Old English, but it has a contemporary sound. With men like Strawberry making it famous, all its connotations are great. However, parents may wish to note that it might be used as a girl's name, as with actress Daryl Hannah.

Dazzy What can Dazzy be but dazzling? This zingy sports name belonged to Brooklyn Dodgers pitcher Dazzy Vance (born Clarence Arthur Vance) who, starting in 1922, pitched his way into the Baseball Hall of Fame.

Dizzy In some cultures, parents give their infants temporary names with meanings like "ugly" or "stupid" to ward off bad luck and fool jealous spirits. In sports, a name like Dizzy could disarm opponents in the same way. It can also mean "dizzyingly great," like baseball pitchers Dizzy Dean (born Jay Hanna Dean), or Dizzy Trout.

Don On the world's ski slopes, jogging trails, surfing beaches, and playing fields, Dons abound—and there tend to be a lot of them in places like the World Series and the U.S. Open too. In baseball there's slugger Don Mattingly, and of course pitcher Don Drysdale, who until the end of the 1988 season held the record for the most consecutive scoreless innings. In tennis there's Don Budge, the first player to win a Grand Slam. This name is usually short for DONALD.

Early All systems are go for Early. Everyone knows "the early bird gets the worm," and baseball fans know Early Wynn, a great pitcher from 1939–63. Early could be used as a diminutive for EARL.

Eppa This unique and spunky name belonged to Baseball Hall of Famer Eppa Rixey, a great pitcher from 1912–33. The name could be used on its own or as a short form of EPHRAIM.

Gilbert, Gil If he goes by Gilbert he may seem vaguely artistic, but if he uses the short form, Gil, he could bring to mind baseball's Gil Hodges. This Germanic name means "pledge."

Gordon, Gordie With this rough-and-ready name, he just might turn out to be the next Gordie Howe, a great hockey player, and perhaps the best forward in history (records in the NHL for the most seasons, the most games, the most goals, and the most points). The name originated as a Scottish clan name.

Grantland His name has a fine, solid, Midwestern ring, and it is best known because of Grantland Rice, who has been called the patron saint of the sportswriting fraternity. This name could bode well for a career in sports, journalism, and many other areas.

Hank A man known as Hank may have a quiet prowess at whatever he undertakes. This is a top-ranked baseball name, including on the roster home-run king Hank Aaron and the great Hank Greenberg. In football, it is associated with Hank McDonald, the first black admitted to the pros. Hank is usually a nickname for HENRY.

Ivan Physical prowess and power are qualities many Americans associate with this Russian name. To tennis fans it also brings to mind Ivan Lendl (ranked number one in the world until late in 1988). The name is pronounced EE-von. It is the Russian form of JOHN.

Jackie A great sportsman, gentleman, and entertainer: Jackie could be any or all of these. The name is legendary in baseball because of Jackie Robinson, the first black admitted to the major leagues. In boxing it recalls Jackie Fields. Jackie is a diminutive of JACK.

Jimmy, Jimbo His real name is probably JAMES, but if he aspires to greatness in sports he'd do well to go by Jimmy. Tennis star Jimmy "Jimbo" Connors has lent the name a winning cachet.

Joe Toughness, gallantry, and savoir faire all combine in this name, which is linked with four sports greats: Joe DiMaggio, Joe Louis, Joe Frazier, and Joe Namath. The name is usually used as a short form of JOSEPH.

Johnny In any sport he could be Johnny-on-the-spot, doing whatever needs to be done. In baseball the name is famous because of the great catcher and all-around player Johnny Bench. Johnny is usually a nickname for JOHN.

Julius As an athlete he could achieve classic greatness, like basketball's incredible Julius Irving. Julius is an ancient Roman clan name.

Junior A boy named for his father is often saddled with the nickname Junior. Those who endure Junior status can take heart from the successful career of baseball's James "Junior" Gilliam.

Kareem, Karim He could be a towering giant in the world of sports—like basketball's Kareem Abdul-Jabbar (born Ferdinand Lewis ["Lew"] Alcindor). To most Americans, the name Kareem means simply "one of the most valuable basketball players ever." In Arabic, Kareem has a positive meaning too: "generous."

Kenesaw You can bet that a child named Kenesaw comes from a family that loves baseball. The name Kenesaw was linked with the sport from 1920 to 1944 in the form of Kenesaw Mountain Landis, the first commissioner of baseball.

Knute The name Knute says forward pass, winning team, and the best of college football in the United States—all because of the Norwegian-born player and coach Knute Rockne, who established Notre Dame's great football tradition. One drawback to this name is that in English it is pronounced like "newt," a type of salamander.

Lefty In business, it would not be easy to trust a man named Lefty. In sports, however, players like baseball's Lefty Grove (born Robert Grove) have given the left-hander's nickname a positive connotation.

Leon His name means "lion," but most people sense that lions (and Leons) can be both roaring fighters and gentle pussycats. In sports the name became famous because of heavyweight boxer Leon Spinks, who defeated Muhammad Ali in 1978, then lost to him later that same year. It is also the real name of baseball's Goose Goslin.

Lou, Lew Like many great sports names (Al, Cy, Gil, Ty), Lou is a brief yet graceful form of a longer name. Lou Gehrig and Lou Brock made the name famous in baseball. Lew Hoad brought it to tennis, and Lew Alcindor (later known as Kareem Abdul-Jabbar) brought it to basketball. For more on the origins and meanings of these forms of Louis and Lewis, see LOUIS.

Magic His name promises someone charming, surprising, emotional, fun, and gifted with a winning touch. When Earvin "Magic" Johnson was given his nickname in high school, his mother sensibly worried that it might one day give him too much to live up to. But Magic Johnson went on to bring more ability, creativity, and panache to basketball than practically any other player.

Mario A dramatic flair and a strong competitive streak can take Mario racing to the front of the pack. He could be a race car driver like Mario Andretti . . . or find his own fast track to the top. Like MARK and MARCUS, Mario (the Italian and Spanish form) comes from the name of the Roman god of war, Mars.

Meadowlark He may sing, fly, or play basketball like a charm—like the great Meadowlark Lemon, "court jester" and incredible player for the Harlem Globetrotters. Meadowlark is Lemon's real first name; his father's first name was Meadow. The meadowlark is a type of bird noted for its beautiful songs.

Mickey His name suggests a popular winner—like sports hero Mickey Mantle. Mickey is also known for baseball's great Mickey Cochrane (born Gordon Cochrane) and Mickey Welch (born Michael Welch). Any parent considering the name MICHAEL (the most popular boy's name in the late 1980s) should consider the happy alternative of Mickey, either as the official name, as it was for Mantle, or as a nickname.

Muhammad A powerful individual with strong beliefs is the image of Muhammad. When Cassius Clay became a Black Muslim he changed his name to Muhammad Ali to signify his new life. Muhammad was the chief prophet of Islam, and believers throughout the Islamic world and in the Black Muslim movement are named in his honor.

O. J. Like running back O. J. Simpson, he could be headed for sports superstardom. The Juice's full name is Orenthal James Simpson. Parents may wish to consider these names or others beginning with "O" and "J" to make the initials O. J.

Orel This name suggests a modest and appealing fellow—whose tenacity and talent just might take him all the way to the World Series, like the Dodgers' record-breaking pitcher Orel Hershiser.

Pelé He could be just what U.S. soccer needs—a Pelé of its own. Pelé may be the most well-known sports name in the world. It is the nickname of soccer superhero Edson Arantes do Nascimento.

Pete He's someone to count on, if he lives up to his name. Pete Rose exemplified the player to count on in baseball, breaking records and winning three batting titles throughout his career. Pete is a short form of PETER, which means "a rock."

Pie Like many whimsical names, this one may designate a great baseball player. Baseball Hall of Famer Pie Traynor (born Harold Traynor) won distinction as a great batter and third baseman with the Pittsburgh Pirates.

Rafer Rafer sounds like a one-of-a-kind. In sports he might be a track star like Rafer Johnson, Olympic decathlon champion in 1960. The name could be a nickname for RAPHAEL.

Red In the wide world of sports there is probably no name more universally esteemed than Red. A boy called Red will have heroes to look up to in many areas, including football (halfback Red Grange); basketball (coach and general manager Red Auerbach); baseball (pitcher Red Ruffing); and reporting (sportswriter Red Smith). For all these men, Red was a nickname. It is often given as a nickname to people with red hair.

Reggie, Reginald He may have crowd-pleasing energy, coordination, and what it takes to become a baseball star like Reggie Jackson. Jackson is fast doing away with the old stereotype of Reggie/Reginald as a stuffy English aristocrat. Reginald developed from two Old English words meaning "power" and "force."

Rocky, Rocco Brutality mixed with compassion, courage

mixed with kindness: these are the stereotypes that surround Rocky. The great boxer Rocky Marciano was indeed brutal in the ring and gentle outside it.

Roy Ability and endurance are two qualities associated with Roy. For the Brooklyn Dodgers, Roy meant catcher Roy Campanella, three times Most Valuable Player in the National League. When Bernard Malamud chose the name Roy Hobbs for the baseball-player hero of his novel *The Natural*, he indicated his choice for a typically American baseball name. Roy means "red" in Gaelic and "king" in Old French.

Sanford, Sandy The casual assurance of this name makes it a great one for sports, all the more because Dodgers pitcher Sandy Koufax made it a legend. Traditionally, Sandy is considered a nickname for ALEXANDER, but baseball fans will know that Koufax's full name was Sanford.

Satchel His name is part of baseball legend, but when Woody Allen named his son Satchel, nonbaseball fans thought of the dictionary definition: "a small valise or bag." Those in the know realized that what the name *really* refers to is the great baseball player Satchel Paige (born Leroy Robert Paige).

Spalding This bouncy sporting name could take him to success in many fields. Baseball's Albert Spalding is known not only as a player and an important force in the early years of professional baseball, but as the founder of the sporting goods company that bears his name.

Stanley, Stan In life, and above all in baseball, this name promises someone brave, trustworthy, and true. Baseball's great Stan Musial ("Stan the Man") went down in history as one of the great hitters of all time. Stanley originated in England as a last name. In the nineteenth century it came into popular use as a first name, and, with the fame of Stan Musial and others, Stan gradually came to seem almost as American as baseball.

Sterling, Stirling The perfect name for the truly precious baby, Sterling means "of highest quality." The name brings to mind not only sterling silver, but Stirling Moss, the great race car driver.

Sugar Ray He'll have a lot to live up to with this name, associated with the great boxers Sugar Ray Robinson (born Walker Smith) and Sugar Ray Leonard (born Ray Charles Leonard). It might be used as a nickname for RAY or RAYMOND.

Tristram, Tristan Intelligent, agile, adaptable—that is Tristram at his best. At his *very* best he might take after the great baseball legend, Tristram (Tris) Speaker. The name has its origin in the legend of a valiant knight named Tristram. Still, the Baseball Hall of Fame may be the name's best reference. Short form: Tris.

Tyrus, Ty It's almost a guarantee that Ty is gallant, talented, daring, and a natural for baseball. Tyrus Raymond Cobb ("the Georgia Peach") has been called the greatest player in the game's history, with a lifetime batting-average record that still stands. The name comes from the ancient seaport of Tyre or Tyrus, which is mentioned in the Bible.

Tyson With the rise of Mike Tyson as the world's undisputed heavyweight champion at the age of only twenty-two, the name Tyson became a part of boxing history. This last name has been used occasionally as a first name.

Waite He could be a blue-blooded, nearsighted lawyer or business executive. Or, he could be a baseball wonder like the great pitcher Waite Hoyt. Waite is a family name, occasionally used as a first name.

Willie If his name is Willie he's likely on a journey—from rookie to renown, in the incomparable tradition of Willie Mays, Willie Stargell, and Willie McCovey. This top baseball name is usually a diminutive of William, but in the case of

Stargell it stood for Wilver. See WILLIAM for more on the origin and meaning.

Wilton, Wilt As an athlete and in ordinary life, one expects Wilt to be inventive, graceful, dignified—and tall. Wilt Chamberlain (born Wilton) did not like to be called "Wilt the Stilt," but that nickname sticks in people's minds at least as much as his famous slam-dunks. Wilton is an Old English given name and a town in Wiltshire, England.

Wilver See WILLIE.

Yogi If his name is Yogi, he'll certainly bring to mind the great baseball player Yogi Berra (born Lawrence Peter Berra). This name is not likely to be much used as a given name, but it is a fine example of a distinctive nickname.

7
FICTIONAL AND MYTHOLOGICAL CHARACTERS

One of the most popular sources of baby names is the world of fiction and mythology. This includes not only novels and ancient myths, but popular songs, poems, comics, and television shows. So many people have names that their parents took from a book, movie, or song, that this may actually be the most common source of new names and name fashions. Sometimes the character or story associated with the name is important. In other cases, the name is chosen mainly because of its sound. The names that follow are all associated with fictional or mythological characters. Some may be the names of famous real people as well but were popularized by a fictional source or are currently best known for a fictional character. You may find a name here that is right for your child, or you may be inspired to look for the perfect name in the books, movies, songs, or TV shows that are your personal favorites. More than any other type of name in this book, these are the stuff of dreams. . . .

GIRLS' NAMES

Adaline, Adeline Gentle, and feminine, and perhaps a bit grand is the nature of "Sweet Adeline." That song helped make the name popular in the early nineteenth century. The name comes from a Germanic word meaning "noble." A more modern-sounding variation is Aline. Diminutives: Addy, Addie.

Amabel See ANNABEL.

Amanda Grace, intelligence, and beauty are all associated with Amanda. This name is a poetic coinage from the Latin, meaning "worthy to be loved." The author of a love poem would address his beloved as Amanda in order to keep her true identity a secret. The diminutive, Mandy, is associated with Barry Manilow's famous love song, "Mandy."

Amata Like AMANDA, her name was inspired by love and poetry. Amata in Latin means "beloved."

Annabel, Annabelle Her name resounds in poetry as "the beautiful Annabel Lee" of Edgar Allan Poe's famous and tragic love poem. It can be considered a combination of ANNA and BELLE, or a form of the Middle English name Amabel, meaning "lovely, amiable."

Ariadne Beautiful, impetuous, and intrepid is the classic Ariadne. In Greek myth, Ariadne was the daughter of King Minos of Crete. She fell in love with Theseus when he came to kill the minotaur and gave him the thread that helped him escape from the labyrinth. Ariane and Arianna are French forms of the name. Of Greek origin, it means "very holy one."

Artemis, Artemisia Purity, strength, and valor distinguish the legendary nature of Artemis. One of the great goddesses of Greek mythology, Artemis was the virgin goddess of hunting and archery, also a guardian of wild animals and children. (In Roman mythology, DIANA is her counterpart.) The name Artemisia is known for a variety of plant named for the goddess. It was used as a personal name in ancient Greece and occasionally in the nineteenth century.

Ashley Attractive, a bit old-fashioned, genteel, graceful, and upscale: this is the 1980s vision of Ashley. In the 1980s the name became one of the most popular for little girls. This name is well known in literature as a masculine first name: for Scarlett O'Hara's first love, Ashley Wilkes, in *Gone with the Wind.* Originally a surname, Ashley comes from Old English and means "ash tree meadow." Alternative spellings: Ashlie, Ashleigh.

Astraea, Astrea Elegant, fair-minded: this may be Astrea if she is true to her name. Astraea is the Greek goddess of justice, but her name comes from the word for "starry." According to legend, when she departed Earth she became the constellation Virgo. Astra is a modern variation on this name, meaning "star."

Athena An aura of wisdom and power surrounds her name. Daughter of Zeus, and one of the twelve great Olympian gods in Greek mythology, Athena was the goddess of war and of many crafts and skills. Dressed in armor, she would aid men on the battlefield. Her most important temple is the Parthenon in Athens.

Becky She could be a blend of two opposite natures: Mark Twain's all-American Becky Thatcher in *The Adventures of Tom Sawyer*—or William Thackeray's scheming, opportunistic Becky Sharp in the famous English novel *Vanity Fair*. The fine thing for a Becky is that it is really up to her to choose which she'll be like. This sprightly, traditional name is usually a diminutive of REBECCA.

Belinda An aura of good-natured fun and lighthearted sophistication surrounds her name. Alexander Pope used the name for the heroine of his mock-heroic poem *The Rape of the Lock*. The name's origin is obscure; it may include a Germanic word for "serpent."

Blanche Proud, fiery, but a bit on the skids, like Blanche

Dubois in *A Streetcar Named Desire*, is one image of Blanche. This French name comes from Latin and means "white" or "fair."

Brenda Dependable, smart, brave, and true, she could take after Brenda Starr, girl reporter. Familiar because of the old Brenda Starr comics, the origin of this English name is not known; it may have come from the Old Norse word *brand*, meaning "sword."

Camilla, Camille A whirlwind of power could lie behind this noble, gracious name. In Virgil's *Aeneid*, Camilla was a proud and valiant warrior queen who led her troops to battle to aid the hero Aeneas. Camille is the French form of this name, and Camilla is the Latin one.

Carmen She's got love in her heart and a flower in her hair, if she's a typical Carmen. In Bizet's opera of that name, the sultry, irresistible Carmen becomes the passionate love and downfall of a young army corporal, Don José. This romantic, tempestuous Spanish name is derived from the Latin word for "song" or "poem."

Cassandra Her beautiful name has an unfortunate meaning. In Greek legend Cassandra, daughter of the king of Troy, had the gift of prophecy but was fated by Apollo never to be believed. Thus the name is sometimes used to describe someone whose doomsaying goes unheeded. Cassandra can go by the nickname Cassie.

Celia She could be beautiful, desirable, charming—and perhaps a bit unreachable. To Celia, poet Ben Jonson wrote "Drink to me only with thine eyes" and "Come my Celia, let us prove, While we can, the sports of love." Another Celia appears as one of the lovers in Shakespeare's comedy *As You Like It*. The name comes from the same Roman clan name as CECIL and CECILIA.

Charity Kindness, gentleness, and generosity are all encompassed in her name. The Puritans gave this name in honor of the Christian virtue charity, which in modern biblical translations is defined as "brotherly love" or simply "love." In more recent times, the name has become associated with the heroine of the Broadway musical "Sweet Charity."

Charmian Her name may sound a bit like Charleen, with the added bonus of a classical background. Charmian was one of the Egyptian queen Cleopatra's attendants, and Shakespeare made her a character in his play *Antony and Cleopatra.*

Clarice, Clarissa, Clarisse The light and elegant sound of her name makes it attractive and romantic. The superstitious might wish to keep in mind, however, that the name Clarissa was used by Samuel Richardson for the virtuous but sadly unlucky heroine of his 1747 novel, *Clarissa.* The earlier French forms of the name are Clarisse and Clarice, meaning "bright."

Clio Gracious, witty, sharp-tongued, gentle: this name suggests a bundle of paradoxes. It means "to make famous," and in Greek mythology Clio was one of the muses. In modern times, Clio has been adopted as the muse of advertising. Each year the industry gives out its Clio Awards, which are comparable to Oscars in the film industry. (Cleo is not a variation of this name, but a short form of Cleopatra.)

Cordelia "Loyal daughter" is the unofficial meaning of her name, from the faithful, gentle Cordelia, in Shakespeare's *King Lear.* Shakespeare's source for the name and its original meaning are unknown.

Corinna, Corinne Lively, cheerful, and attractive are the traits that come to mind when one hears her name. In literature it is associated with Robert Herrick's pastoral love poem *Corinna's Going A-Maying* and Madame de Staël's novel *Corinne.* Corinna comes from the Greek word for "maiden."

Daisy On a bicycle built for two or dancing the Charleston until dawn, Daisy is lively, carefree, and beloved. Daisy is celebrated in the famous song "Daisy Bell" ("a bicycle built for two"). In F. Scott Fitzgerald's great novel of the Jazz Age, *The Great Gatsby*, Daisy is wealthy, beautiful, and loved. In Henry James's *Daisy Miller*, she is depicted as a typical American girl. And then there's the irrepressible Daisy Mae of the *L'il Abner* comics. Clearly, Daisy is more than an ordinary flower.

Daphne Charming, lovely Daphne in Greek mythology was a nymph and a virgin huntress like Artemis. In the most famous story involving her, Apollo fell in love with her and chased her through the woodlands. Rather than let him catch her, she turned herself into a laurel tree. Thus, the meaning of her name: "laurel."

Deirdre Passionate, regal, beautiful, and steadfast in her ideals—that is the Deirdre of Irish legend. She was a heroine of Irish mythology whose story is retold in the play *Deirdre of the Sorrows* by J. M. Synge. This young Celtic woman was betrothed to marry a king but refused him because of her love for a young soldier. When the young soldier was killed in battle, she killed herself. Thus, this romantic old name is sometimes said to mean "sorrow."

Delia Like the island of Delos in ancient Greece, her name can be seen as both exotic and elemental. Delos was the birthplace of the goddess ARTEMIS, and thus Delia is another name for Artemis.

Delphine She could be mysterious, entrancing, and occasionally surprising. This French name (of Greek origin) may refer to the famous oracle at Delphi in ancient Greece, which was believed to speak the word of the gods. It may also be related to the words "delphinium" and "dolphin."

Demeter, Demetria Gracious, feminine, and strong is the

traditional image of Demeter. Demeter was the Greek goddess of harvest and fertility.

Dolores See LOLA.

Dulcia, Dulcie, Dulcinea Sweetness and innocence are the images that spring to mind when one hears that Dulcie is her name. Dulcie may come from the Latin word for "sweet," and this meaning may also have been what Don Quixote had in mind when he resolved to call his lady Dulcinea, "a name which seemed to him as musical, strange and significant as those others that he had devised for himself and his possessions" (*Don Quixote* by Miguel de Cervantes).

Elaine An ancient aura of romance clings to her very respectable name, from the days when knighthood was in flower. In Mallory's *Morte d'Arthur* two women named Elaine loved Lancelot, the legendary knight who was a friend of King Arthur. One died of unrequited love; the other bore him a son, Galahad. Elaine is an Old French form of HÉLÈNE or HELEN.

Electra Drama and excitement seem to emanate from this name. It means "amber," possibly originally "fire" or "spark." In Greek mythology, Electra was not an entirely happy character: in tragedies by Sophocles and Euripides, she helps her brother Orestes get revenge for their mother's killing of their father.

Eliza Bright, enthusiastic, fun, and a bit grand is Eliza. In the musical *My Fair Lady*, Eliza Doolittle was the cockney flower seller that Henry Higgins set out to make into a high-society lady. Eliza is a short form of Elizabeth, but it has been used as an independent name since the reign of Elizabeth I. For more on origins and meaning, see ELIZABETH.

Emma Her old-fashioned name may sound archaic to some, to others full of style and charm. The name has become very popular in England, possibly due to the character Emma Peel on the television series "The Avengers." On a more elevated cultural plane, Emma Woodhouse is the pretty, lively heroine of Jane Austen's novel *Emma*. Emma comes from Old High German, meaning "whole, universal." It was a popular name among the Normans. Diminutives: Em, Emmy.

Esmé, Esmee, Ismay She will be charming, pretty, and romantic if she fits the popular image of Esmé. The name is associated with the wonderful young heroine of J. D. Salinger's story *For Esmé—With Love and Squalor*. Esmé could be a form of Esmeralda ("emerald"). Esmé and the other forms have also been traced back to England and Scotland as men's names. Today the name is used for women, more often in Britain than in the United States.

Eugénie, Eugenia Grand as a classical statue or a great French novel . . . this could be Eugénie. The name is known because of Balzac's novel *Eugénie Grandet*. It is the feminine form of EUGENE, meaning "well-born."

Fern She could be at home in a Victorian drawing room, a lush tropical garden, or in a charming children's story, like Fern Arable, the child heroine of *Charlotte's Web* by E. B. White. This name was popular in the late nineteenth century, along with other botanical names.

Fiona She could be both refined and strong, like her literary Celtic name. Fiona was coined as a pseudonym by Scottish author William Sharp in the nineteenth century. It comes from a Celtic word meaning "white" or "fair." The name subsequently became very popular in Scotland.

Flora The grace of an ancient Roman garden surrounds her name. Flora was the Roman goddess of flowers, and her name comes from the Latin word for "flower." In the children's stories about Babar the Elephant, by Jean and Laurent de Brunhoff, Flora is one of the three charming royal elephant children: Pom, Flora, and Alexander.

Frannie, Franny Charming, privileged, and perhaps a bit crazy—this is the image of Frannie, at least for readers of J. D. Salinger's novel *Franny and Zooey.* This name originated as a diminutive of FRANCES.

Freya, Freyja Fascinating and adventuresome is the popular image of Freya. In Norse mythology, the goddess Freya represented love, beauty, marriage, and fertility. The Old Norse spelling is Freyja.

Gabriela, Gabriella, Gabrielle Celestial strength and earthly power combine in her name. In Jorge Amado's acclaimed novel *Gabriela, Clove and Cinnamon,* Gabriela was a worldly yet almost supernaturally amazing woman. The name means "man of God" or "strength of God" and is the feminine form of GABRIEL. Diminutives: Gaby, Gabie.

Gerda Strength and vitality are associated with this indomitable-sounding name. In Norse mythology, Gerda was the wife of the god Freyr, known for her dazzling beauty.

Gill, Jill She's somebody's sweetheart, if she's true to the Old English meaning of her name. Jill and Gill are short forms of Gillian, which in Old English used to mean "girl" or "sweetheart," as in the old saying "Every Jack must have his gill." The nursery rhyme *Jack and Jill* has made the name known, generation after generation.

Gillian See JILL.

Gisele, Giselle Her French name not only has a beautiful sound, but a beautiful visual image: the ballet *Giselle* by Gautier. The name came to France from the German name Gisela, meaning "pledge."

Glenda Goodness and magic surround her name, because

of the good witch Glenda in *The Wizard of Oz.* This Welsh name actually means "fair and good."

Gloriana Who could be named Gloriana and be anything but regal and glorious? Gloriana was a poetic name for Elizabeth I, made famous by Edmund Spenser in his epic poem *The Faerie Queene.* As a combination of GLORIA and ANNA, it means "glorious grace."

Guinevere, Guenevere, Gwenevere Beauty and romance combine in the popular image of Guinevere. In Arthurian legend, she was King Arthur's queen, who became the mistress of the knight Lancelot. The name is of Welsh origin, the first syllable meaning "white." The last part may mean "phantom." Crosby, Stills, Nash & Young used the name in their song "Guinnevere." Gwen and Gwynne can be used as independent names or as short forms of Guinevere.

Heidi Cheerfulness, health, and good spirits are all associated with Heidi. This Germanic name is often associated with the little Alpine girl heroine of the children's novel *Heidi.* The name is a form of the German name Adelheid, which like Adelaide means "a noble sort."

Hester Her name's proud beauty comes not only from its biblical source but from the story of Hester Prynne in Nathaniel Hawthorne's famous novel *The Scarlet Letter.* Hester is a form of the Old Testament name ESTHER. It means "star." Diminutive: Hetty.

Hetty See HESTER and MEHETABEL.

Iris She may be a link between friends and enemies, actions and theories, or ideas and dreams. In Greek mythology, Iris carried the messages of the gods. The name in Greek means "rainbow," and Iris was the personification of the rainbow, connecting sky and earth.

Ismay See ESMÉ.

Juliet, Juliette Romantic, beautiful, innocent, passionate: this is the traditional image of Juliet, from the tragic heroine of Shakespeare's *Romeo and Juliet.* Juliet Capulet of Shakespeare's play was an Italian of noble birth; in Italian her name would actually have been Guilietta, the diminutive of Guilia. Juliet is the English version of the name, and Juliette is the French form. They are all based on the Latin name JULIA.

Justine, Justina The scales of justice, or exotic decadence: either can represent Justine. Justine comes from Latin, meaning "just." In Lawrence Durrell's novel *Justine* (Book One of the famous *Alexandria Quartet*), the title character is a woman of irresistible beauty and sensuality.

Layla In the world of rock and roll she's got one of the few truly classic names. The rock classic "Layla" by Eric Clapton is her song, which he wrote as an exuberant expression of his pain over an unrequited love.

Leia In the intergalactic battle against the dark side, she is the princess of all that's good. This name seems to have been coined for the character Princess Leia, played by Carrie Fisher in *Star Wars.* Though the name sounds a bit like LEAH, it has an up-to-date flair.

Leila Graceful, romantic, a bit flowery—these are the images that breeze in with her name. Lord Byron made it popular with his poem *The Giaour.* This Moorish name means "dark as night."

Lenore, Leonore, Leonora A darkly romantic echo follows her melodious name, from the famous poem *Lenore* by Edgar Allan Poe. These three names may have developed from ELEANOR and ELEANORA.

Lois Goodness, sweetness, and beauty are all associated with Lois—along with the possibility that Superman may one day sweep her off her feet. Lois Lane was Superman's girlfriend. The original meaning of this Greek name, which came into use because it appears in the Bible, is not known.

Lola, Lolita Pleasure, passion, and fun hover about her name like cupids. The most famous Lolita was the precocious nymphet in the famous novel *Lolita* by Vladimir Nabokov. In the musical *Damn Yankees* the vamp Lola gets to belt out the glorious lyrics, "Whatever Lola wants, Lola gets." In the kinky, mixed-up world of the Kinks song "Lola," what Lola wants is a bit more dubious. Lola and Lolita are short forms of Dolores, a traditional Spanish name meaning "sorrows," in reference to the Virgin as Maria de los Dolores (Mary of the Sorrows).

Lorelei Beauty, mystery, and a bit of danger mingle in this name. In Germanic mythology, Lorelei was a siren whose lovely songs lured sailors to shipwreck along the Rhine River.

Maia, Maya Newness, creativity, and femininity are all part of the classic image of Maia. Maia was the Roman goddess of spring and new growth; the month of May was dedicated to her. In Latin, Maia means "the great one."

Marcella, Marcelle From an English nursery to an Italian villa, Marcella could be quite at home. In children's literature, Marcella is known as the little girl who keeps the dolls Raggedy Ann and Raggedy Andy in her old-fashioned English nursery. The name is actually an Italian feminine form of MARK. Marcelle is the French form.

Mattie, Matty, Maddie Brains, charm, and beauty—the typical Mattie has them all. She could be a fashion model, a detective, or both—like the character played by Cybill Shepherd on TV's "Moonlighting." Mattie can be a diminutive of MARTHA, MATILDA or Madeleine, or an independent name.

Mehetabel, Mehitabel Her ancient, exotic name practically purrs with good karma. This Hebrew name occurs several times in the Bible and is taken to mean "God is doing good." It was used by the Puritans in colonial America. It is also the name of a wonderful cat in the fanciful stories by Don Marquis, collected in *archy and mehitabel.* The lively and adventuresome Mehitabel's motto was "toujours gai" ("always merry").

Melanie Pretty and sweet: there is no better way to describe the typical Melanie. The most famous one is the gentle Melanie Hamilton in *Gone with the Wind*, who marries Scarlett O'Hara's first love, Ashley Wilkes. The name comes from Melania, a name for the Greek goddess Demeter, and means "black."

Melissa She is as sweet as MELANIE, but she could be hard-working and busy as a bee too. Melissa comes from the Greek word for "honey" or "honey bee," and in Greek myth she was the nymph who helped man discover honey. In Ariosto's epic poem *Orlando Furioso*, Melissa was a prophetess with magic powers.

Michelle, Michele Kindness, gentleness, and a peaceful nature are what one expects to find in Michelle. This French name is the feminine form of Michel (MICHAEL). She is likely to be beloved too, like the Michelle in the Beatles song of the same name.

Millie Her name helps bring an old-fashioned charm and an appealing gusto to whatever she does. Like Julie Andrews in the 1967 movie *Thoroughly Modern Millie*, her old-fangled name will not keep her from making the most of life. The name originated as a short form of Mildred ("mild strength") or Millicent ("strong work").

Minerva Wise and skillful is the popular image of Minerva, who in Roman mythology was the goddess of wisdom, invention, crafts and arts, and prowess in war. (She was the counterpart of the Greek goddess Athena.) A possible diminutive of Minerva is MINNIE.

Minnie Who could be more popular, lively, and lovable than Minnie? It would be hard to find anyone, except perhaps a mouse named Mickey. Minnie Mouse and her name are known all over the world. The name could be a diminutive of WILHELMINA, MINERVA, or MARY, but it is also considered an independent name.

Miranda She may be attractive, graceful, and intelligent—and perhaps a bit of enchantment has rubbed off on her too, from her association with Shakespeare's magical play *The Tempest.* Shakespeare coined this name from a Latin word meaning "to be admired" for the lovely and well-educated heroine of the play.

Molly, Mollie, Moll Lively, earthy, and likable is the popular image of Molly. The name is famous in literature because of Molly Bloom in James Joyce's *Ulysses* and for Daniel Defoe's *Moll Flanders.* And who could forget Debbie Reynolds in *The Unsinkable Molly Brown*? Molly began as a diminutive of MARY but is often considered a separate name.

Mona Like Leonardo da Vinci's immortal painting, the Mona Lisa, she may seem a bit mysterious, a bit happy, and a bit sad. The name comes from a longer Irish name meaning "noble." It also recalls the Nat King Cole standard "Mona Lisa."

Morgan Beautiful and powerful is the traditional image of Morgan. In the legends of King Arthur, the sorceress Morgan le Fay was Arthur's sister and devious enemy. This Welsh name, traditionally used for men, means "great bright." It may also bring to mind the family name, known for such people as the megacapitalist J. P. Morgan.

Nell, Nellie, Nelly Forthright, courageous, and good is the way one might describe Nell. Charles Dickens made the name famous with Little Nell (Nell Trent) in *The Old Curiosity Shop.* Rodgers and Hammerstein picked up on its optimistic, honest ring for Nellie Forbush, the heroine of *South Pacific*. The only negative thing about this name is the expression "nervous Nellie." It originated as a diminutive for HELEN or ELLEN.

Norma In Bellini's opera, *Norma*, she is the tragic heroine, a druid priestess who is wronged by her Roman lover. The name is not druidic, though; it may have been invented by Bellini.

Ophelia Her name is rare, perhaps because of the sad drowning of the young and beautiful Ophelia in Shakespeare's most famous tragedy, *Hamlet*. The name may be of Greek origin.

Oriana Rare and precious as gold is Oriana. The name comes from the Latin word *or*, meaning "gold." It was a literary coinage in the seventeenth century, as a name for Queen Elizabeth I.

Pamela Her name sounds attractive to the ear, and she is likely to be every bit as attractive herself. This name was invented by the poet Philip Sidney in the late sixteenth century for his pastoral poem *Arcadia*, and Samuel Richardson used it for the heroine of his popular 1740 novel, *Pamela*.

Penelope Beautiful and faithful is the traditional image of Penelope. As the wife of Odysseus in Homer's *Odyssey*, she waited virtuously for her husband's return from the Trojan War, using clever wiles to put off would-be suitors. She was also an accomplished weaver and a capable manager of their household. PENNY is a diminutive of Penelope.

Penny Bright and shiny is the popular image of Penny. Penny may be a nickname for a child with copper-colored hair, a diminutive of PENELOPE, or an independent name.

Phoebe, Phebe Her name suggests someone lively, cheerful, and perhaps a bit whimsical. In Greek mythology Phoebe was a Titaness, daughter of Uranus and Gaea, and a protectress of the Delphic oracle. The name means "shining" or "bright" in Greek.

Polly, Pollyanna Sweet, generous, and optimistic is the image of Polly. The 1913 novel *Pollyanna* by Eleanor Porter made the longer variation famous. The heroine, Pollyanna Whittier, was conceived as an admirably optimistic character, but her first name came to be used to describe one who blindly sees *only* the bright side of things. Polly originated as a form of MOLLY, which came from MARY.

Portia Elegant, proud, lively, smart, Portia is the type who could buy a Porsche, drive it like a pro, *and* look great behind the wheel. In Shakespeare's play *The Merchant of Venice*, the beautiful Portia's quick wits save her husband's life and confound the evil Shylock. The name is derived from that of an ancient Roman clan.

Ramona Since the late 1800s, this name has been associated with the romance of Old California. The name was popularized by the romantic novel *Ramona* by Helen Hunt Jackson (published 1884). The story of Ramona continues to be performed as a pageant in Southern California. Ramona is the feminine form of the Spanish name Ramón (RAYMOND).

Regan Her sophisticated-sounding name has one unfavorable literary connection. In Shakespeare's *King Lear*, Regan was one of the two evil daughters who betray their father.

Rhoda She might be excitable, funny, and down-to-earth—like the popular television character Rhoda, played by Valerie Harper. The name comes from the Greek word for "rose."

Rowena She may be a Saxon princess, or simply look like one. The heroine of Sir Walter Scott's novel *Ivanhoe* made the name famous; it was previously lost in the mists of legend.

The name may be of Celtic origin, meaning "white mane." Or, it might come from an Old English name meaning "fame friend."

Roxanne, Roxane, Roxanna She may be a hot number if her name is Roxanne—like the Roxanne celebrated in Sting's 1979 song "Roxanne," performed by The Police. The name is associated in literature with Daniel Defoe's novel *Roxana*. Roxane is the Greek form of a Persian name meaning "dawn." Diminutive: Roxy.

Stella She is sparkling, and a bit unreachable, if she is true to her name. Stella comes from the Latin for "star." It was coined by Sir Philip Sidney for his sonnet cycle *Astrophel and Stella* (1591).

Susanna, Susannah The grace of her beautiful old name cannot help but reflect on her. Best of all, she has a lively song all her own, "O, Susanna," by Stephen Foster. This name was a popular one in colonial America and in England during the same period. Its original source is the Apocrypha of the Bible, and it means "lily" in Hebrew.

Tabitha If she blinks her eyes or wiggles her nose, watch out! She could have supernatural powers like the child Tabitha on the 1960s television show "Bewitched." The name means "gazelle" in Aramaic. Diminutive: Tabby.

Tess Beauty and a hint of sadness can be heard in her name, which is famous for the lovely, exploited peasant girl in Thomas Hardy's famous novel *Tess of the D'Urbervilles*, and the movie based on it starring Nastassia Kinski. The name originated as a diminutive of THERESA.

Theia, Thea Goddesslike power is part of her name. In Greek mythology Theia was a Titaness, a daughter of Uranus and Gaea. The name means "divine."

Thisbe She is lively, gentle, and fun-loving if she fits her name. In Greek myth, however, her story was sad: her lover Pyramus killed himself when he mistakenly believed a lion had killed her. The story is best known through Shakespeare's lighthearted use of it in *A Midsummer Night's Dream*, as the subject for the rustics' play. The name is pronounced THIZ-bee.

Trillian If one of the great publishing corporations of Ursa Minor published a baby-name book, they might define Trillian as "attractive, smart, and probably rather patient and level-headed too." There's no earthly definition of this name—except perhaps in the mind of the writer Douglas Adams, who seems to have invented it for the character Trillian in *The Hitchhiker's Guide to the Galaxy*. Chances are, it is related to the number "trillion."

Trixie, Trix She is loyal and true—it's almost a guarantee if her name is Trixie. The name is often associated with Ed Norton's long-suffering wife on TV's "The Honeymooners." The name is a diminutive for BEATRIX and thus means "one who blesses" or "one who makes happy."

Viola, Violet Pretty and modest is the image that goes along with Violet. Viola was the heroine of Shakespeare's *Twelfth Night*. The names come from the purple woodland flower.

Wendy She is charming, good, and if Peter Pan appears in her nursery, she may even fly! The name was invented by J. M. Barrie for the girl in *Peter Pan* (1904).

Willow If she fits her name, she will be lithe and graceful as a willow tree. She could be the center of momentous events, like the heroine of the George Lucas movie, *Willow*. As a botanical name (like Daisy, Rose, etc.), Willow has a particularly idyllic, peaceful sound.

BOYS' NAMES

Achilles Heroic, powerful, and nearly invincible is the mythical image of Achilles. In Homer's *Iliad* he was the hero of the Trojan War. According to Greek myth, he was invulnerable to injury except in his heel (thus the phrase "Achilles heel," meaning a minor but fatal weakness). The name is used more often in French (spelled Achille) than in English.

Aeneas "Noble, brave" might be an apt definition of his name. The Latin poet Virgil's *Aeneid* describes the wanderings of Aeneas after the destruction of Troy in the Trojan War. His settlement in Italy marked the founding of Rome. Of Greek origin, the name means "praiseworthy."

Apollo He could be a golden boy of godlike powers if he fits his name. In Greek mythology, Apollo was the god of the sun, who each day drove his fiery chariot across the sky. He was also the god of medicine, music, prophecy, and poetry.

Archie, Archy If his name is Archie, he is bound to be a memorable character. This name is famous for the fun-loving teenager Archie of *The Archies* comics and TV cartoon, and for Archie Bunker of TV's "All in the Family." Archie is used as an independent name or as a diminutive of ARCHIBALD.

Arthur His name is tied to medieval legend, for the earliest Arthur of renown was King Arthur, founder of the Round Table and leader of the chivalrous knights for which it has long been celebrated. Short form: Art. The original meaning of the name is unknown.

Barnabas, Barnaby, Barney This name belongs to several fictional characters, including the main characters of the TV show "Barnaby Jones" and Charles Dickens's novel *Barnaby Rudge.* The nickname often brings to mind cartoon character Fred Flintstone's next-door neighbor, Barney Rubble. Of Hebrew origin, the name is interpreted as meaning "son of encouragement" or "one who encourages."

Britt He may seem at first to be simply a refined and civilized guy, but underneath his calm exterior he could be a powerhouse of positive energy—like Britt Reid, alias the Green Hornet. In comic books, on radio, and on TV, Britt Reid lived the life of a wealthy newspaper publisher . . . except when he became the Green Hornet, battling evil with the Hornet's sting. This name may be a form of BRET, which means "a Breton" ("one from Brittany"). It may also be taken to mean "a Briton."

Buck He could be a gallant charmer, a strong young whippersnapper, or an intergalactic hero like Buck Rogers. As a noun, "buck" can mean "a male deer," "a robust young man," "a dandy," or "a dollar."

Caspar, Casper Good-hearted is one stereotype of Casper—from the cartoon character Casper the Friendly Ghost, and the biblical story of the three wise men. (They are not named in the Bible, but according to legend one was named Caspar.) This name comes from Persian and is traditionally said to mean "treasure." Gaspar is another form of the name. For more on the short form, see CAP.

Cedric Good looks, gallantry, and generosity are all qualities that might be associated with Cedric. The name became well known in the late nineteenth century because of the charming child hero of the popular novel *Little Lord Fauntleroy*, by Frances Hodgson Burnett. Cedric seems to be a variation on an ancient Celtic name. Alternative spelling: Cedrick.

Conan Power is the watchword for Conan. The name is usually associated with the fictional hero Conan the Barbarian, played in the movies by Arnold Schwarzenegger (*Conan* *the Barbarian, Conan the Destroyer*). This ancient Celtic name is said to mean "high" or "wisdom."

Damon Loyalty and friendship are traditionally associated with this name, from an ancient Roman myth in which Damon pledged his life as a hostage for his condemned friend Pythias. The name comes originally from Greek. Damien and Damian are variations on the name, but fans of horror movies may associate them with the evil "son of Satan" Damien Thorn in *The Omen* and its sequels.

Dermot See KERMIT.

Diarmid See KERMIT.

Ebenezer If his name is Ebenezer, he will very likely *not* be a scrooge. He's more apt to spend his life making up for the reputation of Ebenezer Scrooge in Dickens's *A Christmas Carol.* It is worth remembering, too, that by the end of the story Scrooge repented and gave Tiny Tim his best Christmas ever. In Hebrew, the name means "stone of help." The name was extremely popular in colonial New England. Short form: Eben.

Ellery He may be hard to fool, if his name is Ellery. The great fictional detective Ellery Queen made this name famous in mystery novels, movies, and a TV series. The meaning of this smart and popular-sounding name is unclear; it is more common as a surname than a first name.

Elmer He has two strikes against his name, but that may just mean that Elmer tries harder. This name is associated mainly with cartoon character Elmer Fudd, and with the hypocritical preacher named in the title of Sinclair Lewis's novel *Elmer Gantry.* Around the turn of the century, however, the name was quite popular in the United States. Of Old English origin, it means "noble famous."

Ferris Good-looking, charming, and born to privilege is

the image created by this name. This last name was used as a first name for the wealthy, fun-loving teenager played by Matthew Broderick in the film *Ferris Bueller's Day Off.* The name may also bring to mind the Ferris wheel; the first one was designed by George W. G. Ferris in 1893.

Godfrey He's as aristocratic as they come—and as wonderful—if he's a true Godfrey. Anyone who has seen William Powell in the title role of the 1936 film *My Man Godfrey* will have a warm, fond feeling for this name. (Godfrey is a millionaire who disguises himself as an unemployed "forgotten man." While working as a servant to a wealthy family, he wreaks havoc—and sows seeds of charity and goodwill.) Of Germanic origin, the name is derived from the words for "god" and "peace."

Gray, Grayson This aristocratic-sounding name suggests a life of wealth and privilege, and enough wits and charm to see him through many a scrape—like Dick Grayson, the real name of Batman's sidekick Robin. As Bruce Wayne's young charge, Dick Grayson enjoyed the high life in Wayne Manor, then turned into Robin when the crimefighting began. Grayson is an English surname that is sometimes used as a first name. Alternative forms: Graydon, Gray.

Hamlet Intelligence and sensitivity are associated with Hamlet—from the appealing, tragic hero of Shakespeare's play of that name. This name was a common one in England at the time of Shakespeare. It came from the same source as the noun "hamlet," signifying a small village. Related names, which do not immediately bring to mind the Shakespeare play, include Hammet, Hamlin, Hammet, and Hammond.

Han Courageous, reckless, handsome: this is Han, as created by Harrison Ford in the role of Han Solo in the *Star Wars* movies. This name was apparently coined for the films. It is similar to the German name HANS, a diminutive of Johannes or JOHN.

Hector Bold, proud, and strong is the traditional image of Hector. In Homer's *Iliad*, Hector is the valiant Trojan warrior who taunted Achilles from the walls of Troy. (Thus, "to hector" someone means to intimidate or dominate him or her in a blustering way.) The name comes from Greek; its meaning is something like "hold fast" or "steadfast."

Hercule, Hercules Extraordinary physical strength is associated with Hercules. In Greek mythology, Hercules was a son of Zeus who won immortality by performing a dozen mighty labors. The original meaning of this Greek name is not known. The French form of the name is associated with the intrepid Belgian detective Hercule Poirot of Agatha Christie's mystery novels.

Huckleberry What boy could be more all-American than Huckleberry? This name was coined by Mark Twain for the hero of *Huckleberry Finn*. The huckleberry plant is a uniquely American species as well. Short form: Huck.

Ichabod The many undesirable nicknames that children could fashion from his name could scar Ichabod for life. The name is known because of the character Ichabod Crane in Washington Irving's *The Legend of Sleepy Hollow*. Surprisingly, this name was actually used in colonial America. In Hebrew the name means "where is the glory?" or "no glory."

Jason Handsome, courageous, modest: this is the ideal Jason. In Greek mythology, Jason was one of the most heroic figures, best known because of his quest for the Golden Fleece, his many adventures with the Argonauts, and his turbulent relationship with his wife Medea. The name is of Greek origin and was widely used at the time of Jesus.

Jody Youthful, charming, and friendly is the popular image of Jody. On the 1960s TV show "Family Affair," Jody was the little boy—Buffy's brother. As a masculine name, Jody could be considered a diminutive of JOSEPH, Judah, or JUDE. Jody is also often a feminine name (see JODIE).

Jude His name may be considered vaguely unlucky, for in Thomas Hardy's famous novel *Jude the Obscure* the title character endured a long series of hardships. The Beatles song "Hey Jude" is an anthem to encourage a lovelorn person named Jude (actually Julian Lennon, who was upset by the breakup of his parents). Like Judas and Judah, Jude is a common Hebrew name, traditionally interpreted as meaning "praised."

Kermit Smart, lively, and likable is the popular image of Kermit. The best-known bearer of this Irish name is the very charming Muppet, Kermit the Frog. It is a form of the Gaelic names Dermot and Diarmid, meaning "free of envy." Diminutive (coined by Miss Piggy): Kermie.

Lance, Lancelot Masculine good looks and gallantry are integral parts of his name, which is famous because of a legendary knight of the Round Table. In the Arthurian legend, Lancelot's love affair with Queen Guinevere resulted in war with King Arthur. The name Lance is a modern shortening of this name. Lance brings to mind the ancient weapon used in jousts, though Lancelot actually means "one who serves." Launcelot is an alternative spelling.

Leroy, LeRoi, LeRoy A tough dude is one image of Leroy—in part from the Jim Croce song about an infamous inhabitant of the South Side of Chicago, "Bad, Bad Leroy Brown." This name comes from Old French and means "the king."

Kimball, Kim Lighthearted, self-sufficient, and boyish is the popular image of Kim—from the boy Kim (full name, Kimball O'Hara) in Rudyard Kipling's famous 1901 novel *Kim*. Later Kim came into use as a girl's name; for more, see the listing under "Girls' Names" in "Creators."

Merlin Magical powers are associated with Merlin, for in the Arthurian legends Merlin was the resident sorcerer and prophet in the court of King Arthur. The name is of Celtic origin, perhaps meaning "sea hill." Mervin and Mervyn are other forms of the name.

Nathan Dash, guts, and bravado are all part of the image of Nathan—because of the high-rolling Nathan Detroit in the musical *Guys and Dolls*. The name is a short version of NATHANIEL.

Nick He's apt to be popular, masculine, loyal, and cool, like three great Nicks of literature: Nick Carraway, the wealthy narrator of Fitzgerald's *The Great Gatsby*; Nick Adams, a hero in Hemingway's short stories; and Nick Charles, the hard-boiled detective in Dashiell Hammett's *The Thin Man*. Nick is short for NICHOLAS.

Odysseus See ULYSSES.

Oliver Charming, dashing, and quick-witted is the stereotype of Oliver. Charles Dickens's Oliver Twist has to be the world's most famous Oliver. The origin of the name is unknown. Diminutive: Ollie.

Orion Strong, big-hearted, and perhaps a bit old-fashioned or romantic: this is one way of picturing Orion. In Greek mythology, Orion was a giant hunter who pursued the Pleiades (the seven daughters of Atlas, who turned into stars) and was the lover of Eos, the goddess of dawn. Today the constellation Orion is a familiar sight in the night sky.

Orlando Emotional, dramatic, romantic: this is the traditional image of Orlando. This Italian form of ROLAND is associated with the hero of Ariosto's famous epic poem *Orlando Furioso*. The name means "fame land."

Perry He is likely to be attractive, bright, and hard-working if he is a typical Perry. He might even become a lawyer who almost never loses a case—like the incredible Perry Mason (played on TV by Raymond Burr). Perry Mason's defense of the underdog gives this name an egalitarian, idealistic ring. The name comes from the Old English surname Perry, meaning "pear tree." It can also be interpreted as a diminutive of Peregrine, a name of Latin origin meaning "traveler," or as a form of Pierre or PETER.

Quentin His rare name may sound quaintly British or Scottish to some, Southern to others, or perhaps vaguely menacing. Readers of Sir Walter Scott will recall the hero of the novel *Quentin Durward*; fans of William Faulkner will think of Quentin Compson, a main character in *The Sound and the Fury*; veteran couch potatoes may be reminded of the vampire Quentin on "Dark Shadows." Of Latin origin, it means "the fifth."

Ralph This name seems to herald a down-to-earth person, but with a fighting spirit. In television history, the name is immortal for hotheaded Ralph Kramden, played by Jackie Gleason on "The Honeymooners." This English name comes originally from Old Norse words meaning "counsel" and "wolf."

Randal, Randall A serious, dramatic personality may be associated with Randal. "O where have you been, Lord Randal my son?" is a line famous in English literature, from the ancient ballad *Lord Randal* (also called *Lord Rendal*) about a young lord's poisoning by his lady love. The name comes from Old English and means "shield wolf." Alternative spellings: Randle, Randel, Randell. See RANDY for more on the diminutive.

Rhett Handsome, suave, and perhaps a bit dangerous: this is how one might picture Rhett. In *Gone with the Wind*, Rhett Butler (played in the film by Clark Gable) has the cool and daring of a riverboat gambler, and an instinct for business and women.

Ricky, Rickey In sports or the lively arts, a popular,

extroverted Ricky seems to have an edge. The name is known in TV-land for the voluble bandleader Ricky Ricardo (played by Desi Arnaz on "I Love Lucy") and the budding rock musician Ricky Nelson on "Ozzie and Harriett." Ricky may be a diminutive for RICHARD or FREDERICK, or it may be used as an independent name.

Robinson Civilized is the stereotype of Robinson. As a first name, Robinson is best known for the castaway Robinson Crusoe, in Daniel Defoe's novel of the same name. More common as a surname, Robinson means "son of ROBERT."

Roger His name had a proud and serious history . . . and then along came lovable Roger Rabbit. Roger (Hrothgar in Old English) originated from Old High German words meaning "fame" and "spear." Today the name might imply fame, but not of a warlike sort.

Roland Bravery, loyalty, and romance are all associated with Roland. The name is known as that of the legendary nephew of Charlemagne who was killed in battle at Roncevaux in the year 778. His story was later enshrined in the epic poems *La Chanson de Roland* and *Orlando Furioso.* The name is more common in France than in the United States. Of Germanic origin, the name means "fame land." Alternative spelling: Rowland.

Shane Strong, self-reliant, heroic, and wonderful is the stereotype of Shane. This name is best known through the great western movie *Shane,* in which the title character is a mysterious gunfighter who befriends and aids a pioneer family. Shane is a variation of SEAN.

Sherman Cool, calculating, and maybe even a bit ruthless is one way to picture Sherman. He might even be a rich young investment banker in New York City, like Sherman McCoy, the main character of Tom Wolfe's novel *The Bonfire of the Vanities.* It is a last name brought into use as a first name.

Theo Cheerful, resilient, and fun-loving is the contemporary image of Theo. This old-fashioned name has a new popular slant—from the TV character Theo Huxtable, the lively son of Cliff and Clair Huxtable on "The Cosby Show." Theo is given as an independent name, or as a short form of THEOPHILUS or THEODORE.

Thor, Thorhall Powerful and elemental as rain, wind, and sea is the ancient image of Thor. Thor was the Norse god of thunder and battle; he was also a patron of marriage, agriculture, and the home. Thorhall was a legendary Norse explorer.

Thorstein, Thurston Upper-class all the way is the popular image of Thurston. He could even seem like a millionaire—without actually spending any money—like the castaway Thurston Howell III (played by Jim Backus) on the sitcom "Gilligan's Island." Of Scandinavian origin, Thurston and Thorstein mean "Thor's stone." See also THOR.

Tim This brief and sympathetic name is famous in literature for little Tiny Tim, the beloved crippled boy in Charles Dickens's *A Christmas Carol.* Tim is a short form of TIMOTHY.

Toby He's bound to be gregarious and amusing if he fits the traditional image of Toby. The name is known in literature for Uncle Toby in *Tristram Shandy* and for the raucous life of the party, Sir Toby Belch, in Shakespeare's *Twelfth Night.* The name came into use as a diminutive of TOBIAS.

Ulysses, Odysseus A great and heroic adventurer: this is the classic Ulysses or Odysseus. In Greek mythology, Odysseus was the king of Ithaca and a leader of the Greeks in the Trojan War, who journeyed for ten years after the war to reach home. His adventures were immortalized in Homer's epic poem, the *Odyssey.* James Joyce used the Latin form of the name, Ulysses, as the title for his great modernist novel. The original meaning of the name is unknown.

Wade A masculine, resolute individual—quite possibly from a privileged background—is how one might picture Wade. This name is usually interpreted as a surname of Anglo-Saxon origin, meaning "a ford" (as in a river crossing) or "wanderer." Wade is also a sea giant in Norse, Danish, and Anglo-Saxon mythology, associated both with the ocean and with stone ruins.

8
BIBLICAL CHARACTERS

The Bible is the Western world's most venerable source of names—names of inspiration, honesty, courage, righteousness, and faith that have endured for thousands of years. An exhaustive chapter on biblical names could fill a book in itself! Many of the Bible's most important names and beloved names (such as John, Thomas, Mary, and Elizabeth) have been used for so many centuries that most people no longer think of them as biblical. Thus, many of those names have been discussed in other parts of this book. By contrast, the names featured in this chapter are readily associated with the Bible. A few of them are rarely used today but hearken back to the days in America's past when they were in vogue. Many of these names (such as Joshua, Zechariah, and Sarah) have become popular once more in the 1980s—not only because of their fine biblical meanings but because of their suggestion of early American ideals and lore. Take a look in this chapter, and in your own Bible, and you may well find a name that truly inspires you.

GIRLS' NAMES

Drusilla Even in ancient Rome, this name was associated with blue blood. According to historians, Drusilla was a beautiful daughter of Herod the king (he is mentioned in Acts 12:1), who came to hear Paul preach (Acts 24:24). Short form: Dru.

Esther Courage and talent are associated with Esther, one of the Bible's great heroines. She was a Hebrew woman who married a Persian king and risked her life to prevent the killing of the Jews within her empire (Book of Esther). Esther is a Persian name meaning "star." (The biblical Esther's Hebrew name was Hadassah.)

Eva, Eve This name has a wonderful meaning. It is said to mean "life," for Adam called his wife Eve "because she was the mother of all living" (Genesis 3:20). However, because of Eve's association with humankind's fall from grace into sin, the name has not been as popular as many other biblical names throughout history.

Hannah A mother's love and courage are associated with this old-fashioned name, famous because of the Bible's Hannah, the mother of Samuel (1 Samuel 1–2). It was a very popular early American name, from colonial days to the early nineteenth century. From Hebrew, it means "grace." Other forms of the name are ANNA and ANNE. Nan is sometimes a nickname for Hannah.

Jemima Jemima was one of the three daughters given to Job after the Lord returned him to prosperity, and "in all the land there were no women so fair as Job's daughters; and their father gave them inheritance among their brothers" (Job 42:15). In light of the current popularity of "J" names, such as Jennifer and Jessica, Jemima is certainly worth consideration.

Kezia, Keziah Like JEMIMA, she was one of the three

daughters given to Job at the end of his troubles. From Hebrew, the name means "cassia," a type of tree.

Leah Diligence, strength of purpose, and faithfulness are part of the popular image of Leah. The name's renown originated with the wife of Jacob, who as the mother of Reuben, Simeon, Levi, Judah, Issachar, Zebulun, and Dinah, is honored as one of the builders of the house of Israel. However, Jacob always preferred Leah's beautiful sister, Rachel. (Their story is in Genesis 29–35.) The name is of Hebrew origin, meaning "wild cow," often also interpreted as "weary."

Miriam A lively and intelligent person is suggested by this name. Miriam was a prophetess and the sister of Moses and Aaron, who danced to celebrate Israel's deliverance through the Red Sea (Exodus 15:20–21). The name's original meaning is unknown. "Bitter," "rebellion," and "star of the sea" have been suggested as possible meanings. The name comes from the same ancient root word as MARY.

Naomi Kindness, thoughtfulness, and forbearance are part of the image of Naomi, from the heartwarming biblical story of Ruth and Naomi, told in the Book of Ruth. In Hebrew the name means "my delight."

Priscilla This old-fashioned-sounding name is known because of an early Christian woman. Priscilla and her husband Aquila received the apostle Paul in their home (Acts 18:1–4), and all three worked together at their trade of tentmaking. The name comes from Latin and means "old," "ancient," or "strict." Diminutive: Prissy.

Rachel Love at first sight may be in store for Rachel. In the book of Genesis, Jacob fell in love with the young Rachel on their first meeting, waited fourteen years before her father would let them marry, and adored her until her death (Genesis 29–35). As his wife, she became the ancestress of three tribes of Israel. Today the name still implies a woman of great natural beauty and grace. In Hebrew, the name means "ewe." Short forms: Rae, Ray.

Rebecca, Rebekah A strong will and ambition are associated with this name. As Isaac's wife, Rebekah was the mother of Jacob and Esau. On behalf of her favorite son, Jacob, she helped trick Isaac into giving his blessing to Jacob rather than Esau (Genesis 24–27). This ancient name means "a looped cord for tying young animals," thus "a snare." Short forms: BECKY, REBA.

Ruth Compassion, generosity, love: these are attributes associated with Ruth. The Book of Ruth in the Old Testament describes the widow Ruth's selfless devotion to her mother-in-law Naomi, and how her generosity was ultimately rewarded. The meaning of the name is uncertain; it comes from Hebrew and is sometimes said to mean "companion."

Sara, Sarah, Sarai This ancient name has a noble and dramatic air, for it is associated with some of the most dramatic stories in the Bible (Genesis 12–23). Sarah was the wife of the patriarch Abraham, known for her beauty, and for becoming the mother of Isaac in her old age. (Her original name, Sarai, was changed to Sarah as a sign of God's covenant.) Sarah was a popular name in colonial America and throughout the nineteenth century, and in recent years it has become a favorite again. In Hebrew the name means "princess." Diminutives: Sallie, SALLY, Sadie.

Veronica This lively, romantic name does not appear in the Bible, but it is famous as part of Christian tradition. Saint Veronica stood by the road as Jesus walked toward Calvary, and she wiped his brow with her towel, on which a permanent image of his face then appeared. Veronica in Latin means "true image."

BOYS' NAMES

Aaron He might be a restless individual with lots of ambition. As the first High Priest of Israel, the biblical Aaron was Moses's right hand man, and at times a rival to his leadership. Scholars believe the name is of Egyptian origin; the meaning is unknown.

Abner He could be a valiant fighter if he lives up to the tradition of his name. The biblical Abner was Saul's cousin and commander-in-chief of his army, and after Saul's death a courageous leader in the fight of Saul's house to retain control over Israel (2 Samuel 2–3). Of Hebrew origin, the name means something like "father of light."

Adam This name embodies both earth and God's breath of life, as the name of the first man created from the dust of the ground. In the Hebrew Bible, *adam* means simply "man" or "mankind."

Amos A harsh reality is evoked in the meaning of this name: "burden bearer." Amos is one of the prophets of the Old Testament.

Caleb In a Western, Caleb would be one of the good guys. Faithful, trustworthy, and a good man to have in a tight situation is his stereotype. In the Bible, Caleb and many other men were sent to explore the promised land. They saw it was an excellent land, and advised the Israelites to go in and take it. When others mutinied, Caleb stood firm (Numbers 13–14). This Hebrew name means "like a dog," thus, "faithful."

Daniel He could have the courage and bravado of Daniel in the lion's den if he bears this name. Daniel means "God is my judge," and there are several Daniels in the Bible, including the prophet Daniel, who served as a high-level advisor to King Nebuchadnezzar, miraculously survived the lion's den, and prophesied the future triumph of the Messianic kingdom (Book of Daniel). Dan is the short form, and the name of one of the twelve tribes of Israel.

Eleasar, Eleazar, Eliezar Several people in the Bible share this name, which means "God is my help." The most important was Aaron's son, who succeeded his father as chief priest of the Israelites (Numbers 20:22–29).

Elijah He could be a man of action *and* a man of spirit, if he takes after the prophet Elijah, who performed fiery proofs of God's existence and ascended to heaven in a whirlwind (1 Kings 17–29; 2 Kings 1–2). This Hebrew name means "Yahweh is God." Short form: Lige.

Elisha Like the prophet Elisha, he may have an important mission and a sixth sense for the future. Elisha was selected as the successor to the great prophet Elijah (1 Kings 19) and received his powers. The name means "God is salvation."

Emanuel, Emmanuel, Immanuel This is one name that is truly divine. Immanuel originated as one of the names of Christ given by the prophet Isaiah (Isaiah 7:14). Of Hebrew origin, it means "God is with us." The Spanish form is Manuel. Diminutive: Manny.

Ezekiel, Zeke Visionary Ezekiel and down-to-earth Zeke are the two sides of this ancient name. Ezekiel was the prophet of the Old Testament whose visions of dry bones (Ezekiel 37) and of wheels in the air (Ezekiel 1) are celebrated in American folk songs, in addition to being important messages to God's people. The name means "God strengthens." Zeke is the short form.

Ezra A stern, old-fashioned character is what one imagines when hearing his name. This name is associated with a book of the Bible and the biblical character Ezra. He was an Israelite and a high official in the Persian government, charged with enforcing the Jewish laws (Ezra 7; Nehemiah 8).

Gabriel This name bespeaks some of heaven's and earth's greatest mysteries. The archangel Gabriel is the most important angel in the Bible, the one who was sent to Mary to announce that she would be the mother of Jesus (Luke 1:26–37). Gabriel appeared to interpret Daniel's vision and give him prophecy (Daniel 8:15–27; 9:20–27), and is traditionally believed to be one of the angels who will blow the trumpets at the Last Judgment (Revelation 8). In Hebrew the name means "man of God" or "strength of God." Short form: Gabe.

Gideon Dauntless courage and faith are associated with Gideon. In one of the Bible's most exciting episodes, Gideon led a sudden night attack with a small band of men, winning a victory over incredible odds (Judges 7). This Hebrew name means "hewer" or "smiter."

Hiram This old-fashioned name is known from ancient history because of Hiram, King of Tyre, whose friendly dealings with kings David and Solomon are recorded in the Bible (1 Kings 5, 9). In bygone days in America the name was used far more than it is today. This name is of Phoenician origin. Short form: Hi.

Hosea This name is associated with the prophet Hosea, and with the recent popularity of the name Joshua, it is interesting to note that Hosea comes from the same Hebrew root. It means "salvation."

Isaac This name might be given to a long-awaited and beloved son, for it belonged to Abraham and Sarah's son Isaac, who was promised by God, but not born until their old age. The name also has a wonderful meaning: "he laughs," or "laughter." His mother first laughed in disbelief that she should bear a son (Genesis 18:12–15), and then laughed in joy upon his birth (Genesis 21:6). Carrying out God's promise to make of Israel a great nation, Isaac became the father of Jacob and Esau.

Isaiah Wisdom and hope are linked with this name, which

is known because of the great prophet Isaiah, whose prophecies included the good news of the Messiah to come (Isaiah 11–12). Of Hebrew origin, the name means "Yahweh is salvation."

Ishmael A sense of power and foreboding surrounds his name. In the Bible, Ishmael was the son of Abraham and the maid Hagar. He became an outcast from Abraham's household but the father of a nation in his own right (Genesis 16 and 21).

Jacob His name bespeaks tenacity and ingenuity. Known because of the patriarch Jacob, it may bring to mind his fourteen-year wait to marry his beloved Rachel, or his great success as a herdsman, which made him rich. He wrestled with an angel, and he was the father of twelve sons, whose descendants became the members of the twelve tribes of Israel. His story is found in Genesis 5–50. The meaning of the name in Hebrew is unclear, but it is sometimes said to mean "supplanter," for Jacob's role in taking the birthright of his brother Esau.

Jared His name has a hard-as-nails toughness about it that could serve him well in many fields. In the Bible, only Methuselah lived longer than Jared (Genesis 5:8–19).

Jeremiah Strength, courage, and sincerity seem a part of this name, which is associated with one of the great prophets. The name comes from Hebrew and means "exalted." For more on the diminutives, see JERRY and JEREMY.

Jonah, Jonas He could have a stubborn streak, if he takes after the unwilling prophet Jonah, who rebelled against God and only agreed to obey after being swallowed by a whale (Book of Jonah). However, peace is part of the literal meaning of this name, which is of Hebrew origin and means "dove." It was also the name of the father of Simon Peter (Matthew 16:17). Jonas is the Latin form of the name.

Jonathan He will be gallant, loyal, and much loved if he fits his name. The Bible's most famous Jonathan was King Saul's son, a courageous warrior (2 Samuel 1:17–27), known especially for his loyalty to his friend David, for whom he risked his life in spite of the opposition of his father (1 Samuel 18–19). The name comes from Hebrew and means "the Lord has given," sometimes interpreted as "gift of God." Short form: Jon.

Joshua Honesty, strength, and courage are associated with this once old-fashioned name, which in recent years has become extremely popular. The Joshua of the Bible was both valorous and holy; he was Moses's successor as leader of the Israelites, and the story of how he led the battle of Jericho (Joshua 6) is one of the Bible's most dramatic tales. The name comes from Hebrew and means "salvation." Short form: Josh.

Josiah Justice and righteousness are part of the history of this name, known because of the seventeenth king of Judah, who led political and religious reform (2 Chronicles 34–35). This Hebrew name means "may the Lord give."

Luke Sympathy, faith, realism, and intelligence are all associated with this name and with Saint Luke, author of the Gospel of Luke and the Acts of the Apostles. He is believed to have been a physician. The name comes from Greek and means "of Lucania" (a region in southern Italy).

Marc, Mark His name may sound easygoing and placid, but he may have a fiery side too: the name is associated with the god Mars, the Roman god of war. Mark (MARCUS in Latin) was the secular name used by Saint Mark, believed to be the author of the Gospel of Mark, as he made his way about the Roman Empire spreading the word of Christ. (In the Acts of the Apostles and the Epistles he is referred to as John Mark or John, John being the translation of his Hebrew name.) He was a companion of Paul, Barnabas, and Peter at various times.

Matthew Linked with the author of the first Gospel, this name suggests a man of quiet integrity and strength. Matthew was one of the Twelve Apostles; his is the most widely read gospel and includes the Sermon on the Mount. He is believed to have been a tax collector when he was called to follow Jesus (Matthew 9:9). The name comes from Hebrew and means "gift of God."

Micah His name has a jaunty ring that could serve him well. It appears several times in the Bible; the most notable Micah was a prophet who was a contemporary of Isaiah (Book of Micah). With its similarity in sound to Michael, Micah might be a fine alternative to that very popular name. Like MICHAEL, it means "who is like God?"

Moses An aura of strength and righteousness surrounds Moses. The name recalls the man who led the Israelites out of Egypt to the Promised Land (in Exodus, Leviticus, Numbers, and Deuteronomy), parted the Red Sea (Exodus 14), and brought down the Ten Commandments from Mount Sinai (Exodus 20). Moses has rarely been used as a first name in the twentieth century. Scholars are not sure whether the name is Hebrew or Egyptian; it may mean "to draw forth." Short forms: Mose, Moe.

Nehemiah A thoughtful man of action is the Nehemiah of the Bible, a governor who led the reconstruction of the walls of Jerusalem in fifty-two days (Nehemiah 6:15). His history is recorded in the Book of Nehemiah. The name, of Hebrew origin, means "whom God hath comforted."

Noah A hard-working and righteous man is suggested by this name, famous because of the man who took God at his word and built an ark before the flood. Scholars disagree on the meaning of this ancient name; "to rest" and "comfort" have been suggested. (Genesis 6–9).

Paul "Most likely to succeed" is the award most likely to be given to dedicated, zealous Paul. The biblical Paul was known as Saul of Tarsus, Saul being his Hebrew name, and he was first known as a persecutor of Christians. After his conversion to Christianity (Acts 9), he became the greatest missionary of the early church. The name comes from Latin and means "small."

Peter Faithful, honest, and good-hearted: that is one popular image of Peter, a name that came into use in honor of the apostle Peter. Actually named Simon, he was nicknamed Peter by Jesus himself, who declared that upon the rock of his faith he would build his church (Matthew 16:18). The name comes from Greek and means "stone" or "rock." For more on the short form, see PETE.

Philip Innovative, interesting, personable may be the contemporary image of Philip. In the New Testament there are two notable Philips: one of the Twelve Apostles and one of the important early evangelists (Acts 8). Of Greek origin, the name means "lover of horses." Alternative spelling: Phillip. Short form: Phil.

Reuben His name suggests a natural leader, such as the biblical Reuben, the eldest of Jacob's twelve sons, whose descendants became one of Israel's twelve tribes. Reuben himself was compassionate but not always blameless in his actions (Genesis 37 and 35:22). Of Hebrew origin, the name means "behold, a son." Rube is the usual nickname of Reuben; unfortunately, the slang term "rube" means "hick" or "country bumpkin."

Saul A strong, fascinating personality is Saul's traditional image. Saul was the name of the first king of Israel (1 Samuel 8–31). It was also the Hebrew name of Saul of Tarsus, best known by his Latin name, Paul. In Hebrew the name means "asked."

Silas A friendly and able companion is the traditional

image of Silas, who accompanied the apostle Paul on many of his travels (Acts 15–18). The exact origin of the name is obscure; it is often associated with the Latin name Silvanus, meaning "of the woods."

Simeon This pleasant-sounding name has two important references in the Bible. Simeon was the second son of Jacob, and his descendants formed one of the twelve tribes of Israel. Another Simeon was a devout man who was waiting for the Messiah. On seeing the infant Jesus in the temple, he recognized him and offered a hymn of praise, prophesying on the role of Christ (Luke 2:25–35). This Hebrew name comes from a word meaning "to hear."

Theophilus Scholarly and kindly is how one might picture Theophilus. The Gospel of Luke and the Acts of the Apostles are dedicated to Theophilus. This may be taken as a literary reference to all potential readers, for the name in Greek means "lover of God" or "loved by God." For more on the name's jaunty short form, see THEO.

Tobias His old-fashioned name may sound a bit quaint, but it could herald a very interesting person. In the Book of Tobit in the Protestant Apocrypha, Tobias is one of the characters, and it is because of him that the name came into use. In Hebrew the name means "God is good." In the standard Bible, Tobiah is an unadmirable character who, apparently opposing God's will, resisted rebuilding the wall of Jerusalem—so the name is not given in his honor. For more on the diminutive, see TOBY.

Zacchaeus Determination may be the hallmark of Zacchaeus. The Bible's Zacchaeus is famous for his short stature and for climbing a tree in order to see Jesus when he passed by. Later, he received Jesus in his home and repented of his sins, giving half of his riches to the poor (Luke 19:1–10). The name is a form of ZECHARIAH.

Zachariah, Zacharias, Zechariah Honesty, uniqueness, and an upstanding character are implied by this old name, which in recent years has come back in style. Twenty-eight men in the Bible bear this name; the two most important are the prophet Zechariah and the father of John the Baptist (Luke 1:5). This Hebrew name means "God has remembered." Short forms: Zach, Zack. For a variation of the name, see ZACHARY.

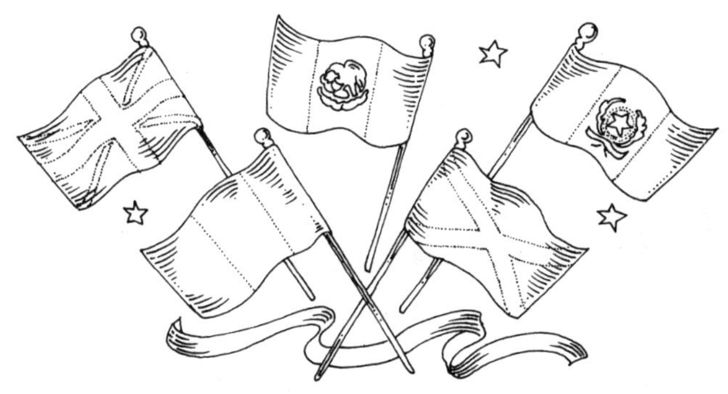

9
INTERNATIONAL FAVORITES

The world is rich in wonderful names, and as it grows smaller, names from one nation become familiar in a country halfway around the globe; customs are shared, styles swapped, and horizons broadened. In this chapter are selections of names from thirteen countries. Many of them are described more fully in other parts of this book, and you can locate them by checking the index.

CANADA

In a country as large as Canada, naming styles and customs may differ a great deal from province to province. Naturally, French names and French spellings are used more in Quebec than in other provinces. Other differences reflect the country's history as well. For example, in 1988 *The Gazette* (Montreal) named Shane and Kayla as among the top ten names in Newfoundland, reflecting the region's Celtic roots. In New Brunswick and Prince Edward Island, Mary and Marie were both in the top four most popular names, a fact attributed to the many Roman Catholics in those provinces. In the

Yukon and the Northwest Territories, Lauren, Natasha, Amber, and Crystal were popular names. Tracking the national average more closely was the province of Manitoba, with the *Winnipeg Free Press* listing Ashley and Michael as the most popular baby names in 1987. In March 1988 *The Gazette* listed the following names as Canada's most popular overall.

	GIRLS' NAMES	BOYS' NAMES
1.	**Ashley**	**Christopher**
2.	**Amanda**	**Andrew**
3.	**Jessica**	**Michael**
4.	**Jennifer**	**Matthew**
5.	**Sarah**	**David**
6.	**Stephanie**	**Ryan**
7.	**Melissa**	**Kyle**
8.	**Nicole**	**Tyler**
9.	**Laura**	**Daniel**
10.	**Megan**	**Justin**

ENGLAND

Out of 5,477 births announced in *The Times* of London in 1987, the following first names were the most popular. Generally, parents whose baby's arrival is announced in *The Times* represent an upscale sector of society. A similar group in the United States would include couples whose marriages are announced in the *New York Times*.

	GIRLS' NAMES	BOYS' NAMES
1.	**Emma**	**James**
2.	**Charlotte**	**Thomas**
3.	**Sophie**	**William**
4.	**Emily**	**Alexander**
5.	**Alice**	**Edward**
6.	**Rebecca**	**Charles**
7.	**Lucy**	**Nicholas**
8.	**Alexandra**	**Benjamin**
9.	**Harriet**	**George**
10.	**Sarah**	**Oliver**

Close runners-up for the top ten first names were Frederick, Georgina, Hannah, and Olivia.

FRANCE

Unlike citizens of the United States and Canada, the people of France cannot name their children whatever they please. Since the time of the French Revolution, civil law has regulated the naming of French citizens, placing a number of restrictions on parents and granting civil authorities the right to refuse choices that they find inappropriate. In recent years, for example, a couple was unable to name their child Jennifer because the local official found it "bizarre." Even so, the choice of names is far from small. Parents may choose names from the Catholic calendar of saints, mythology, and known personages from ancient history. They may also choose double names (like Jean-Pierre or Marie-France), which have been very popular in recent years. However, triple names are not allowed (no Jean-Paul-Yves!). Civil authorities may authorize (but with prudence) certain diminutives (like Ginette for Genevieve) and contractions of double names (like Sylviane for Sylvie-Anne).

In practice, most people do not feel constrained by these rules. Often a Catholic saint's name is chosen, and the child may celebrate the saint's feast day, and invoke that saint in prayers or moments of crisis throughout life. The enunciation and musicality of names count for a great deal too. A name may be chosen largely for its sound, which in itself can be an indicator of class or sophistication.

The following names are well used in France. The English equivalent is given in parentheses if it differs from the French form.

GIRLS' NAMES

Anne
Catherine
Cécile
Claire
Françoise (Frances)
Geneviève
Hélène
Jeanne
Marie
Martine (Martina)
Michèle
Sylvie

BOYS' NAMES

Alain
André (Andrew)
Charles
Claude
François (Francis)
Jean (John)
Louis
Michel (Michael)
Paul
Philippe (Philip)
Pierre (Peter)
René

GERMANY

In Germany, name choices are regulated by the state, and this practice has discouraged the free-wheeling inventiveness in naming that is possible in some countries. The most limiting factor is that surnames are prohibited as first names. Other names that by their nature are not first names (for instance, common nouns) are prohibited as well. However, name fashions do change with each generation. The names that follow are a selection of traditional German names.

GIRLS' NAMES

Anna
Barbara
Bärbel (a form of Barbara)
Berta
Charlotte
Christa (a form of Christiane)
Christiane (Christine)
Edith
Elisabeth
Elke
Erika
Frieda (a form of Friederike)

GIRLS' NAMES

Friederike

Gabriele

Greta, Grete, Gretel

Gretchen

Hedwig

Helga

Hilda, Hilde (forms of Hildegard)

Hildegard

Johanna

Katharina (Katherine)

Käthe (a form of Katherina)

Klara, Clara

Lise (a form of Elisabeth)

Lotte (a form of Charlotte)

Maria

Marianne

Rosalinde

Rosamunde

Sabina

Ursula

Wilhelmine

BOYS' NAMES

Adolf

Albrecht (Albert)

Andreas (Andrew)

Bruno

Eduard, Edvard (Edward)

Ernst (Ernest)

BOYS' NAMES (continued)

Erwin
Franz (Francis)
Friedrich (Frederick)
Fritz (a diminutive of Friedrich)
Georg (George)
Gottfried (Godfrey)
Gunter
Gustav
Hans (a diminutive of Johannes)
Heinrich (Henry)
Heinz (a diminutive of Heinrich)
Helmut
Hermann
Johann, Johannes (John)
Josef (Joseph)
Jurgen
Karl
Klaus
Konrad
Kurt
Ludwig (Louis)
Martin
Max
Oskar (Oscar)
Otto
Peter
Walter
Werner
Wilhelm (William)
Wolfgang

GREECE

Greece is often called the cradle of western civilization, and the names of the ancient Greek gods, goddesses, heroes, and heroines have long been a popular source of names throughout the world. Some of those names are in fact among the most familiar names in Greece today. Below are some of the most common names in modern Greece.

GIRLS' NAMES

Anna
Antigone
Artemis
Athena
Catarina, Katarina (Katherine)
Christina
Eleni
Maria
Zoe

BOYS' NAMES

Alexandros (Alexander)
Alexis
Andreas (Andrew)
Constantinos (Constantine)
Christos (Christ, "the anointed one")
Michalis (Michael)
Yiorgos (George)

IRELAND

Some of the names that follow are uniquely Irish. They come from Irish Gaelic, which, like Welsh and Scottish Gaelic, is of Celtic origin. Others, while used elsewhere, have been taken up so enthusiastically in Ireland that they have become a special part of Irish tradition as well.

GIRLS' NAMES

Aisling
Bridget, Brigid
Clare
Deirdre
Eileen
Erin
Frances
Gertrude, Gertie
Grania
Kate
Katherine
Kathleen
Kitty
Maeve
Maire (Mary)
Margaret
Maud
Maureen
Molly
Nora
Noreen
Patricia
Rose
Rosemary
Sheila
Sinead
Siobhan, Shivaun
Una

BOYS' NAMES

Aloysius
Benedict
Brendan
Brian
Colman, Colm, Colum
Conor
Desmond
Donagh
Donal
Donheh
Eamon
Eoin
Fergus
Flann
Francis
George
Gerald
Hugh
Joseph, Joe
Liam
Malachy
Myles
Niall (Neil)
Padraic
Patrick
Phelam
Seamus
Sean

ISRAEL

In modern Israel, name fashions vary greatly between religious sects, regions, and generations. For example, Hasidic naming customs differ from Orthodox ones, and various groups of immigrants and native-born Israelis each have their own name fashions. What is more, these styles often change very quickly. The unifying element is the use of Hebrew names and spellings. There is even a Commission for Hebrew Nomenclature, and guidelines have been established for returning names to their original Hebrew forms. Naturally, many names from the Bible are used. Another trend has been the use of names invented from phrases (like Aliyah, meaning "wave of immigration") or common nouns. Following are a few names of this type that have been used in Israel in recent years, and which would also not be too difficult for non-Hebrew speakers to spell and pronounce. Their Hebrew meanings are given as well.

GIRLS' NAMES

Avivah "spring"
Avivit "lilac"
Azah "strong" or "bright"
Dafne "laurel," the equivalent of Daphne (Greek) or Laurel (Latin)
Daliah "dahlia"
Dalit "trailing vine"
Galiah "wave"
Hillah "halo"
Ilanah "tree"
Leorah "light to me"
Mirit "sweet wine"
Neimah "pleasant"

GIRLS' NAMES (continued)

Netah "plant"
Orah "light"
Ornah "pine"
Ramah "high"
Roni "song"
Zivah "radiant"

BOYS' NAMES

Amir "tree top"
Ari a popular short form of Aryeh, which means "lion"
Doron "gift"
Dov "bear"
Gil "joy"
Gili "my joy"
Noam "delight"
Omer "sheaf"
Oran "pine"
Orli "my light"
Ron "sing"
Ronen "sing"
Shai "gift" (this also happens to be a nickname for Shaya, the Yiddish diminutive of Isaiah)
Tal "dew"

ITALY

In Italy, name fashions change from year to year as parents seemingly vie to have the most beautiful and interesting names for their children. Nicknames and diminutives are seldom used either for children or adults, which means that the real name is even more significant than it is in English-speaking countries where a William is often known as Bill, and so on. In recent years there was a trend toward foreign-sounding names, many with a Russian flavor. That rage is past, but in some of the names below one can still detect an exotic ring. According to the Italian Cultural Institute, the following names are some of the best known and most popular children's names in the late 1980s. If their English counterparts differ from the Italian, they follow in parentheses.

GIRLS' NAMES

Alessandra (Alexandra)
Alessia (Alicia)
Barbara
Cristina (Christina)
Federica (Fredrika)
Francesca (Frances)
Giulia (Julia)
Ludovica (Louisa)
Monica
Serena
Silvia
Valeria (Valerie)

BOYS' NAMES

Alberto (Albert)
Alessandro (Alexander)
Andrea (Andrew)
Cristiano (Christian)
Gabriele (Gabriel)
Luca (Luke)
Matteo (Matthew)
Michele (Michael)
Roberto (Robert)

JAPAN

In Japan, names are not spelled out in Roman letters but written in the Japanese pictographic alphabet. A great variety of names is used, many more than in America and Europe, which makes it difficult to establish a group of traditional favorites. In the past, Japanese parents were more concerned about the meanings of their children's names. Now they are more apt to name a child after a movie star or other popular figure. The following names are both traditional and popular in Japan in the late 1980s.

GIRLS' NAMES	BOYS' NAMES
Michiko	**Ichiro**
Naomi	**Makoto**
Yoko	**Yoichi**

MEXICO

Tradition rather than fad or fashion tends to dominate naming customs in Mexico, according to the New York office of the Mexican Consulate General. Of all the girls' names, Maria is the favorite. Frequently, variety is achieved by using two names, one of them Maria. Maria Teresa, Maria Louisa, Maria Guadalupe, Maria Rosa, and Rosa Maria are all popular combinations. Nicknames and diminutives are much used as well.

The names of Mexico are extremely common in the American Southwest, where Spanish has been part of the culture longer than any other European language. Through immigration, Hispanic first names have become common in many other parts of the United States as well. For example, in 1981–83 the Stanford University School of Business Administration had five graduates named José; three named Enrique;

two each named Carlos, Luis, and Gerardo; and one each named Jesus, Alberto, Ildelfonso, Alejandro, Raúl, Rodolfo, Jorge, Antonio, Pedro, and Miguel.

Here are some of the most widely used names in Mexico, some followed by their traditional diminutives or nicknames. The English equivalent is given in parentheses.

GIRLS' NAMES

Carlota (Charlotte)
Catalina, Cata (Catherine)
Dolores, Lola
Enriqueta (Henriette)
Guadalupe, Lupe
Juana, Juanita (Jane or Joan)
Luisa (Louisa)
Maria
Rosa
Teresa, Tere

BOYS' NAMES

Alberto, Beto (Albert)
Carlos (Charles)
Eduardo (Edward)
Enrique (Henry)
Ernesto (Ernest)
Francisco, Paco
José, Pepe (Joseph)
Luis (Louis)
Juan (John)
Pedro (Peter)
Raúl (Ralph, Rudolph)
Ricardo (Richard)

RUSSIA

Here are some of the most famous Russian names from history, culture, and literature. They happen to be some of the world's most striking and romantic names as well. Since Russian names are written in the Russian (Cyrillic) alphabet, many of them do not have exact counterparts in English. Thus, spellings can vary, for instance: Vasili or Vassily, Tanya or Tania.

GIRLS' NAMES

Alexandra
Anna, Anya
Elena
Galina
Irina
Marina
Nadezhda, Nadia
Natalia, Nataly
Natasha
Nina
Olga
Sofia, Sophia
Sonia, Sonya
Tamara
Tatiana, Tanya, Tania
Valentina
Vera

BOYS' NAMES

Alexander, Alexei, Alexey, Alexis

Anton

Boris

Dmitry

Fyodor

Georgi (George)

Grigory (Gregory)

Igor

Ilya

Ivan

Konstantin (Constantine)

Leonid (Leonard)

Mikhail (Michael)

Nikolai, Nikita (Nicholas)

Sasha (a diminutive of Alexander)

Sergei

Vanya (a diminutive of Ivan)

Vasili, Vassily

Vladimir

Yuri

SCOTLAND

For centuries, Scotland has exchanged names with England and Ireland. However, many names may still be considered typically Scottish, either because they originated in Scotland or because historically they have been much more popular there than anywhere else. Many of the homegrown Scottish names have Gaelic origins (like many Irish names) and have become popular in Ireland, even as some Irish names have come into use in Scotland. One uniquely Scottish practice is to add a suffix ending in "a" to a masculine name to create a feminine form. Thus, Andrew becomes Andreana, and James becomes Jamesina. The following names may be considered typically Scottish.

GIRLS' NAMES

Agnes (and the diminutive Nessie)
Andreana, Andreena, Andrena, Andrene, Andriene, Andrina
Elsie
Elspeth
Fiona
Jamesina
Janet
Janice, Janis
Janie, Janey
Janine
Jeanette, Janette, Janetta
Jeanne, Jeanie
Johanna
Kirstie (a diminutive of Christine or Christina)
Lesley
Lindsay, Lindsey, Linsay, Lyndsay, Lyndsey
Maisie (a variation of Margaret)

GIRLS' NAMES (continued)

Moira (a Gaelic form of Mary)
Seona, Sheona, Shiona
Shauna, Shonagh, Shonah

BOYS' NAMES

Alan
Alistair, Alasdair, Alisdair, Alastair
Angus
Donald
Douglas
Dugald, Dougal
Duncan
Ewan, Euan
Fionn, Fionnan
Graham, Graeme
Hamish
Ian, Iain
Jamie (a diminutive of James)
Kenneth
Leslie
Lindsay
Malcolm
Ronald
Seamus
Sean, Shane, Shaun

SWEDEN

In the seventeenth century, lovely, brilliant Queen Christina of Sweden entranced the courts of Europe, and ever since then Sweden has been known as a land of good-looking and talented people. In the nineteenth century, a singer named Jenny Lind enchanted audiences everywhere and was dubbed "the Swedish Nightingale." In the twentieth century, this northern country brought the world tennis stars Bjorn Borg and Stefan Edberg, film director Ingmar Bergman, and the film star Ingrid Bergman. Many Swedish names also occur in English; others differ mainly in the spelling. Following are some typical and common Swedish first names.

GIRLS' NAMES

Agneta (Agnes)
Alexandra
Amanda
Anita
Ann
Anna
Annette
Annika
Astrid
Barbro
Berit
Birgit, Birgitta (Bridget)
Britt, Britta (Bridget)
Cecilia
Charlotta
Dagmar
Ebba
Edit
Eleonora
Elin
Elisabeth
Elsa
Emma
Erika
Ester (Esther)
Eva
Gabriella
Gertrud
Gudrun
Gunilla
Gunnel
Harriet
Hedvig (Hedwig)
Helena
Helga
Inga

GIRLS' NAMES (continued)

Ingalill
Ingeborg
Ingegerd
Inger
Ingrid
Isabella
Jenny
Karin (Karen)
Katarina (Katherine)
Kerstin
Kristina (Christina)
Lena
Lisbet (Elizabeth)
Lotta (Lottie)
Magdalena (Marlena)
Maj
Malin
Margareta (Margaret)
Maria
Marianne
Mona
Monika (Monica)
Petronella
Pia
Rebecka (Rebecca)
Rigmor
Silvia, Sylvia
Solveig
Stina
Susanna
Ulla
Ulrika
Viktoria (Victoria)
Viveka

BOYS' NAMES

Adam
Alexander
Alf
Anders (Andrew)
Arne
Axel
Bengt
Bertil
Bjorn
Bo
Daniel
David
Edvard (Edward)
Edvin (Edwin)
Emil
Erland
Ernst (Ernest)
Eskil
Evert
Folke
Fredrik (Frederick)
Gabriel

BOYS' NAMES (continued)

Greger (Gregory)
Gunnar
Gustav
Hans
Helge
Henrik
Herbert
Ingemar
Ingvar
Jakob (Jacob)
Jan
Jesper
Joakim
Johan (John)
Jonas
Kalle
Karl
Kjell
Klas
Krister
Lars
Leif
Lennart
Magnus
Markus (Marcus)
Martin
Mats
Mikael (Michael)
Niklas, Nils (Nicholas)
Olof
Oskar (Oscar)
Ove
Patrik (Patrick)
Per
Pontus
Rolf (Randolf)
Rune
Staffan (Stephen)
Stig
Sture
Sven
Tobias
Tomas (Thomas)
Ulf
Urban
Yngve

10
GREAT PLACES

Names of places have long been used as personal names. In fact, many traditional names originally indicated that the bearer came from a certain town or region. The name Laurence, for example, means "from Laurentium," a town in ancient Rome. The name Magdalene derives from Magdala, a town in Galilee. With the passing of centuries, however, these particular places have ceased to be important in themselves, and the names are used for other reasons.

Some of the names listed below immediately bring to mind a geographical place. Others are derived from place names, but they have become so familiar as personal names that the original meanings are nearly forgotten. What they have in common is that the places themselves are important to people today.

A simple place name can invoke strong emotions and images better than practically any type of word. Many of them are strikingly beautiful as well. Perhaps one of these will strike a chord with you.

GIRLS' NAMES

Bethany This town in Galilee figures importantly in the New Testament and was a special one in the life of Jesus. It was the home of his friends Mary, Martha, and Lazarus; it was also the place where Jesus was anointed (Mark 14:3–9).

Bethel Bethel was a sacred location in the days of the biblical patriarchs, for it was the place where Abraham built an altar to God (Genesis 12:8) and the site Jacob associated with the presence and power of God (Genesis 31:13, 35:6–7). In Hebrew the name means "house of God." A similar name is Bethia, which means "daughter of God." Short form: Beth.

Brittany This picturesque region in northwestern France was actually settled by people from Britain around A.D. 500. Though a part of France since 1532, the inhabitants long retained many of their unique customs, and even today the Bretons are known as proud and independent-minded people. This name became a very popular one for girls born in the 1980s, perhaps because it also brings to mind Great Britain. Thus, it may have seemed to have both a vaguely English sound (like Ashley, Grayson, and other popular names), along with the distinction of being a brand new name.

Carmel, Carmelle, Carmela, Carmella These names all refer to Mount Carmel in Israel, which figures prominently in the Bible. The Carmelite order of nuns and monks took their name from this mountain. In Hebrew, the name means "garden land" or "fruitful land."

Carolina A comforting place or a loving person—like in James Taylor's song "Carolina in My Mind"—is what may come to mind with this name. Like the name Caroline, Carolina is a feminine form of CHARLES. The states North Carolina and South Carolina were named for Charles I and Charles II of England.

Dixie "I wish I was in the land of cotton, Old times there are not forgotten," goes the famous song, "Dixie." For those who have had similar longings to be back home, "away down South in Dixie," this name might be attractive. It has been given as a girls' name from time to time in the South.

Eden Paradise, the garden God prepared for the first man and woman to live in, was located in the land of Eden (Genesis 2:8). The name derived from a Hebrew word meaning "delight."

Erin This poetic name for Ireland is a favorite among those whose hearts belong to the Emerald Isle. In Gaelic the name means "western island."

Iona The small island of Iona off the northwest coast of Scotland is not only a beautiful place but was important to the spread of Christianity. A famous monastery was founded there by Saint Columba in 563.

Jamaica The Caribbean island country of Jamaica, known for its misty Blue Mountains and white sand beaches, inspires use of this name.

Kimberley Diamonds and gold helped make this name known around the world. Kimberley, South Africa, is a famous diamond mining center. Kimberley is also the name of a gold field in Western Australia. For more on this name, see KIM.

Lorraine This beautiful name belongs to a region in eastern France. It is best known as part of the Alsace-Lorraine region that was annexed by Germany and then returned to France after World War I.

Neva The Neva is one of the great rivers of Russia, and this name recalls its distant, exotic grandeur. The name also brings to mind the Spanish word for "snowfall," which is part of the names of some great American places, such as the Sierra Nevada.

Odessa The city of Odessa in Russia has for centuries been a vital port on the Black Sea and a center of culture for the Ukraine. There is also a city named Odessa in west central Texas.

Olympia What can Olympia be but the nearest thing on earth to a living, lively Greek goddess? The name recalls two great places from classical history and mythology: the legendary abode of the Greek gods on Mount Olympus and the Olympia plain in Greece where the first Olympic Games were held.

Roma *La dolce vita* and the grandeur of ancient civilizations are part of this name. Roma is the Italian word for Rome.

Shannon The River Shannon is one of the most famous in Ireland. As a first name, Shannon has been used for boys as well as girls.

Sharon Sharon is a coastal plain in Israel, mentioned several times in the Bible. The flocks of King David pastured there (1 Chronicles 27:29), and the rose of Sharon is mentioned in the Song of Solomon (2:1–3). The name comes from a Hebrew word meaning "level place" or "plain."

BOYS' NAMES

Austin This name was once best known as a surname, but it has become most famous for Austin, Texas, the capital of the Lone Star State. The city was named for the "father of Texas," Stephen Fuller Austin.

Bryce Bryce Canyon in Utah is one of the wonders of the American West. For more on this name, see BRICE.

Clyde The River Clyde is one of the most famous rivers in Scotland. It runs through the Clyde Valley, which is where the great Clydesdale horses originated.

Dallas This name is best known because of Dallas, Texas. The city itself was named for a U.S. vice president, George Mifflin Dallas.

Everest The highest mountain in the world is Mount Everest, on the border of Tibet and Nepal. It was named for the British explorer of the Himalayas, Sir George Everest.

Houston Houston, the largest city in the Southwest, was named for one of Texas's great heroes, Sam Houston, the first president of the Republic of Texas and later a governor of the state.

Israel "God strives" is the Hebrew meaning of Israel. This name refers both to the modern country Israel and to the people of Israel, or Israelites, descended from the twelve sons of Jacob. Israel was a name given Jacob by God (Genesis 32:28).

Jordan The most significant river in the Bible is the Jordan. It is mentioned many times, most notably as the site of Jesus's baptism by John the Baptist (Matthew 3).

Tennessee This Southern state is one of the most popular when it comes to inspiring first names.

Troy The ancient city of Troy, immortalized in Homer's epic poem the *Iliad*, brings to mind the mighty Greek and Trojan warriors. The site of the ancient city has actually been discovered in Turkey.

11
MORE NAMES FOR GREAT BEGINNINGS

Many parents throughout American history have given their sons (and occasionally their daughters) last names as first names. Often the mother's maiden name is used, or occasionally another family surname. Humphrey Bogart was one such son; Humphrey was his mother's last name. With the right last name, all sorts of favorable things can be implied—including wealth, sophistication, family connections, and education. In recent years, this type of name has become very fashionable for boys *and* girls all over the United States.

This chapter is full of last names that could be used as first names—and have great connotations. There are also a number of traditional first names, many of which are described more fully in other parts of the book. As you read, look at both the last names and the first names, and let your imagination go!

MAYFLOWER NAMES AND OTHER GREAT NAMES FROM EARLY AMERICA

It has long been considered a mark of prestige to be able to trace one's heritage back to one of America's "first families," those who arrived on the *Mayflower* on December 26, 1620. Their names, however, are available to anyone! Following are the names of the men who signed the Mayflower Compact on behalf of themselves and their families.

John Alden
Isaac Allerton
John Allerton
John Billington
William Bradford
William Brewster
Richard Britteridge
Peter Brown
John Carver
James Chilton
Richard Clarke
Francis Cooke
John Crackston
Edward Doty
Francis Eaton
Thomas English
Moses Fletcher
Edward Fuller
Samuel Fuller
Richard Gardiner
John Goodman
Stephen Hopkins
John Howland
Edward Liester
Edmund Margeson
Christopher Martin

William Mullins
Digery Priest
John Rigdale
Thomas Rogers
George Soule
Miles Standish
Edward Tilly
John Tilly
Thomas Tinker
John Turner
Richard Warren
William White
Thomas Williams
Edward Winslow
Gilbert Winslow

The following last names were all associated with particularly prominent families and individuals in the New England colonies, and with their blue-blooded heritage they could make distinctive first names today.

Ames
Bradford
Bradstreet
Brattle
Bulkeley
Colman
Cotton
Cushman
Davenport
Dudley
Dummer

Franklin
Keayne
Mather
Morton
Norton
Rowlandson
Sewall
Shepard
Stoddard
Vane
Ward
Williams
Winthrop
Wise

A little over 150 years after the *Mayflower*'s landing, the Declaration of Independence was signed. On that historic document, the first names most often appearing were George, William, John, and Thomas in a four-way tie. Tied for second place were Samuel, Francis, and Benjamin, and tied for third place were Richard, Robert, and James.

Among signers of the Mayflower Compact, the Declaration of Independence, the Articles of Confederation, and the Constitution, these were the ten most popular names—the most distinguished first names in colonial America:

1. **John**
2. **William**
3. **Thomas**
4. **George**
5. **Edward** (tie)
   James (tie)
   Richard (tie)
8. **Francis**
9. **Samuel**
10. **Daniel**

THE VIRTUES

Among the New England Puritans, Christian virtues provided inspiration for many popular names. Some of these names were given to boys as well as to girls. Currently they are considered girls' names, and they retain an attractive, old-fashioned charm. Following are some of the best.

Charity
Chastity
Comfort
Constance
Faith
Fidelity
Hope
Mercy
Patience
Peace
Prudence
Temperance
Welcome

THE IVY LEAGUE AND OTHER ELITE INSTITUTIONS

Many of America's top universities and prep schools were named for distinguished and wealthy Americans, from colonial days through the nineteenth century. Now, they are great places to look for a name with an obviously blue-blooded or preppy ring. The following names are some of the best and the brightest.

Berkeley University of California, Berkeley
Brearley The Brearley School

Brown Brown University
Bryn Bryn Mawr College
Choate Choate Rosemary Hall
Cornell Cornell University
Dalton The Dalton School
Dartmouth Dartmouth College
Juilliard The Juilliard School
Princeton Princeton University
Radcliffe Radcliffe College
Reed Reed College
Smith Smith College
Spence The Spence School
Stanford Stanford University
Vanderbilt Vanderbilt University
Vassar Vassar College
Wellesley Wellesley College
Yale Yale University

Another fine source of names steeped in history is the Harvard residence houses. Named for eminent figures in colonial America, they provide a subtle link to Harvard as well. The names of the Harvard houses:

Adams
Cabot
Currier
Dudley
Dunster
Eliot
Kirkland
Leverett
Lowell
Mather
North
Quincy
Winthrop

AMERICA'S TOP TEN CORPORATE NAMES

How to name for success in corporate America? For girls, the question is tricky. For boys, one answer is to look to the names of the men who run America's businesses.

In 1987, more than 40 percent of the chief executive officers of America's Corporate 1000 companies (similar to the *Fortune* 500) went by one of the following ten names. More than 20 percent used one of the first three.

1. **John**
2. **William**
3. **Robert**
4. **James**
5. **David**
6. **Charles**
7. **Thomas**
8. **Richard**
9. **Donald**
10. **Paul**

Close runners-up for the top ten were George and Joseph/Joe.

GREAT AMERICAN CAPITALISTS OF THE NINETEENTH CENTURY

In the days when guests left calling cards and men of substance dressed for dinner, men of means also enjoyed substantial names. While some of their names may sound a bit ponderous today, there is no denying their solidity. Parents looking for a substantial name for a son would do well to consider these examples.

Andrew Carnegie
Andrew William Mellon

Collis Porter Huntington
Cornelius Vanderbilt
Edward Henry Harriman
Harrison Gray Otis
Harvey Samuel Firestone
Henry Clay Frick
Henry Edwards Huntington
James Buchanan "Diamond Jim" Brady
Jay Gould
John Jacob Astor
John Pierpont Morgan
Junius Spencer Morgan
Amasa Leland Stanford
Marshall Field
Nicholas Biddle
Phineas Banning

AMERICA'S FIRST LADIES

The women who have lived in the White House as first lady of the land have often been as different from each other as apple pie and Tiffany diamonds. Interestingly, what some of them *have* had in common are their first names. Three were named Elizabeth, and two each were named Abigail, Julia, or Edith. Since Eliza is actually a short form of Elizabeth, one could actually say that four of them have gone by forms of that regal-sounding name. The names Anne or Anna occur three times as first names, but Anna Eleanor Roosevelt and Anne Frances (Nancy) Reagan did not use their given first names. To show how name fashions have changed in two hundred years—and perhaps inspire you to revive an old style—the names are given in chronological order, with the presidents' last names in parentheses.

Martha Dandridge Custis (Washington)
Abigail Smith (Adams)
Dorothea ("Dolley") Payne Todd (Madison)
Elizabeth Kortright (Monroe)
Louisa Catherine Johnson (Adams)
Anna Symmes (Harrison)
Letitia Christian (Tyler)
Julia Gardiner (Tyler)
Sarah Childress (Polk)
Margaret Smith (Taylor)
Abigail Powers (Fillmore)
Jane Means Appleton (Pierce)
Mary Todd (Lincoln)
Eliza McCardle (Johnson)
Julia Dent (Grant)
Lucy Ware Webb (Hayes)
Lucretia Rudolph (Garfield)

Frances Folsom (Cleveland)
Caroline Lavinia Scott (Harrison)
Ida Saxton (McKinley)
Edith Kermit Carow (Roosevelt)
Helen Herron (Taft)
Ellen Louise Axson (Wilson)
Edith Bolling Galt (Wilson)
Florence Kling De Wolfe (Harding)
Grace Anna Goodhue (Coolidge)
Lou Henry (Hoover)
Anna Eleanor Roosevelt (Roosevelt)
Elizabeth Virginia Wallace (Truman)
Mamie Geneva Doud (Eisenhower)
Jacqueline Lee Bouvier (Kennedy)
Claudia ("Lady Bird") Alta Taylor (Johnson)
Thelma Catherine Patricia Ryan (Nixon)
Elizabeth ("Betty") Bloomer (Ford)
Rosalynn Smith (Carter)
Anne Frances ("Nancy") Davis (Reagan)

As for the men in the White House, five have been named James, four John, three William, two Andrew, and two Franklin.

FLOWERS

In the late nineteenth century, flower names such as Rose, Lily, Daisy, and Hazel came into vogue, and now that this Victorian fashion is far in the past, some of these names may be due for a revival. Daffodil and Eglantine, both used by the Victorians, may always sound rather artificial. However, other favorites like Ivy, Iris, and Fern could fit in well in the late twentieth-century name climate. Several other flower names have always stood nicely alone, not overly associated with any period (Laurel, Marguerite). Heather became popular in the 1970s.

Here is a garden of old-fashioned favorites, hardy perennials, and a few exotic varieties:

Blossom
Bryony
Clover
Daffodil
Dahlia
Daisy
Fern
Hazel
Heather
Holly
Iris
Ivy
Laurel
Lily
Magnolia
Marguerite
Myrtle
Olivia, Olive

Pansy
Poppy
Rose, Rosa, Rosemary, Rosemarie, Rosalie, Rosanna, Rosabel, Rosabelle
Sage
Violet, Viola
Willow

Themes of springtime beauty and new life are expressed in the following names.

April
Dawn
Flora
June
May, Mae, Maya, Maia
Summer

JEWELS

Jewels have long provided a rich source of names, favored for their suggestions of beauty, rarity, and precious worth. Like the jewels themselves, some of the names are subtle (Beryl, Jade), some glitter and flash (Ruby, Diamond), some are brash and aggressive (Topaz, Jet). Others—not strictly jewels, but similarly valued—are more humble in origin (Crystal, Coral). The jewel names BERYL, CRYSTAL, PEARL, JASPER are described in the "Creators" chapter, along with the famous people who bear those names. Below is a small trove of additional gem names.

GIRLS' NAMES

Amber Prized for jewelry and decorative objects, this yellow, orange, or yellow-brown translucent stone is found mainly along the Baltic Sea. Amber is also a color, like the color of whiskey, or of "amber fields of grain" (as in the song "America the Beautiful").

Coral Built up by the skeletons of tiny sea animals, coral has formed whole islands and reefs. It is white, pinkish, or red-orange. There is also a rare black coral. A precious red coral is prized for jewelry.

Diamond "Diamonds are forever" and "Diamonds are a girl's best friend" are phrases this name brings to mind. The diamond is the birthstone for April.

Esmeralda This is the Spanish word for emerald, the brilliant, green transparent jewel. The emerald is the birthstone for May.

Gem, Gemma Gemma is the Italian word for "gem," and it has long been used in Italy as a feminine name. Both Gemma and Gem have also been used in English-speaking countries. The implied meaning of these names is "rare, precious."

Jacinth In modern English, jacinth is a reddish-orange variety of zircon. In the Bible, however, jacinth is mentioned many times, probably in reference to a bluish stone, like turquoise or aquamarine. The ancient Greek word for bluebell or hyacinth was jacinth, and jacinth is also an old-fashioned English name for the hyacinth flower.

Jade This beautiful pale green stone is generally associated with the Orient. In addition to jewelry, elaborate carvings may be made of jade. A "jade" may also be a broken-down horse or a worthless woman, but these two meanings are nearly obsolete.

Jewel A jewel is not only a precious stone, but an object or person that is much treasured or esteemed, as in the phrase "She is a jewel."

Opal This lustrous stone is known for the rainbow of colors that can be seen in it. It is the birthstone for October.

Ruby In *The Wizard of Oz*, Dorothy's magic ruby slippers were what returned her home again. The brilliant red ruby is the birthstone for December.

Sapphire Brilliant blue is the usual color of this lovely gem. The word "sapphire" may also mean a blue color, as in "her beautiful sapphire eyes."

Topaz This translucent yellow stone usually comes from Brazil, Burma, or Sri Lanka. Some varieties may also be blue, brown, or pink. It is the birthstone for November.

BOYS' NAME

Jet This deep black type of coal can be highly polished and is used for jewelry. Jet can also mean "a deep black color."

DESIGNER NAMES

Style, sophistication, money, incredible good looks: these are all associated with the names of some of the world's most popular designers. Not surprisingly, some designers' names (Ashley, Chanel) have become popular first names in recent years. Your child could look great in one of the names that follow.

Chanel Chanel No. 5 perfume and the simple elegance of a Chanel suit are associated with this name, made famous by the designer Coco Chanel.

Churchill After recalling the great Prime Minister Winston Churchill, the minds of the style-conscious may turn to Jane Churchill's designer fabrics, wallpapers, and accessories. This is a name for those who wish to seem on top of the world.

Ellis A casual dignity is associated with this name because of designer Perry Ellis.

Estée Classic glamour and rags-to-riches success are associated with this name, known for one of the business world's great success stories, Estée Lauder and her cosmetics company.

Giorgio On Madison Avenue or Rodeo Drive, this name seems right at home, along with designer Giorgio Armani.

Halston American elegance is associated with Halston. The famous designer's full name is Roy Halston Frowick.

Issey A flair for luxury and a chic popular appeal go along with this name, which is associated with fashion designer Issey Miyake.

Karan As an alternate to Karen, why not try Karan, the name of the brilliantly successful and popular women's fashion designer Donna Karan?

Klein Anne Klein and Calvin Klein give this name a double dose of style power.

Rodeo Pronounced Ro-DAY-oh, this brings to mind one of the truly legendary, luxurious shopping streets of the world—Rodeo Drive in Beverly Hills.

Sloane Born to wealth and born to shop is a definition of Sloane. Fashionable Sloane Street in London is known not only for the designer shops that line it but for its young and wealthy clientele. Lady Di's old set was called the Sloane Rangers.

Steuben Clear superiority is associated with Steuben—the name of the world's most luxurious purveyor of crystal and glass.

Waterford Quality, taste, and old-fashioned craftsmanship are associated with this name because of famous Waterford crystal.

Willi Youthful, colorful, and up-to-the-minute is the message behind this name, associated with designer Willi Smith, creator of WilliWear. For more on this name in its traditional spelling, see WILLIE.

12
NEWS FROM THE TOP

THE TOP TEN NAMES IN THE UNITED STATES

In 1957 the *New York Herald Tribune* ran an article headlined " 'Linda' Passes 'Mary' as Most Popular Name." It told readers that if they wanted to win a bet from their friends, they should ask them to guess the most popular name for baby girls in America. They would probably guess Mary, Elizabeth, Margaret, or Anne—and lose. According to a Gallup poll, the most popular name for girls born from 1946 to 1956 was Linda. Mary was included on the top ten list, however, along with Deborah, Susan, Carol, Margaret, Barbara, and Karen. The article cautioned readers not to make any bets on the most popular name for boys. Gallup found that for boys born from 1946 to 1956, the most-used name was still John, as it had been for ages. The article made the point that in naming daughters, parents tend to follow fads and fashions much more than in naming sons.

The Gallup pollsters of 1956 might be astounded to see the most popular names thirty years later. Girls' names have always tended to change with the times. But in the mid-1980s, for the first time in American history, John, William,

Charles, and James were not among the top ten names for baby boys. Only Robert (which according to one study did not become one of the top five names until around 1900) held onto a spot in the top ten (ninth place in 1986). The following names were the most popular ones given to babies born in the United States in 1986.

	GIRLS' NAMES	BOYS' NAMES
1.	**Jessica**	**Christopher**
2.	**Sara**	**Michael**
3.	**Amanda**	**Matthew**
4.	**Ashley**	**Ryan**
5.	**Jennifer**	**Andrew**
6.	**Brittany**	**Joshua**
7.	**Kristen**	**Nicholas**
8.	**Heather**	**Brandon**
9.	**Stephanie**	**Robert**
10.	**Lindsay**	**Daniel**

Naturally, the most popular names vary from region to region and even town to town. For example, in the borough of the Bronx, in New York City, José was the fourth most popular boys' name in 1987. Even though the order of popularity may differ, and a few names may have a special local appeal, a similar *type* of name is often popular throughout the country. Listed below are the most popular names given to babies born in New York City's five boroughs in 1987 (data from the New York City Department of Health). Though the list differs in some respects from the national list above, the feeling is similar.

	GIRLS' NAMES	BOYS' NAMES
1.	**Jessica**	**Michael**
2.	**Jennifer**	**Christopher**
3.	**Stephanie**	**Jonathan**
4.	**Melissa**	**Daniel**
5.	**Christina**	**David**
6.	**Nicole**	**Anthony**
7.	**Amanda**	**Joseph**
8.	**Ashley**	**Matthew**
9.	**Tiffany**	**John**
10.	**Samantha**	**Andrew**

HIT SONGS, OLD AND NEW

Many popular songs of the past and present include personal names. From nursery rhymes to classic rock-and-roll hits, the songs—and the names in them—are an important part of popular culture. Some songs have inspired parents in naming their children. Others, while not directly inspiring namesakes, have brought particular names into the public consciousness and helped keep them there. For children and adults whose names are part of great songs, it is a special pleasure to be able to say, "They're playing *my* song."

Here are some names that have top billing in the history of popular music:

Adeline "Sweet Adeline"

Alexander "Alexander's Ragtime Band"

Alfie "Alfie" (Hal David, Burt Bacharach)

Alice "Sweet Alice"; "Alice's Restaurant" (Arlo Guthrie)

Angie "Angie" (Rolling Stones); "Angie Baby" (Helen Reddy)

Annie "Annie Laurie"; "Annie's Song" (John Denver); *Annie* (the musical)

Betsy "Sweet Betsy From Pike"

Bill "Bill Bailey, Won't You Please Come Home?"; "Steamboat Bill"

Billy "Billy Boy"

Bobby "Bobby Shaftoe"

Bonnie "My Bonnie Lies Over the Ocean"

Brian "Brian's Song"

Caroline "Sweet Caroline" (Neil Diamond)

Casey ("Casey Would Waltz with the Strawberry Blonde While) The Band Played On"; "Casey Jones"

Cathy "Cathy's Clown" (Everly Brothers)

Charlie "Charlie Is My Darling"

Charlotte "Hush Hush Sweet Charlotte"

Chuck "Chuck E.'s in Love" (Rickie Lee Jones)

Clementine "My Darling Clementine"

Daisy "Daisy Bell (A Bicycle Built for Two)"

Dan "Old Dan Tucker"

Daniel "Daniel" (Elton John)

Danny "Danny Deever"; "Danny Boy"

Diana "Diana" (Paul Anka)

Dinah "Dinah"

Dolly "Hello, Dolly!"

Ezekiel "Ezekiel Saw the Wheel"

Frankie "Frankie and Johnny"

Georgia "Sweet Georgia Brown"

Guinnevere "Guinnevere" (Crosby, Stills, Nash & Young)

Harry "I'm Just Wild About Harry" (music by Eubie Blake)

Hernando "Hernando's Hideaway"

Holly "Deck the Halls with Boughs of Holly"

Huckleberry "Do, Do, My Huckleberry Do"

Irene "Irene" (from the 1919 musical *Irene*)

Jack "Jack and Jill"; "Little Jack Horner"

Jean "Jean" (Oliver)

Jeanie "Jeanie with the Light Brown Hair"

Jill "Jack and Jill"

Johnny "When Johnny Comes Marching Home"; "Frankie and Johnny"; "Johnny Get Your Gun"; "Oh, Johnny, Oh, Johnny, Oh!"; "Johnny One Note"

Josephine, Jo "Josephine, My Jo"

Joshua "Joshua Fit the Battle of Jericho"

Juanita "Juanita"

Jude "Hey Jude" (Beatles)

Judy "Suite: Judy Blue Eyes" (Crosby, Stills, Nash & Young)

Julie "When Julie Comes Around"

Kathleen "Kathleen Mavourneen"

Lara "Lara's Theme (Somewhere My Love)" (from *Doctor Zhivago*)

Layla "Layla" (Eric Clapton)

Leroy "Bad, Bad Leroy Brown" (Jim Croce)

Lili "Lili Marlene"

Liza Jane "Good-bye, Liza Jane"; "Li'l Liza Jane"

Lou "Skip to My Lou"

Louis "Meet Me in St. Louis, Louis"

Lucy "Lucy in the Sky with Diamonds" (Beatles)

Lulu "Lulu's Back in Town"

Maggie "When You and I Were Young, Maggie"

Mandy "Mandy" (Barry Manilow)

Margery "Seesaw, Margery Daw"

Maria "Maria" (from *West Side Story*); "Maria" (from *The Sound of Music*)

Marlene "Lili Marlene"

Mary "Oh, Mary, Don't You Weep, Don't You Mourn"; "Mary Had a Little Lamb"

Mary Ann "Mary Ann" (Calypso song)

Matilda "Waltzing Matilda"

Michelle "Michelle" (Beatles)

Mona "Mona Lisa" (Nat King Cole)

Moses "Go Down, Moses"

Ned "(Old) Uncle Ned"

Nellie, Nelly "Nelly Bly"; "Nelly Was a Lady"; "When I Saw Sweet Nellie Home"

Oliver *Oliver* (the musical based on Charles Dickens's novel *Oliver Twist*)

Pearl "My Pearl's a Bowery Girl"

Peg "Peg o' My Heart"; "Peg" (Steely Dan)

Peggy "Peggy"; "Peggy Sue" (Buddy Holly)

Peter "Peter, Peter Pumpkin-Eater"

Polly "Polly, Put the Kettle On"

Ramona "Ramona"

Rhonda "Help Me, Rhonda" (Beach Boys)

Rose Marie "Rose Marie"

Rosie "Sweet Rosie O'Grady"

Sally "Lay Down Sally" (Eric Clapton)

Sandra "Look At Me, I'm Sandra Dee"

Sara "Sara Smile" (Darryl Hall, John Oates)

Sherry "Sherry" (Four Seasons)

Simon "Simple Simon"

Sue "I Love You in the Same Old Way—Darling Sue"; "Sweet Sue (Just You)"

Susanna "O, Susanna"

Susie "If You Knew Susie, Like I Know Susie"; "Wake Up Little Susie" (Everly Brothers)

Tom "Tom, Tom, the Piper's Son"; "Tom Dooley"

Tommy *Tommy* (the rock musical by The Who)

NAMES OF CELEBRITIES' CHILDREN

While ordinary folks often follow the fashions set by popular celebrities, the naming of children is one area that proves a slight exception to this. In recent years, some celebrities have chosen such outrageous names for their children that it seems they are daring others to follow. Others have chosen very traditional names, which may actually become more popular through their influence, but whose popularity could not be attributed solely to them.

For those who wish to emulate and those who simply wish to be entertained, here is what some notable people in the public eye have named their babies:

Alan Alda **Eve, Elizabeth, Beatrice**

Woody Allen and Mia Farrow **Satchel**

Prince Andrew and Sarah, the Duchess of York **Beatrice Elizabeth Mary**

Lisa Bonet **Zoe**

Prince Charles and the Princess of Wales **William, Harry**

Cher and Greg Allman **Elijah Blue**

Cher and Sonny Bono **Chastity**

Bill Cosby **Erika Ranee, Erinn Charlene, Ennis William, Ensa Camille, Evin Harrah**

Joan Didion and John Gregory Dunne **Quintana Roo**

Kirk Douglas **Michael, Joel, Peter, Eric**

Michael Douglas **Cameron**

Mia Farrow In addition to Woody Allen's son **Satchel**, her children are **Matthew Phineas, Sascha Villiers, Lark Song, Fletcher Farrow, Summer Song, Gigi Soon Mi, and Misha**

Mick Jagger **Jade, Karis, Elizabeth Scarlett, James Leroy Augustine**

John Fitzgerald Kennedy and Jacqueline Lee Bouvier **Caroline Bouvier, John Fitzgerald, Patrick Bouvier** (died in infancy)

Tom Landry **Thomas, Kitty, Lisa**

Sugar Ray (Ray Charles) Leonard **Ray Charles**

Bette Midler **Sophie**

Chuck Norris **Mike, Eric**

Ryan O'Neal **Tatum, Griffin**

Marie Osmond **Stephen James**

James Danforth Quayle **Tucker Danforth, Benjamin Eugene, Mary Corinne**

Caroline Kennedy Schlossberg **Rose Kennedy**

Cybill Shepherd **Clementine ("Clemmy")**, and twins **Ariel** and **Cyrus Zachariah ("Zack")**

Grace Slick **China**

Sylvester Stallone **Sage, Seth**

Barbra Streisand **Jason Emanuel**

Kathleen Turner **Rachel Ann**

Robin Williams **Zachary**

Bruce Willis and Demi Moore **Rumer Glenn**

Stevie Wonder **Aisha, Keita, Mumtaz**

Frank Zappa **Moon Unit, Dweezil, Ahmet**

INDEX

Aaron, 187
Abby, 85-86
Abe, 101
Abigail, 85-86, 233
Abner, 187
Abraham, 3, 9, 101
Abram, 101
Achilles, 171
Ada, 119-20
Adaline, 153-54
Adam, 3, 187, 216
Adams, 230
Addie, 154
Addison, 3
Addy, 154
Adela, 120
Adelaide, 120, 162
Adele, 120
Adelheid, 162
Adeline, 60, 120, 153-54, 244
Aden, 101
Adlai, 101
Adolf, 202
Adria, 14
Adrian, 5, 14, 48, 143
Adrienne, 14
Aeneas, 171
Aggie, 120
Agnes, 120, 213
Agneta, 215
Aidan, 101
Aiden, 101
Aileen, 120, 121
Aimee, 14
Aisha, 249
Aisling, 205
Akira, 48
Al, 124, 142, 147
Alain, 123, 201
Alan, 31, 123, 214
Alana, 14, 31
Alasdair, 49, 214
Alastair, 49, 214
Albert, 51, 123-24, 142
Alberto, 208, 210
Albrecht, 202
Aldis, 48
Aldo, 48
Aldous, 48
Aldus, 48
Alec, 48
Aleck, 48
Alejandro, 210
Alessandra, 98, 208
Alessandro, 78, 208
Alessia, 208
Alex, 101
Alexa, 120
Alexander, 48, 78, 98, 101, 120, 142, 150, 161, 199, 212, 216, 244
Alexandra, 14, 120, 199, 211, 215

Alexandria, 120
Alexandrina, 120
Alexandros, 204
Alexei, 212
Alexey, 212
Alexis, 120, 124, 204, 212
Alf, 216
Alfie, 244
Alfred, 124
Ali, 14
Alic, 48
Alice, 8, 14, 199, 244
Alicia, 14
Alick, 48
Aline, 154
Alisdair, 49, 214
Alison, 14
Alistair, 48-49, 214
Alix, 120
Allan, 123
Allaster, 49
Allegra, 15
Allen, 123
Allistair, 49
Allister, 49
Ally, 14
Aloysius, 205
Althaea, 137-38
Althea, 137-38
Alvan, 49
Alvar, 49
Alvin, 49
Alwin, 49
Alwyn, 49
Amabel, 154
Amanda, 154, 198, 215, 242, 243, 249
Amata, 154
Amber, 198, 237
Ambrose, 49
Amelia, 121
Amerigo, 124
Ames, 227
Amir, 207
Amnon, 10
Amos, 187
Amy, 14
Ana, 15
Anais, 15
Anders, 102, 216
Andre, 201
Andrea, 41, 102, 208
Andreana, 213
Andreas, 102, 202, 204
Andreena, 213
Andrena, 213
Andrene, 213
Andrew, 5, 6, 10, 101-2, 198, 213, 234, 242, 243
Andriene, 213
Andrina, 213
Andy, 10, 102
Angela, 86
Angelina, 86
Angeline, 86
Angie, 86, 244
Angus, 49, 214
Anita, 15, 215
Ann, 86, 97, 215
Anna, 3, 15, 39, 41, 86, 154, 162, 184, 201, 204, 211, 215, 233
Annabel, 154
Annabelle, 154
Anne, 3, 15, 39, 86, 97, 184, 200, 233, 241
Annette, 15, 86, 215
Annice, 121
Annie, 86, 121, 244
Annika, 215
Annis, 121
Anouk, 15
Ansel, 49
Anselm, 49
Anthony, 49-50, 86, 243
Antigone, 204
Antoine, 86
Antoinette, 86
Anton, 50, 212
Antonio, 210
Antony, 49-50
Anya, 211
Aphra, 15-16
Apolla, 171
April, 236
Archibald, 50, 171
Archie, 50, 171
Archy, 171
Aretha, 16
Ari, 10, 207
Ariadne, 154
Arianna, 9
Ariel, 249
Aristotle, 124
Arleen, 121

Arlene, 121
Arline, 121
Arlo, 50
Arne, 216
Aron, 59
Art, 171
Artemis, 154, 158, 204
Artemisia, 154
Arthur, 171
Asa, 124
Asher, 50
Ashleigh, 155
Ashley, 50, 155, 198, 220, 238, 242
Ashlie, 155
Astra, 155
Astraea, 16, 155
Astrea, 155
Astred, 16
Astrid, 16, 215
Athena, 155, 204
Athol, 50
Aubrey, 50-51
Audrey, 16
August, 102
Augusta, 16, 87
Auguste, 102
Augustin, 102
Augustina, 16
Augustine, 16, 102, 248
Augustus, 3, 16, 102
Austin, 223
Ava, 16
Averell, 102
Averil, 102
Averill, 102
Avivah, 206
Avivit, 206
Axel, 216
Ayleen, 121
Azah, 206

Bab, 87
Babe, 138, 142
Babette, 87
Babs, 87
Ban, 142
Bancroft, 142
Barbara, 87, 201, 208, 241
Barbel, 201
Barbro, 215
Barnabas, 171, 172
Barnaby, 171-72
Barnard, 125
Barnet, 51
Barnett, 51
Barney, 125, 171-72
Barrie, 87
Barry, 102
Bart, 8, 54, 124, 142
Bartholomew, 10, 124, 142
Bartlett, 10, 142
Barton, 10, 51, 142
Basil, 51, 80
Bea, 17
Bearrach, 102
Beatrice, 16-17, 248
Beatrix, 16-17, 170
Beau, 51
Becky, 155, 186
Bee, 17
Belinda, 34, 155
Bell, 87
Bella, 87
Belle, 87, 154
Ben, 51, 103
Benedict, 102, 103, 205
Bengt, 216
Benjamin, 51, 103, 199
Benjamin Eugene, 249
Bennet, 103
Bennett, 51, 103
Benson, 51
Benton, 51
Berenice, 87
Berit, 215
Berkeley, 3, 229
Bernadette, 121
Bernard, 121, 125
Bernice, 87
Bernie, 125
Berrach, 102
Berry, 87
Bert, 51, 109, 124
Berta, 201
Bertie, 124
Bertil, 216
Bertram, 51, 125
Bertrand, 125
Beryl, 17, 236
Bess, 87, 91
Beth, 10, 87, 91, 220
Bethany, 220
Bethel, 220
Beto, 210

Betsey, 87
Betsy, 2, 10, 87, 91, 244
Bette, 17, 91
Betty, 17
Bill, 10, 82, 116, 244
Billie Jean, 138
Billy, 10, 116, 244
Birgit, 18, 215
Birgitta, 18, 215
Bjorn, 142, 216
Blaise, 125
Blake, 51-52
Blanche, 155-56
Bliss, 52
Blossom, 235
Bo, 216
Bob, 114
Bobbie, 41
Bobby, 114, 244
Bonnie, 17, 244
Bonny, 17
Booth, 52
Boris, 7, 9, 142, 212
Bouvier, 249Brad, 143
Bradford, 143, 227
Bradley, 143
Bradstreet, 227
Bradwell, 143
Brandon, 52, 242
Brattle, 227
Brean, 53
Brearley, 229
Brenda, 156
Brendan, 52, 205
Bret, 52
Brett, 52
Brian, 52-53, 205, 244
Brice, 53, 223
Bridget, 3, 17-18, 205
Brigham, 103
Brighid, 18
Brigid, 17-18, 205
Brigit, 17-18
Brigitta, 18
Brigitte, 17-18
Brita, 18
Britt, 172, 215
Britta, 18, 215
Brittany, 4, 220, 242
Bronko, 143
Bronson, 125
Brook, 88
Brooke, 88
Brooklyn, 249
Brooks, 53
Brown, 230
Bruce, 8, 53
Bruno, 125, 202
Bryan, 53
Bryce, 53, 223
Bryn, 230
Bryon, 53
Bryony, 235
Buck, 172
Buckminster, 125
Bucky, 125
Bud, 54
Buddy, 53-54
Bulkeley, 227
Burgess, 54
Burt, 51, 54
Burton, 54
Buster, 54
Buzz, 126
Byron, 54-55

Cabot, 230
Cal, 103
Caleb, 187
Calvin, 103
Cameron, 248
Camilla, 156
Camille, 17, 156
Candace, 18
Candi, 18
Candice, 18
Candy, 18
Cap, 143
Carew, 55
Carey, 55
Carl, 104, 126, 131
Carla, 6, 41, 88
Carlos, 210
Carlota, 210
Carlotta, 19
Carmel, 220
Carmela, 220
Carmella, 220
Carmelle, 220
Carmen, 156
Carol, 18, 41, 241
Carole, 18
Carolina, 32, 88, 220
Caroline, 88, 220, 244, 249

Carolyn, 34, 88
Carrie, 88
Carry, 88
Carson, 18, 24
Carter, 103
Cary, 55
Casey, 143, 244
Caspar, 143, 172
Casper, 172
Cassandra, 156
Cassie, 156
Cassius, 143-44
Cata, 210
Catalina, 210
Catarina, 204
Catherine, 88, 95, 200
Cathy, 95, 244
Cecil, 55, 156
C;aaecile, 10, 18, 200
Cecilia, 18, 156, 215
Cecily, 18
Cedric, 172
Cedrick, 172
Celia, 123, 156
Chanel, 238
Charity, 3, 26, 89, 156-57, 229
Charleen, 19
Charlene, 19, 248
Charles, 3, 18, 19, 88, 103-4, 126, 199, 201, 220, 231, 242, 249
Charlie, 244
Charlotta, 215
Charlotte, 18-19, 140, 199, 201, 245
Charmian, 157
Chastity, 229, 248
Cher, 19
Chere, 19
Cheri, 19
Cherie, 19
Cherilyn, 19
Cherrill, 19
Cheryl, 19
Cheryll, 19
Chester, 55, 104
Chet, 55
China, 249
Choate, 230
Chris, 89, 138
Chrissie, 138
Chrissy, 89
Christa, 201
Christiaan, 126
Christian, 126
Christiane, 201
Christina, 30, 45, 138, 204, 243
Christine, 30, 88-89, 138
Christopher, 126, 131, 198, 242, 243
Christos, 204
Christy, 89
Chuck, 104, 126, 245
Churchill, 238-39
Cicely, 18
Cindy, 19
City, 243
Claiborne, 104
Clair, 89
Claire, 89, 200
Clara, 19-20, 202
Clare, 89, 205
Clarence, 126-27
Clarice, 157
Clarissa, 157
Clarisse, 157
Clark, 55
Claud, 55-56
Claude, 20, 55-56, 201
Claudette, 20, 89
Claudia, 20, 89
Claudine, 20
Clay, 104
Clayborn, 104
Clayborne, 104
Clayton, 104
Clementine, 245, 249
Clemmy, 249
Cleo, 157
Cleopatra, 157
Cliff, 56
Clifford, 56
Clint, 6, 56
Clinton, 56
Clio, 157
Clive, 56
Clover, 235
Clyde, 223
Colette, 6, 20
Collette, 20
Colm, 56, 205
Colman, 56, 205, 227
Colum, 56, 205
Columbus, 127
Comfort, 229

Conan, 172-73
Connie, 89
Conor, 205
Conrad, 56, 131
Constance, 89, 229
Constantine, 104
Constantinos, 204
Cora, 89
Coral, 236, 237
Cordelia, 157
Coretta, 89
Corinna, 157
Corinne, 157, 248
Cornell, 230
Cotton, 104, 227
Cristiano, 208
Cristina, 208
Crystal, 20, 198, 236
Currier, 230
Curtis, 57
Cushman, 227
Cuynthia, 20
Cy, 105, 144, 147
Cybill, 20, 42
Cyndi, 7, 19
Cyndy, 19
Cynthia, 19, 20
Cyrus, 105, 144, 249

Daffodil, 235
Dafne, 206
Dagmar, 215
Dahlia, 235
Daisy, 3, 158, 235, 245
Dale, 57
Daliah, 206
Dalit, 206
Dallas, 223
Dalton, 230
Damaris, 90
Damon, 173
Dan, 245
Dana, 127
Dane, 127
Daniel, 187-88, 198, 216, 228, 242, 243, 245
Daniela, 127
Danny, 245
Dante, 57
Daphne, 9, 158
Darius, 105
Darlene, 20
Darrell, 144
Darryl, 144
Dartmouth, 230
Darwin, 127
Daryl, 20, 144
Dashiell, 57
Davenport, 227
Davi, 105, 127
David, 105, 127, 198, 216, 231, 243
Davy, 105, 127
Dawn, 138, 236
Dazzy, 144
Dean, 57
Deanna, 21
Deb, 90
Debbie, 90
Deborah, 90, 241
Debra, 90
Deirdre, 158, 205
Delia, 158
Delphine, 158
Demeter, 21, 158-59
Demetria, 21, 158-59
Demi, 8, 20-21
Deneice, 21
Denese, 21
Denice, 21
Deniece, 21
Denis, 127
Denise, 21
Dennis, 21, 127
Dennise, 21
Denyse, 21
Dereck, 57
Derek, 57, 58
Derick, 57
Dermot, 173
Derrek, 57
Derrick, 57
Desmond, 205
De Witt, 105
Diamond, 236, 237
Diana, 21, 90, 154, 245
Diane, 90
Diarmid, 173
Dick, 113
Dietrich, 57, 58
Dina, 21
Dinah, 21, 245
Dione, 21
Dionne, 21

Dirk, 57, 58
Dixie, 221
Dizzy, 144
Djuna, 21
Dmitry, 212
Doll, 22, 91
Dolley, 91
Dollie, 21
Dolly, 21, 22, 91, 245
Dolores, 159, 210
Don, 105, 144
Donagh, 205
Donal, 205
Donald, 8, 105, 144, 214, 231
Donheh, 205
Donna, 21-22
Dorcas, 90
Doris, 22
Doron, 207
Dorothea, 21, 22, 90-91, 99
Dorothy, 21, 22, 91
Dot, 22, 91
Dottie, 22, 91
Doug, 106
Dougal, 214
Douglas, 7-8, 106, 214
Dov, 207
Drew, 22
Dru, 184
Drusilla, 184
Dudley, 58, 227, 230
Dugald, 214
Dulcia, 159
Dulcie, 159
Dulcinea, 159
Dummer, 227
Duncan, 214
Dunstan, 106
Dunster, 230
Dustin, 7, 58
Dweezil, 249
Dwight, 106
Dylan, 58

Eamon, 205
Earl, 106, 145
Early, 106, 145
Ebba, 215
Eben, 173
Ebenezer, 173
Ed, 106, 128
Eddie, 58, 106
Eden, 221
Edgar, 59
Edie, 22
Edison, 127-28
Edit, 215
Edith, 22, 201, 233
Edna, 22
Eduard, 202
Eduardo, 210
Edvard, 202, 216
Edvin, 216
Edward, 58, 106, 115, 199, 228
Edwin, 128
Efrem, 60
Eileen, 121, 205
Elaine, 159
Eleanor, 91, 163
Eleanora, 91, 163
Eleasar, 188
Eleazar, 188
Electra, 159
Elena, 211
Eleni, 204
Eleonora, 91, 215
Eli, 128
Elias, 128
Eliezar, 188
Elijah, 188
Elijah Blue, 248
Elin, 215
Elinor, 91
Eliot, 128, 230
Elisabeth, 91, 215
Elise, 91
Elisha, 188
Eliza, 91, 159, 233
Elizabeth, 2, 3, 5, 9, 10, 17, 32, 33, 87, 91, 94, 122, 159, 183, 201, 233, 241, 248
Elizabeth Scarlett, 248
Elke, 201
Ella, 23
Ellen, 91-92, 167
Ellery, 173
Ellie, 91
Elliot, 128
Elliott, 128
Ellis, 239
Elly, 91
Elmer, 173
Elmo, 128
Elmore, 59

Elsa, 215
Elsie, 91, 213
Elspeth, 213
Elvin, 49, 59
Elvis, 59
Elwin, 49, 59
Elwyn, 49, 59
Em, 92
Emanuel, 71, 188, 249
Emeline, 92
Emerson, 59
Emil, 59, 216
Emile, 59-60
Emilie, 23
Emily, 6, 23, 199
Emma, 159-60, 199, 215
Emmanuel, 188
Emmeline, 92
Emmy, 92
Engelbert, 9
Ennis, 248
Enoch, 3
Enrique, 209, 210
Enriqueta, 210
Ensa, 248
Eoin, 205
Ephraim, 60, 145
Eppa, 145
Erasmus, 128
Eric, 3, 23, 128, 248, 249
Erica, 23
Erik, 128
Erika, 23, 201, 215, 248
Erin, 205, 221
Erinn, 248
Erland, 216
Erle, 106
Erma, 23
Ermina, 23
Ernest, 60
Ernestine, 60
Ernesto, 210
Ernst, 60, 202, 216
Errol, 60
Erskine, 60
Erwin, 129, 203
Eskil, 216
Esme, 160
Esmee, 160
Esmeralda, 237
Estee, 239
Estelle, 23
Ester, 215
Esther, 162, 184
Ethan, 107
Ethel, 23
Euan, 214
Eubie, 60
Euclid, 129
Eudora, 23-24
Eugene, 8, 60-61, 62, 160
Eugenia, 160
Eugenie, 160
Eva, 16, 184, 215
Eve, 184, 248
Evelyn, 61, 138
Everest, 223
Evert, 216
Evin Harrah, 248
Evonne, 139, 141
Ewan, 214
Ezekiel, 188, 245
Ezra, 188

Fae, 24
Faith, 26, 229
Farley, 61
Farrow, 248Fay, 24
Faye, 8, 24
Federica, 208
Felix, 107
Ferdinand, 129
Fergus, 205
Fern, 160, 235
Fernand, 129
Ferris, 173-74
Fidelity, 229
Fiona, 160, 213
Fionn, 214
Fionnan, 214
Fitzgerald, 249
Flann, 205
Flannery, 24
Fletcher, 248
Flo, 139
Flora, 160-61, 161, 236
Florence, 2, 139
Florie, 139
Florrie, 139
Flory, 139
Floss, 139
Flossie, 139
Folke, 216
Ford, 61

Fran, 92
Frances, 92, 161, 205
Francesca, 92, 208
Francesco, 129
Francis, 61, 92, 129, 130, 205, 228
Francisco, 129, 210
Francois, 201
Francoise, 200
Frank, 61, 107
Frankie, 245
Franklin, 107, 228, 234
Frannie, 161
Franny, 161
Franz, 129, 130, 203
Fred, 8, 61-62, 107
Frederick, 107, 179, 199
Fredrik, 216
Freya, 161
Freyja, 161
Frieda, 201
Friederike, 202
Friedrich, 203
Fritz, 203
Fyodor, 212

Gabe, 189
Gabie, 161
Gabriel, 161, 189, 216
Gabriela, 161
Gabriele, 202, 208
Gabriella, 9, 161, 215
Gabrielle, 161
Gaby, 161
Galiah, 206
Galileo, 130
Galina, 211
Galway, 62
Garrett, 62
Garrick, 62
Garrison, 62
Garry, 62
Gary, 62
Gaspar, 172
Gem, 237
Gemma, 237
Gene, 61, 62
Genevieve, 92, 200
Geoff, 63
Geoffrey, 62-63, 67
Georg, 203
George, 8, 107, 135, 199, 205, 228
Georgi, 212
Georgia, 24, 245
Georgiana, 24
Georgina, 199
Gerald, 67, 130, 205
Gerard, 63
Gerardo, 210
Gerda, 161
Germaine, 122
Gertie, 24, 205
Gertrud, 215
Gertrude, 8, 24, 205
Gideon, 189
Gigi Soon Mi, 248
Gil, 145, 147, 207
Gilbert, 145
Gilda, 24
Gili, 207
Gill, 161
Gillian, 161
Ginger, 7, 24-25
Giorgio, 239
Giovanni, 110-11
Gisele, 161
Giselle, 161
Giulia, 208
Gladys, 25
Glenda, 161-62
Gloria, 9, 93, 162
Gloriana, 162
Godfrey, 174
Gordie, 145
Gordon, 145
Gottfried, 203
Grace, 25
Gracie, 25
Graeme, 63, 214
Graham, 63, 214
Grahame, 63
Grania, 205
Grant, 63
Grantland, 145
Gray, 3, 174
Graydon, 174
Grayson, 174, 220
Greer, 25
Greg, 63
Greger, 217
Gregg, 63
Gregor, 25
Gregory, 25, 63
Greta, 25, 202
Gretchen, 3, 202

Grete, 202
Gretel, 202
Griffin, 249
Grigory, 212
Griselda, 47
Gudrun, 215
Guedolen, 25-26
Guenevere, 162
Guinevere, 27, 162
Guinnevere, 245
Gunilla, 215
Gunnar, 217
Gunnel, 215
Gunter, 203
Gussie, 16
Gustav, 63, 203, 217
Gustave, 63
Gustavus, 63
Gwen, 26, 162
Gwendolin, 25, 26
Gwendolyn, 25, 26
Gwenevere, 162
Gwenn, 26
Gwyn, 26
Gwynne, 26, 162

Hadassah, 184
Hadrian, 14, 48
Hal, 64, 109
Halston, 239
Hamilton, 108
Hamish, 214
Hamlet, 174
Hamlin, 174
Hammet, 174
Hammond, 174
Han, 174
Hana, 139
Hank, 109, 145
Hannah, 15, 86, 97, 139, 184, 199
Hannibal, 3, 108
Hans, 110-11, 130, 174, 203, 217
Harlan, 108
Harland, 108
Harlow, 50
Harold, 64
Harriet, 93, 199, 215
Harrison, 64
Harry, 8, 64, 108, 245, 248
Hart, 64
Hattie, 93
Hatty, 93
Hayden, 64
Haydn, 64
Haydon, 64
Hazel, 235
Heather, 26, 235, 242
Hector, 175
Hedvig, 215
Hedwig, 8, 202
Hedy, 26
Heidi, 162
Heinrich, 203
Heinz, 203
Helen, 91, 92, 93, 121, 159, 167
Helena, 31-32, 93, 215
Hélène, 159
Helene, 93, 200
Helga, 140, 202, 215
Helge, 217
Helmut, 203
Henri, 109
Henrik, 217
Henry, 64, 93, 108-9, 145
Herb, 109
Herbert, 109, 217
Herbie, 109
Hercule, 175
Hercules, 175
Herman, 64
Hermann, 203
Hermione, 23
Hernando, 245
Hester, 162
Hetty, 162
Hilda, 26, 202
Hilde, 202
Hildegard, 202
Hillah, 206
Hiram, 189
Holly, 26, 235, 245
Homer, 65
Honor, 122
Honora, 39, 122
Honour, 122
Hope, 26, 229
Horace, 3, 65
Horatio, 109
Hortense, 26
Hosea, 189
Houston, 223
Howard, 130
Howie, 130
Hubert, 60, 109

Huck, 175
Huckleberry, 175, 245
Hugh, 109, 205
Hughie, 109
Hugo, 130-31
Humphrey, 65, 225
Humphry, 65
Hunter, 65

Iain, 214
Ian, 65, 110-11, 214
Ichabod, 3, 175
Ichiro, 209
Idelfonso, 210
Ignace, 131
Ignatius, 66, 131
Igor, 212
Ilanah, 206
Ilene, 121
Ili, 189
Ilya, 212
Immanuel, 188
Imogen, 27
Imogene, 27
Inga, 215
Ingalill, 216
Ingeborg, 216
Ingegerd, 216
Ingemar, 217
Inger, 216
Ingmar, 65
Ingrid, 27, 216
Ingvar, 217
Inigo, 66
Iona, 221
Irene, 122, 139, 245
Irina, 139, 211
Iris, 162, 235
Irma, 23, 27
Irmina, 23, 27
Irvin, 66
Irvine, 66
Irving, 66
Irwin, 131
Irwyn, 129
Isaac, 3, 8, 189
Isabel, 93-94
Isabell, 87
Isabella, 87, 93-94, 216
Isadora, 27
Isaiah, 189-90
Ishmael, 190
Isidora, 27
Ismay, 160, 162
Isobel, 93-94
Israel, 223
Issey, 239
Ivan, 110-11, 145-46, 212
Ivonne, 141
Ivy, 27, 235

Jacinth, 237
Jack, 66, 146, 245
Jackie, 2, 94, 139, 146
Jackson, 66
Jacob, 109-10, 190
Jacqueline, 94, 139
Jacquelyn, 94
Jade, 236, 237, 248
Jakob, 217
Jamaica, 221
James, 10, 78, 94, 109-10, 131, 146, 199, 213, 228, 231, 234, 242, 248, 249
Jamesina, 213
Jamie, 214
Jan, 217
Jane, 41, 94, 139
Janet, 139, 213
Janetta, 213
Janette, 213
Janey, 213
Janice, 213
Janie, 213
Janine, 213
Janis, 213
Jared, 190
Jasmine, 27, 28
Jason, 175, 249
Jasper, 66, 236
Jay, 66
Jean, 41, 94, 110-11, 201, 245
Jeanette, 94-95, 213
Jeanie, 94, 213, 245
Jeanne, 94, 95, 200, 213
Jeannette, 94-95
Jeannie, 94
Jean-Pierre, 200
Jed, 131
Jedidiah, 131
Jeff, 66-67, 110
Jefferson, 67, 110
Jeffrey, 62-63, 66-67
Jemima, 184

Jennie, 27-28
Jennifer, 27, 28, 184, 198, 242, 243
Jenny, 27-28, 216
Jeremiah, 6, 67, 190
Jeremy, 67, 190
Jerome, 67
Jerry, 67, 130, 190
Jersey, 4
Jesper, 217
Jess, 28
Jessamine, 28
Jessamyn, 28
Jesse, 110
Jessica, 28, 184, 198, 242, 243
Jessie, 28
Jesus, 210
Jet, 236, 238
Jewel, 238
Jill, 161, 245
Jim, 10, 110, 131
Jimbo, 146
Jimi, 131
Jimmy, 110, 131, 146
Jo, 95, 245
Joakim, 217
Joan, 28, 29, 41, 42
Jo Ann, 29
Joanna, 28-29, 139
Joanne, 29
Jodie, 29, 175
Jody, 29, 175
Joe, 146, 205, 231
Joel, 67, 248
Johan, 217
Johann, 203
Johanna, 28-29, 202, 213
Johannes, 110-11, 203
John, 3, 9, 10, 28, 65, 66, 78, 94, 110-11, 146, 174, 183, 228, 231, 234, 241, 243, 249
Johnny, 10, 111, 146, 245
Joi, 122
Joie, 122
Jon, 191
Jonah, 190
Jonas, 190, 217
Jonathan, 5, 110-11, 191, 243
Joni, 8, 29
Jordan, 223
Jorge, 210
José, 209, 210
Josef, 203
Joseph, 95, 111, 146, 175, 205, 243
Josephine, 95, 245
Josh, 191
Joshua, 3, 50, 183, 191, 242, 245
Josiah, 191
Joy, 122
Joya, 122
Juan, 210
Juana, 210
Juanita, 210, 245
Judah, 175, 176
Judas, 176
Jude, 175, 176, 245
Judia, 233
Judith, 29, 122
Judy, 29, 122, 245
Juilliard, 230
Julia, 3, 95, 163
Julian, 67-68
Juliana, 95
Julie, 95, 246
Juliet, 163
Juliette, 163
Julius, 3, 68, 95, 146
June, 29, 236
Junior, 146
Jurgen, 203
Justin, 111, 198
Justina, 163
Justine, 163
Justinian, 111
Justus, 111

Kalle, 217
Karan, 239
Kareem, 146
Karen, 29, 241
Karim, 146
Karin, 29, 216
Karis, 248
Karl, 104, 126, 131, 203, 217
Katarina, 204, 216
Kate, 95, 205
Katharina, 202
Katharine, 95
Kathe, 202
Katherine, 29, 30, 95, 205
Kathleen, 29, 95, 205, 246
Kathryn, 95
Kathy, 95
Katie, 95
Katrina, 95

Katy, 95
Kay, 95
Kayla, 197
Keayne, 228
Keir, 68
Keirstan, 30
Keita, 249
Keith, 68
Ken, 10, 68
Kenesaw, 147
Kenneth, 10, 68, 214
Kermie, 176
Kermit, 176
Kersten, 30
Kerstin, 30, 216
Kezia, 184-85
Keziah, 184-85
Kim, 29-30, 176, 221
Kimball, 176
Kimberley, 30, 221
Kimberly, 30
Kingsley, 68
Kiri, 30
Kirk, 68-69
Kirkland, 230
Kirsteen, 30
Kirsten, 30
Kirsti, 30
Kirstie, 30, 213
Kirstin, 30
Kirsty, 30
Kirstyn, 30
Kit, 95, 131
Kitty, 30, 95, 205, 249
Kjell, 217
Klara, 202
Klas, 217
Klaus, 203
Klein, 239
Knox, 111
Knute, 147
Konrad, 56, 203
Konstantin, 212
Kristen, 30, 242
Krister, 217
Kristi, 31
Kristie, 31
Kristin, 30
Kristina, 30-31, 216
Kristy, 30
Kurt, 131, 203
Kyle, 198
Kyra, 31

Lana, 31
Lance, 176
Lancelot, 176
Lanford, 69
Lara, 246
Larissa, 139-40
Lark Song, 248
Larry, 69
Lars, 217
Laura, 31, 139-40, 198
Laurel, 235
Lauren, 31, 198
Laurence, 31, 69
Laurie, 31
Lavinia, 3
Lawrence, 69
Layla, 163
Leah, 163, 185
Learned, 132
Lee, 31, 69
Lefty, 147
Leia, 163
Leif, 132, 217
Leigh, 31
Leila, 163
Leland, 111
Lena, 31, 216
Lennart, 217
Lenny, 69
Lenore, 163
Leo, 69, 70
Leon, 147
Leonard, 69-70, 70
Leonardo, 69-70
Leonid, 212
Leonora, 163
Leonore, 163
Leontine, 32
Leontyne, 32
Leorah, 206
LeRoi, 176
Leroy, 176, 246, 248
Les, 70
Lesley, 213
Leslie, 214
Lester, 70
Leverett, 230
Lew, 70, 147
Lewis, 70, 147
Liam, 70, 205

Lil, 32
Lila, 32
Lilah, 32
Lili, 32, 246
Liliane, 32
Lille, 32
Lillian, 32
Lillie, 32
Lily, 32, 235
Lina, 31, 32
Lincoln, 111
Linda, 32, 241
Lindsay, 32, 213, 214, 242
Lindsey, 32, 213
Lindsy, 32
Linsay, 32, 213
Linsey, 32
Linus, 132
Lionel, 70
Lisa, 33, 140, 249
Lisbet, 216
Lise, 91, 122, 202
Liv, 33
Livia, 33, 95-96
Liz, 2, 10, 91
Liza, 33, 91
Liza Jane, 246
Lizzie, 91
Lloyd, 111-12
Lois, 163-64
Lola, 164, 210
Lolita, 164
Lorelei, 164
Loretta, 33
Lorette, 33
Lorraine, 221
Lotta, 19, 216
Lotte, 19, 202
Lottie, 19, 140
Lotty, 19
Lou, 70, 147, 246
Louis, 33, 70, 147, 201, 246
Louisa, 33
Louise, 33
Lowell, 230
Luca, 208
Lucille, 33
Lucinda, 33-34
Lucy, 33, 34, 96, 199, 246
Ludovica, 208
Ludwig, 203
Luis, 70, 210
Luisa, 210
Luke, 191
Lulu, 246
Luther, 132
Lyde, 96
Lydia, 96
Lyndon, 112
Lyndsay, 213
Lyndsey, 32, 213
Lynn, 34, 35
Lynne, 34
Lynsey, 32
Lytton, 71

Maddie, 164
Madeleine, 164
Madison, 112
Mae, 36, 37, 236
Maeve, 34, 205
Magdalena, 216
Magdalene, 219
Maggie, 96, 246
Magic, 147-48
Magnolia, 235
Magnus, 217
Mahala, 34
Mahalia, 9, 34
Maia, 37, 164, 236
Maire, 205
Maisie, 213
Maj, 216
Makoto, 209
Malachy, 205
Malcolm, 112, 214
Malin, 216
Mamie, 36, 96
Man, 71
Mandy, 154, 246
Manfred, 71
Manny, 188
Manuel, 71, 188
Marc, 191
Marcella, 164
Marcelle, 164
Marcia, 34
Marco, 132
Marcus, 34, 112, 113, 148
Margaret, 25, 35, 37, 40, 41, 96, 205, 241
Margareta, 216
Margarete, 25
Margarita, 41

Margaux, 34
Margery, 246
Margo, 34-35, 36
Margot, 34-35
Marguerite, 35, 235
Maria, 35, 36, 202, 204, 210, 216, 246
Marian, 35
Marianne, 36, 202, 216
Marie, 35, 36, 122-23, 197, 200
Marie-France, 200
Mariel, 35, 36
Marilyn, 35
Marina, 211
Mario, 113, 148
Marion, 35
Mark, 34, 112, 113, 132, 148, 164, 191
Markus, 217
Marlena, 35-36
Marlene, 35-36, 246
Marlin, 71
Marlo, 36
Marlon, 71
Marsden, 71
Marsha, 34
Marshall, 112
Martha, 97, 164
Marti, 97
Martie, 97
Martin, 113, 140, 203, 217
Martina, 140
Martine, 140, 200
Marty, 97, 113
Mary, 3, 35, 36, 37, 96, 98, 166, 168, 183, 185, 197, 241, 246, 248
Mary Ann, 36, 246
Mary Anne, 36
Mary Corinne, 249
Mather, 228, 230
Matilda, 45, 97, 164, 246
Mats, 217
Matt, 10
Matteo, 208
Matthew, 10, 192, 198, 242, 243, 248
Mattie, 97, 164
Matty, 97, 164
Maud, 205
Maureen, 140, 205
Maurice, 71
Maven, 34, 36
Mavin, 34
Mavine, 34
Mavis, 37
Max, 3, 132, 203
Maxime, 97
Maxine, 97
May, 37, 236
Maya, 164, 236
Meadowlark, 148
Medgar, 113
Meg, 96
Megan, 198
Mehetabel, 3, 162, 164-65
Mehitabel, 164-65
Mel, 6-7, 71
Melanie, 165
Melbourne, 71
Meldon, 71
Melissa, 7, 165, 198, 243
Melville, 71
Melvin, 71
Merce, 71-72
Mercer, 72
Mercy, 3, 229
Meredith, 37
Meret, 37
Merideth, 37
Meridith, 37
Meriwether, 132-33
Merle, 37, 72
Merlin, 176-77
Merv, 72
Mervin, 72, 177
Mervyn, 72, 177
Meryl, 37-38
Mia, 38
Micah, 72, 192
Michael, 8, 72, 73, 148, 165, 192, 198, 242, 243, 248
Michalis, 204
Michel, 201
Michelangelo, 72-73
Michele, 165, 200, 208
Michelle, 165, 246
Michiko, 209
Mick, 72, 73
Mickey, 72, 148
Miguel, 210
Mikael, 217
Mike, 72, 249
Mikhail, 212

Milan, 73
Mildred, 138, 165
Miles, 38, 73
Millie, 165
Milt, 73
Milton, 73
Mimi, 249
Mina, 100
Minerva, 165, 166
Minnie, 36, 100, 165-66
Miranda, 166
Mireille, 10
Miriam, 36, 185
Mirit, 206
Misha, 248
Moe, 192
Moira, 36
Moll, 166
Mollie, 166
Molly, 36, 166, 168, 205
Mona, 166, 216, 246
Monica, 208
Monika, 216
Montgomery, 73
Monty, 73
Moon Unit, 249
Morgan, 166
Moria, 214
Morris, 71, 73
Morton, 228
Mose, 192
Moses, 192, 246
Muhammad, 148
Mumtaz, 249
Muriel, 38
Myles, 73, 205
Myrtle, 235

Nadezhda, 211
Nadia, 140, 211
Nadine, 38, 140
Nan, 184
Nancy, 97
Naomi, 185, 209
Nastassia, 39
Nastassja, 39
Nat, 74
Natala, 38
Natalia, 38, 39, 211
Natalie, 38
Nataly, 211
Natasha, 39, 198, 211
Nathan, 74, 177
Nathanael, 74
Nathaniel, 3, 74, 177
Neal, 133
Ned, 246
Nehemiah, 192
Neil, 74, 133
Neimah, 206
Nell, 91, 166-67
Nellie, 91, 166-67, 246
Nelly, 91, 166-67, 246
Nelson, 113
Nessie, 120
Netah, 207
Nettie, 15
Neva, 221
Niall, 133, 205
Nicholas, 133, 177, 199, 242
Nick, 133, 177
Nicolas, 133
Nicolaus, 133
Nicole, 198, 243
Niels, 133
Nigel, 74
Nikita, 212
Niklas, 217
Nikolai, 212
Nils, 217
Nina, 39, 211
Ninon, 39
Noah, 192
Noam, 133, 207
Noel, 74, 97
Noelle, 97
Nora, 39, 205
Norah, 39
Norbert, 133
Noreen, 39, 205
Norma, 167
Norman, 133
North, 230
Norton, 228
Nowell, 97

Odessa, 222
Odysseus, 177, 180
O.J., 148
Olga, 140, 211
Olive, 39, 235
Oliver, 177, 199, 246
Olivia, 33, 39, 96, 199, 235
Ollie, 177

Olof, 217
Olympia, 222
Omar, 74
Omer, 207
Opal, 238
Ophelia, 167
Oprah, 39
Orah, 207
Oran, 207
Orel, 148-49
Oriana, 167
Orion, 177
Orlando, 177
Orli, 207
Ornah, 207
Orson, 74-75
Oscar, 75
Oskar, 203, 217
Otto, 203
Ove, 217
Owen, 75

Pablo, 75
Paco, 210
Padraic, 75, 205
Paloma, 39-40
Pamela, 167
Pansy, 236
Pat, 98, 113
Patience, 3, 89, 229
Patricia, 97-98, 205
Patrick, 98, 113, 205, 249
Patrik, 217
Patti, 98
Patty, 98
Paul, 75, 192-93, 201, 231
Paulette, 40
Paulina, 32, 40
Pauline, 40
Peace, 229
Pearl, 40, 236, 246
Pedro, 210
Peg, 40, 96, 247
Peggy, 40, 96, 247
Pele, 149
Penelope, 167
Penny, 167
Pepe, 210
Per, 217
Percy, 3, 75
Peregrine, 178
Perry, 177-78
Pete, 149, 193
Peter, 149, 178, 193, 203, 247, 248
Petronella, 216
Phebe, 167-68
Phelam, 205
Phil, 193
Philip, 193
Philippe, 201
Phillip, 193
Phineas, 75, 248
Phoebe, 167-68
Phyliss, 98
Pia, 216
Pie, 149
Pierre, 178, 201
Plato, 133-34
Platon, 134
Polly, 36, 168, 247
Pollyanna, 168
Pom, 161
Pontus, 217
Poppy, 236
Portia, 168
Presley, 59
Princeton, 230
Priscilla, 185
Prissy, 185
Prudence, 229

Quentin, 178
Quincy, 230
Quintana, 248

Rachel, 40, 185-86
Rachel Ann, 249
Radcliffe, 230
Rae, 186
Rafael, 76
Rafer, 149
Ralph, 178
Ramah, 207
Ramón, 168
Ramona, 168, 247
Randal, 178
Randall, 178
Randel, 178
Randell, 178
Randle, 178
Randolf, 75-76
Randolph, 75-76
Randy, 8, 75-76, 178
Ranee, 248

Raphael, 76, 149
Raquel, 40
Raúl, 210
Ray, 76, 151, 186, 249
Raymond, 76, 151
Reba, 40, 186
Rebecca, 3, 155, 186, 199
Rebecka, 216
Rebekah, 186
Red, 149
Reed, 230
Regan, 168
Reggie, 149
Reginald, 149
Rene, 134, 201
Reuben, 193
Rex, 76
Reynold, 76
Reynolds, 76
Rhett, 178
Rhoda, 168
Rhonda, 247
Ricardo, 210
Richard, 113, 179, 228, 231
Rickey, 178-79
Ricky, 107, 178-79
Rigmor, 216
Rita, 40-41
Roald, 134
Rob, 114
Robbie, 114
Robert, 77, 113-114, 231, 242
Roberta, 41
Roberto, 208
Robin, 76-77, 114
Robinson, 179
Rocco, 149-50
Rocky, 149-50
Rod, 77
Rodeo, 239
Rodney, 77
Rodolfo, 210
Roger, 179
Roland, 179
Rolf, 217
Roma, 222
Roman, 77
Romanus, 77
Ron, 114, 207
Ronald, 8, 114, 214
Ronen, 207
Roni, 207
Roo, 248
Rosa, 41, 98, 210, 236
Rosabel, 236
Rosabelle, 236
Rosalie, 236
Rosalind, 41, 98, 123
Rosalinde, 202
Rosalyn, 41, 98
Rosalynn, 98
Rosamunde, 202
Rosanna, 41, 236
Rose, 3, 41, 98, 205, 236, 249
Rosemarie, 236, 247
Rosemary, 205, 236
Rosie, 247
Ross, 77
Rowena, 168-69
Rowland, 179
Rowlandson, 228
Roxane, 169
Roxanna, 169
Roxanne, 169
Roxy, 169
Roy, 150
Roz, 41
Roza, 41
Rube, 193
Ruby, 236, 238
Rudolf, 77
Rudolph, 77
Rudy, 77
Rufus, 114
Rumer Glenn, 249
Rune, 217
Russ, 77
Russell, 77
Rust, 77
Rusty, 77
Ruth, 186
Ryan, 8, 78, 198, 242

Sabina, 202
Sadie, 186
Sage, 236, 249
Sallie, 123, 186
Sally, 8, 10, 123, 186, 247
Salmon, 114
Sam, 114
Samantha, 243
Sammy, 114
Samuel, 3, 114, 228
Sandra, 98, 120, 247

Sandro, 78
Sandy, 41, 98, 120, 150
Sanford, 150
Sapphire, 238
Sara, 186, 242, 247
Sarah, 3, 10, 123, 183, 186, 198, 199
Sarai, 186
Sascha, 248
Sasha, 212
Satchel, 150, 248
Saul, 193
Scarlett, 248
Scot, 78
Scott, 11, 78
Seamus, 78, 205, 214
Sean, 2, 8, 42, 78, 110-11, 179, 205, 214
Seona, 214
Serena, 208
Sergei, 212
Seth, 249
Sewall, 228
Shai, 207
Shamus, 78
Shane, 179, 197, 214
Shannon, 222
Shari, 19, 41
Sharon, 222
Shaun, 78, 214
Shauna, 214
Shavon, 42
Shavonne, 42
Shawn, 78
Sheena, 41
Sheila, 123, 205
Shelley, 41-42
Sheona, 214
Shepard, 228
Shere, 19, 42
Sheri, 19, 42
Sherley, 99
Sherline, 99
Sherman, 179
Sherrill, 19
Sherry, 19, 42, 247
Sherwood, 78
Sheryl, 19, 42
Shiona, 214
Shirlee, 99
Shirleen, 99
Shirley, 98-99
Shirly, 99
Shivaun, 42, 205
Shonagh, 214
Shonah, 214
Shurly, 99
Sian, 42
Sibyl, 42
Sid, 79
Sidney, 3, 78-79
Siegmund, 134
Sigmund, 134
Sigourney, 42
Silas, 193-94
Silvester, 79
Silvia, 43, 208, 216
Simeon, 194
Simon, 42, 247
Simone, 42
Sinead, 205
Siobhan, 42, 205
Sloane, 239
Sly, 79
Smith, 230
Sofia, 43, 211
Solveig, 216
Somerset, 79
Sonia, 42-43, 211
Sonja, 42-43
Sonny, 79
Sonya, 42-43, 211
Sophia, 43, 211
Sophie, 43, 199, 249
Spalding, 150
Spence, 230
Stacey, 2
Staffan, 217
Stan, 150
Standish, 114-15
Stanford, 230
Stanislaus, 134
Stanislaw, 134
Stanley, 150
Stefanie, 141
Steffi, 9, 141
Stella, 169
Stephanie, 141, 198, 242, 243
Stephen, 43, 79, 141, 249
Stephie, 141
Sterling, 151
Steuben, 240
Steve, 79
Steven, 79

Stevie, 43, 79
Stig, 217
Stina, 216
Stirling, 151
Stoddard, 228
Sture, 217
Sue, 43, 247
Sugar Ray, 151
Summer, 236
Summer Song, 248
Susan, 43, 99, 241
Susanna, 43, 169, 216, 247
Susannah, 99, 169
Susie, 43, 99, 247
Susy, 43
Suzanne, 43
Suzy, 99
Sven, 217
Sybil, 42, 43
Sydney, 79
Sylvester, 79
Sylvia, 43, 216
Sylviane, 200
Sylvie, 200

Tabby, 169
Tabitha, 169
Taite, 44
Tal, 207
Tallulah, 43-44
Tama, 44
Tamar, 44
Tamara, 44, 211
Tammie, 44
Tammy, 44
Tamsin, 44
Tania, 44, 211
Tanya, 44, 211
Tate, 44
Tatiana, 44, 211
Tatum, 44, 249
Ted, 115
Temperance, 229
Tennessee, 223
Tere, 210
Terence, 79
Teresa, 99, 210
Teri, 99
Terrence, 79
Terri, 99
Terry, 79, 99
Tess, 99, 169
Tessa, 99
Thea, 169
Theia, 169
Thelonious, 79-80
Theo, 180, 194
Theodora, 99
Theodore, 99, 115, 180
Theodoric, 57, 58
Theodosia, 99
Theophilus, 180, 194
Theresa, 99, 169
Therese, 99
Thisbe, 169-70
Thomas, 44, 115, 183, 199, 228, 231, 249
Thomasin, 44
Thor, 180
Thorhall, 180
Thorstein, 180
Thorton, 80
Thurgood, 115
Thurston, 180
Tifani, 45
Tifanie, 45
Tiffani, 45
Tiffanie, 45
Tiffany, 44-45, 243
Tilda, 45, 97
Tillie, 45
Tilly, 45, 97
Tim, 80, 180
Timothy, 80, 180
Tina, 45
Tobias, 180, 194, 217
Toby, 180, 194
Tom, 115, 247
Tomas, 217
Tommy, 115, 247
Toni, 100
Tony, 50
Topaz, 236, 238
Tracey, 141
Traci, 141
Tracie, 141
Tracy, 141
Treat, 80
Trevor, 80
Tricia, 98
Trillian, 170
Tris, 151
Tristan, 151
Tristram, 151

Trix, 17, 170
Trixie, 17, 170
Trixy, 17
Troy, 224
Trudy, 24, 45
Truman, 115-16
Tucker Danforth, 249
Twyla, 45
Ty, 147, 151
Tycho, 134
Tyler, 198
Tyron, 80
Tyrone, 80
Tyrus, 151
Tyson, 151

Ulf, 217
Ulla, 216
Ulrika, 216
Ulysses, 180
Una, 205
Urban, 217
Ursula, 100, 202

Val, 45
Valentina, 47, 211
Valeria, 208
Valerie, 45
Vanderbilt, 230
Vane, 228
Vanessa, 45, 46
Vanna, 45-46
Vanya, 212
Vasco, 134
Vasili, 80, 211, 212
Vasily, 80
Vassar, 230
Vassily, 211, 212
Vaughan, 80-81
Vaughn, 80-81
Vera, 211
Veronica, 186
Vicki, 100
Vickie, 100
Vicky, 100
Victoria, 100
Vikki, 100
Viktoria, 216
Villiers, 248
Vince, 81
Vincent, 81
Vincente, 81
Viola, 47, 170, 236
Violet, 170, 236
Virgil, 81
Virginia, 25, 46
Vita, 46
Viveka, 216
Vivian, 46
Vivien, 46
Vivienne, 46
Vladimir, 212

Wade, 181
Waite, 151
Wallace, 81
Wallis, 100
Walter, 81, 203
Wanda, 46
Ward, 228
Warren, 116
Washington, 81
Wassily, 80
Waterford, 240
Wayne, 82
Welcome, 229
Wellesley, 230
Wendy, 170
Werner, 134, 203
Wernher, 134
Whitney, 46
Wilfred, 82
Wilfrid, 82
Wilhelm, 100, 203
Wilhelmina, 46, 100, 141, 166
Wilhelmine, 202
Will, 10, 82, 116
Willa, 46, 100
Willi, 240
William, 3, 8, 10, 70, 116, 151-52, 199, 228, 231, 234, 241, 248
Williamina, 100
Williams, 228
Willie, 116, 151-52, 240
Willis, 82
Willow, 170, 236
Willy, 10
Willye, 141
Wilma, 100, 141
Wilson, 116
Wilt, 152
Wilton, 152
Wilver, 152

Win, 82
Winifred, 100
Winnie, 100
Winslow, 82
Winston, 82, 116-17
Winthrop, 117, 228, 230
Wise, 228
Wolfgang, 82, 203
Woodrow, 117
Wyndham, 82
Wynton, 82
Wystan, 83

Yale, 230
Yiorgas, 204
Yngve, 217
Yogi, 152
Yoichi, 209
Yoko, 46-47, 209
Yolanda, 47
Yuri, 135, 212
Yvette, 141
Yvonna, 141
Yvonne, 141

Zacchaeus, 194
Zach, 117, 195
Zachariah, 117, 195, 249
Zacharias, 117, 195
Zachary, 117, 195, 249
Zack, 117, 195, 249
Zane, 83
Zebulon, 135
Zebulun, 135
Zechariah, 117, 183, 194, 195
Zeke, 188
Zelda, 47
Zeno, 135
Zivah, 207
Zoe, 204, 248
Zora, 47
Zubin, 83

Agnes
Carol Francene
Dawn Marie
Nikki Lynne
Claudia Lee
Patricia Ann
Patricia Lee
Amelia
Mary
Signey

Clayton
Carl Phillip
Charles Phillip
Karl Philip
James Paul
Henry
Paul
Timothy James
Thomas Siemers
James Donald